JBoss Drools Business Rules

Capture, automate, and reuse your business processes in a clear
English language that your computer can understand

Paul Browne

BIRMINGHAM - MUMBAI

JBoss Drools Business Rules

First published: March 2009

Production Reference: 1260309

Published by Packt Publishing Ltd.
32 Lincoln Road
Olton
Birmingham, B27 6PA, UK.

ISBN 978-1-847196-06-4

www.packtpub.com

Cover Image by Parag Kadam (paragvkadam@gmail.com)

Credits

Author

Paul Browne

Reviewer

Peter Johnson

Acquisition Editor

David Barnes

Development Editor

Usha Iyer

Technical Editor

Aditi Srivastava

Copy Editor

Sneha Kulkarni

Production Editorial Manager

Abhijeet Deobhakta

Project Coordinator

Neelkanth Mehta

Indexer

Hemangini Bari

Proofreader

Dirk Manuel

Production Coordinator

Dolly Dasilva

Cover Work

Dolly Dasilva

Foreword

Drools was co-created by Bob McWhirter and I at Codehaus, a fantastic collaborative environment for open source development. Drools 2.0, the first official release of Drools, was a great volunteer effort from a range of people working tirelessly over evenings and weekends.

There is a long-running joke that much of Drools 2.0 was written while under the influence of beer — much to the chagrin of a CTO who was told this little anecdote just after telling us that transactions worth millions of dollars were processed with Drools 2.0.

The success of Drools 2.0 didn't go unnoticed. I was soon given the opportunity, by Marc Fleury, to work full time on Drools at Jboss — now a division of Red Hat. With the backing of JBoss, I was soon able to hire several of the key Drools community members, of Drools such as Michael Neale, Edson Tirelli, and Kris Verlaenen. Each of them has become an evil genius in his own right, making Drools what it is today. Bob is also employed at JBoss, but has since moved onto other Ruby-based endeavours.

I've known Paul for a number of years, throughout which he's been an active and valued community member. I remember the conversation two years back when Paul talked about his desire to write a Drools book. His initial goal was to write a small e-book, but I guess his ambitions and imagination got the better of him, prompting him to do something much more ambitious. So it's with great pleasure that I see Paul finally achieve this, his first Drools book. We didn't make things easy for him. Drools 5.0 was a continually changing platform during it's development cycle, on which he was trying to base this book. The main focus of this book is the web-based governance system, what other vendors call a BRMS. And luckily, most of the important aspects are here in all their glorious detail.

Previous Drools versions have challenged commercial vendors in this space, allowing people to state what they know and not have to waste time translating this knowledge into a machine-understandable format. Drools 5.0 is about to be released, and is a monumental peace of engineering over Drools 2.0, 3.0, and 4.0. It brings together rules, workflow, and event processing, along with an enterprise governance system, to form the foundations of the what I call a Business Logic Integration Platform.

I've always stated that end business users struggle to understand the differences between rules and processes, and more recently between rules and event processing. They just want to model it using some software. The traditional way of using two vendor offerings forces the business user to work with a process-oriented or rules-oriented approach. But this gets in the way, often with great confusion over which tool they should be using to model which bit. If you combine these technologies in the right way and take a behavioural modelling approach, you form something that is simpler and at the same time much more powerful. This allows the business user to work more naturally, where the full range of approaches is available to him or her, without the tools getting in the way. From being process-oriented to rule-oriented or shades of grey in the middle—whatever suits the problem being modelled at that time. We are taking this one step further and are adding event processing with Drools Fusion. Thus, we are creating a more holistic approach to software development. The term 'holistic' is used for emphasizing the importance of the whole and the interdependence of its parts.

The JBoss Drools community continues to grow at a fantastic rate and we are very lucky to get such great feedback and contributions. First-rate commercial support continues to be available from Red Hat, which helps us to continue what we are doing. Red Hat provides the branded version of Drools, JBoss Rules, which goes through additional QA and testing against the rest of the JBoss products, such as JBoss ESB and JBoss AS, and is available under long term support contracts. Thousands of sites worldwide have used Drools as a part of their solution.

So where does Drools go from 5.0? Our initial focus will now be on services and delivering codeless deployments. We will also focus on further enterprise-based governance enhancements as we continue to move up the stack from a simple embedded engine. In reality, we've only just started, and there's still much more of the vision to put into place. So all I can say is, you ain't seen nothing yet.

Mark Proctor
JBoss Rules Lead

About the author

Paul Browne's first job was selling computers in France and things went steadily downhill from there. He spent millons on behalf of a UK telephone company's procurement department and implemented direct marketing for a well-known Texan computer maker before joining the IT department of a company that builds bright red tractors and other seriously cool machines.

Paul then embraced his techie side (he was writing games in machine code from the age of 11) and started a consultancy that used IT to solve business problems for companies in the financial and public sectors in Ireland, UK , Belgium, and New Zealand. Eight years later, he now works with an Irish government agency that helps similar software companies to grow past their initial teething pains.

More formally, Paul has a bachelor's degree in Business and French from the University of Ulster, a master's degree in Advanced Software from UCD Dublin, a post-grad qualification in Procurement from the Chartered Institute of Procurement and Supply (UK), and will someday complete his ACCA financial exams.

Paul can be found on LinkedIn at `http://www.linkedin.com/in/paulbrowne`, and via the Red Piranha (Business knowledge) project at `http://code.google.com/p/red-piranha/`.

I would like to thank my parents for the gift of learning; my wife and family for the constant encouragement to write this book; the work colleagues that I've had the pleasure to learn from and all the people behind the Drools and other outstanding open software projects.

About the reviewer

Peter Johnson started his computer career in August of 1980, in Burroughs. He programmed mainframes in COBOL and Algol. He started working in Java in 1998, and was the lead designer on projects such as a JDBC driver for the DMSII (Unisys Data Management System II) database that runs on Unisys mainframes. For the past several years he has been the chief architect in a team that does performance analysis of Java applications on large-scale Intel-based machines (8 to 32 CPUs), and evaluates various open source software for enterprise readiness. In addition, Peter is a JBoss committer and is a co-author of the book *JBoss In Action*, published by Manning. Peter often speaks on Java performance and various open source topics at industry conferences such JBossWorld and the annual Computer Measurement Group International Conference.

Table of Contents

Preface

In business, a lot of actions are trigged by rules: "Order more ice cream when the stock is below 100 units and temperature is above 25° C", "Approve credit card application when the credit background check is OK, past relationship with the customer is profitable, and identity is confirmed", and so on. Traditional computer programming languages make it difficult to translate this "natural language" into a software program. But JBoss Rules (also known as Drools) enables anybody with basic IT skills and an understanding of the business to turn statements such as these into running computer code.

This book will teach you to specify business rules using JBoss Drools, and then put them into action in your business. You will be able to create rules that trigger actions and decisions, based on data that comes from a variety of sources and departments right across your business. Regardless of the size of your business, you can make your processes more effective and manageable by adopting JBoss Rules.

Banks use business rules to process your mortgage (home loan) application, and to manage the process through each step (initial indication of amount available, actual application, approval of the total according to strict rules regarding the amount of income, house value, previous repayment record, swapping title deeds, and so on).

Countries such as Australia apply business rules to visa applications (when you want to go and live there)—you get points for your age, whether you have a degree or masters, your occupation, any family members in the country, and a variety of other factors.

Supermarkets apply business rules to what stock they should have on their shelves and where—this depends upon analyzing factors such as how much shelf space there is, what location the supermarket is in, what people have bought the week before, the weather forecast for next week (for example, ice cream in hot weather), and what discounts the manufacturers are giving.

This book shows how you can use similar rules and processes in your business or organization. It begins with a detailed, clear explanation of business rules and how JBoss Rules supports them.

You will then see how to install and get to grips with the essential software required to use JBoss Rules. Once you have mastered the basic tools, you will learn how to build practical and effective of the business rule systems.

The book provides clear explanations of business rule jargon. You will learn how to work with Decision Tables, **Domain-Specific Languages (DSL)**s, the Guvnor and JBoss **Integrated Development Environment (IDE)**, workflow and much more.

By the end of the book you will know exactly how to harness the power of JBoss Rules in your business.

What this book covers

Chapter 1: This chapter gives you a good platform to understand business rules and JBoss rules. We look at the problems that you might have (and why you're probably reading this book). We look at what business rule engines are, and how they evaluate business rules that appear very simple and how they become powerful when multiple rules are combined.

Chapter 2: This chapter explains setting up Java, setting up **Business Rule Management System (BRMS)**/Guvnor running on the JBoss App Server, setting up Eclipse, and installing the Drools Plug-in. It also details the installation of the Drools examples for this book and the Maven to build them.

Chapter 3: Guvnor is the user-friendly web editor that's also powerful enough to test our rules as we write them. We take up an example to make things easier. Then we look at the various Guvnor screens, and see that it can not only write rules (using both guided and advanced editors), but that it can also organize rules and other assets in packages, and also allow us to test and deploy those packages. Finally, we write our very first business rule—the traditional 'Hello World' message announcing to everyone that we are now business rule authors.

Chapter 4: This chapter shows how to use the Guvnor rule editor to write some more sophisticated rules. It also shows how to get information in and out of our rules, and demonstrates how to create the fact model needed to do this. We import our new fact model into the Guvnor and then build a guided rule around it. Finally we test our rule as a way of making sure that it runs correctly.

Chapter 5: This chapter pushes the boundries of what we can do with the Guvnor rule editor, and then brings in the JBoss IDE as an even more powerful way of writing rules. We start by using variables in our rules example. Then we discuss rule attributes (such as salience) to stop our rules from making changes that cause them to fire again and again. After testing this successfully, we look at text-based rules, in both the Guvnor and the JBoss IDE, for running 'Hello World' in the new environment.

Chapter 6: This chapter looks again at the structure of a rule file. At the end of this chapter, we look at some more advanced rules that we can write and run in the IDE.

Chapter 7: This chapter explains how testing is not a standalone activity, but part of an ongoing cycle. In this chapter we see how to test our rules, not only in the Guvnor, but also using FIT for rule testing against requirements documents. This chapter also explains Unit Testing using JUnit.

Chapter 8: This chapter explains how to use Excel Spreadsheets (cells and ranges) as our fact model to hold information, instead of the write-your-own-JavaBean approach we took earlier. Then we use Excel spreadsheets to hold Decision tables, to make repetitive rules easier to write.

Chapter 9: This chapter aims to make our rules both easier to use, and more powerful. We start with DSLs—Domain-Specific Languages. This chapter follows on from the 'easy to write rules' theme from the previous chapter and also discusses both ruleflow and workflow.. It would be great to draw a workflow diagram to see/control what (groups of) rules should fire and when. Rule flow gives us this sort of control.

Chapter 10: This chapter shows you how to deploy your business rules into the real world. We look at the pieces that make up an entire web application, and where rules fit into it. We see the various options to deploy rules as part of our application, and the team involved in doing so. Once they are deployed, we look at the code that would load and run the rules—both home-grown and using the standard RuleAgent. Finally we see how to combine this into a web project using the framework of your choice.

Chapter 11: This chapter looks at what happens under the cover by opening up the internals of the Drools rule engine to understand concepts such as truth maintenance, conflict resolution, pattern matching, and the rules agenda. In this chapter, we explore the Rete algorithm and discuss why it makes rules run faster than most comparable business logic. Finally we see the working memory audit log and the rules debug capabilities of the Drools IDE.

Chapter 12: This chapter deals with the other advanced Drools features that have not yet been covered. This includes Smooks to bulk load data, Complex Event Processing, and Drools solver to provide solutions where traditional techniques would take too long.

What you need for this book

We need four pieces of software for this book. All of these are open source, can be downloaded easily from the Internet, and are available under a business-friendly license.

We need Java as this is the core computer language upon which all of the other tools are built. We need BRMS/Guvnor and JBoss App Server to provide a web-based rules editor aimed at business users. We also need to install Maven, a build tool that takes the various Java scripts (source) and transforms them into a package that we can deploy on a web server. We need Eclipse and the Drools plug-in to edit the Java files that we will use for transporting information around the system. We also need to download Drools examples for this book which are available at `http://code.google.com/p/red-piranha`.

Who this is book for

If you are a business analyst—somebody involved with enterprise IT at a high level, who understands problems and planning solutions, rather than coding in-depth implementations—then this book is for you.

If you are a business user who needs to write rules, or a technical person who needs to support rules, this book is for you.

If you are looking for an introduction to rule engine technology, this book will satisfy your needs.

If you are a business user and want to write rules using Guvnor or the JBoss IDE, this book will be suitable for you.

This book will also suit your need if you are a business user and who wants to understand what Drools can do and how it works, but would rather leave the implementation to a developer.

Conventions

In this book, you will find a number of styles of text that distinguish between different kinds of information. Here are some examples of these styles, and an explanation of their meaning.

Code words in text are shown as follows: "We'll see that one file contains two rules: `Hello World` and `GoodBye`."

A block of code will be set as follows:

```
public void setChocolateOnlyCustomer
(boolean choclateOnlyCustomer) {
this.chocolateOnlyCustomer = chocolateOnlyCustomer;
```

When we wish to draw your attention to a particular part of a code block, the relevant lines or items will be made bold:

```
for ( int i = 0; i < rules.length; i++ ) {
    String ruleFile = rules[i];
    log.info( "Loading file: " + ruleFile );
```

Any command-line input and output is written as follows:

```
cd C:\projects\drools-book-examples
```

New terms and **important words** are introduced in a bold-type font. Words that you see on the screen, in menus or dialog boxes for example, appear in our text like this: "When Eclipse opens (and you've selected the workspace), select **File | New Project** from the menu".

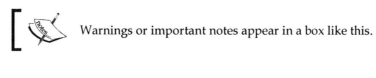

Warnings or important notes appear in a box like this.

Tips and tricks appear like this.

Reader Feedback

Feedback from our readers is always welcome. Let us know what you think about this book, what you liked or may have disliked. Reader feedback is important for us to develop titles that you really get the most out of.

To send us general feedback, simply drop an email to feedback@packtpub.com, making sure to mention the book title in the subject of your message.

If there is a book that you need and would like to see us publish, please send us a note in the **SUGGEST A TITLE** form on www.packtpub.com or email suggest@packtpub.com.

If there is a topic that you have expertise in and you are interested in either writing or contributing to a book, see our author guide on www.packtpub.com/authors.

Customer Support

Now that you are the proud owner of a Packt book, we have a number of things to help you to get the most from your purchase.

Errata

Although we have taken every care to ensure the accuracy of our contents, mistakes do happen. If you find a mistake in one of our books—maybe a mistake in text or code—we would be grateful if you would report this to us. By doing this you can save other readers from frustration, and help to improve subsequent versions of this book. If you find any errata, report them by visiting http://www.packtpub.com/support, selecting your book, clicking on the **let us know** link, and entering the details of your errata. Once your errata are verified, your submission will be accepted and the errata added to the list of existing errata. The existing errata can be viewed by selecting your title from http://www.packtpub.com/support.

Piracy

Piracy of copyright material on the Internet is an ongoing problem across all media. At Packt, we take the protection of our copyright and licenses very seriously. If you come across any illegal copies of our works in any form on the Internet, please provide the location address or website name immediately so we can pursue a remedy.

Please contact us at copyright@packtpub.com with a link to the suspected pirated material.

We appreciate your help in protecting our authors, and our ability to bring you valuable content.

Questions

You can contact us at questions@packtpub.com if you are having a problem with some aspect of the book, and we will do our best to address it.

1
Drooling over JBoss Rules

My grandfather was a docker in Belfast who loaded and unloaded ships. My father was an accountant who tracked and valued the items as they moved around the world. My job is to replace both of them with automated systems, and apply a complex set of business rules that determine what gets loaded first and how much it is worth. For items such as fresh produce, the answer is complex and often changes by the hour.

If you look at your family tree, you'll probably see a similar progression. We've gone from lifting bags of coal to being workers who move knowledge around. We may not have blisters on our hands, but we do get sore heads from the business (medical, legal, financial and similar) problems that we deal with.

How do we know if we're doing a good job? For our grandfather's generation, it was easy to see people and companies who moved the most 'stuff' around. For our generation things are different—We're moving knowledge that we can't see. We often need to apply unclear business rules to our job. To be successful we need to do our job quicker, faster, and better than anybody else.

JBoss Rules can help us become better and faster at managing our knowledge. To explain how, this chapter looks at:

- Who you are and what your problem is
- Life or death business rules
- Business rules in your organization
- Why existing solutions don't cut it
- How rule engines can come to the rescue
- An introduction to JBoss and JBoss Rules
- The bigger picture and parts of the solution
- How to write the rules
- When not to use a rule engine

Who are you? What's your problem?

If you are reading this, you probably know important information. You might be in the medical, legal, or accountancy professions. You may be the only person in the company who understands how to process refunds to tractor dealers in the Chicago area. You may be the most experienced underwriter in the mortgage application department. Or you may be the person who is most capable of talking to 'those guys in IT'. Perhaps you've taken part in one or more Business and IT projects, or maybe this is your first one.

Whoever you are, you've got a problem. Maybe your team is too busy for the workload it has, maybe you can't recruit enough people to work for you, or maybe you can get the people, but it takes too many resources to train them. Whatever the cause, there are not enough minds to go around, and costly or embarrassing mistakes happen as a result.

You've probably already joked about being able to clone your key people. Wouldn't it be great to leave your clone working at the desk while you get some time on the beach; or even just get to go home on time? Although JBoss Rules does not allow you to clone yourself, it does allow you to clone your mind that is, put your knowledge into a computer. Once in the computer, this knowledge can be copied, reviewed, and kept working even after you go home.

Your second thought after hearing the "put your knowledge into a computer" bit is probably, "If the computer knows what I know, will I be out of a job?". Maybe. Or more likely, you'll no longer do the routine 80% of your job that you hate—the rubbish that fills up your day. It means that you will spend more of your time doing the 20% that you enjoy, including talking to people, meeting customers, improving the process, planning your next golf (sorry, "business networking") trip, or whatever you find interesting.

This book is aimed at non-technical users, although it contains a lot of information for people who want to get under the covers of JBoss Rules. Don't worry even if the entire extent of your PC skills is limited to writing a couple of formulae in Excel. You're going to be OK.

Does this sound like where you work?

Everybody complains about his or her job from time to time. You probably have a mug saying "You don't have to be crazy to work here…but it helps". Just try out our 10-question pop quiz and see if it sounds somewhat like the place where you spend most of you working hours:

1. Is Bob, in the corner, the only person who knows how the system really works? Can the business scale only if we have an expert? Is critical knowledge lost when people like Bob leave?

2. If you're Bob (owning the knowledge), are you sick of people asking you stupid questions? Do you think: don't these people know that you've got a job to do?

3. Are your customers getting a different answer every time they call your company (and getting more than slightly irate about it)? Are you at risk of receiving a slap on the wrist (or worse, a fine) from a regulator or other standards body?

4. Do you find yourself working around, rather than with, your computer systems? Have you ever thought of pouring coffee into your computer keyboard in frustration? (Trust me, it doesn't help.)

5. Are things always done by the book, or is there a lot of informal knowledge that is just in people's heads?

6. Did you prepare for a quality (ISO 9001) audit and then leave the process documentation unused on a shelf? Is there anybody around who knows or wants to change this process? Is this the right balance between being too hard to change (and being stuck in a rut) and being too easy (resulting in chaos)? If a change is made, will people know about it and will they take any notice?

7. Does your business knowledge exist in some easily usable format? Is its format easy to update? Can everybody use it from one central location (so that copies are not 'out of sync')? Can you track changes made and roll them back if you get it wrong?

8. Do the right people (and only the right people) have access (both read and update) to this information? Does this access need to change depending on the context of what the user is doing at the time?

9. Do people in your organization work on projects? Do they come together to form goal-driven teams and then go back to their original jobs when the objectives have been achieved? Do you know how to document the outcome of these projects as rules so that they can be reused?

10. Are tasks carried out in isolation? How do we ensure that tasks and team members collaborate effectively? In the old days, everything was done in-house. Now the 'office as a factory' must also seamlessly interlink with other suppliers plugged in as part of the process.

If some of these problems seem familiar, then maybe, just maybe, business rules and JBoss Rules can help. But if you think you've got problems, consider the following example.

Life or death business rules

The health services in Bangladesh (like many elsewhere) can't get enough doctors. Training more doctors is not an answer. Those who do qualify tend to leave for higher rates of pay elsewhere. So, given the desperate need for trained medical staff in rural areas (for example, to curb child mortality rates), what are the health workers to do?

The more qualified a doctor is, the more likely he is to take a flight. The district hospital in Matlab, Bangladesh, boasts an operating table, lamp, oxygen cylinder, and anesthetic machine, all carrying the EU's gift tag. They gleam, partly because they are unused. Several surgeons and anesthetists have been trained, but none so far have been retained. "Other than holding a gun to their head, doctors do not stay here.", comments Shams Arifeen, a researcher in the **International Centre** for **Diarrhoeal Disease Research, Bangladesh (ICDDR, B)**. Doubling their pay is not the answer because they can earn five or ten times as much in private practice. Besides, specialists want to educate their children in the capital Dhaka, not in Bangladesh's backwaters.

What would you do?

Imagine that you were standing in that clinic without medical training, when a mother asks you to look at her sick child. What will you do? The solution that the Bangladesh health workers came up with was **IMCI** or **Integrated Management of Childhood Illness**. IMCI takes the knowledge in a doctor's head and writes it down as a set of rules that health workers can follow. When a sick child is brought into the remote clinic, the health worker is able to follow the simple step-by-step instructions to make quite a sophisticated diagnosis.

The following figure shows IMCI:

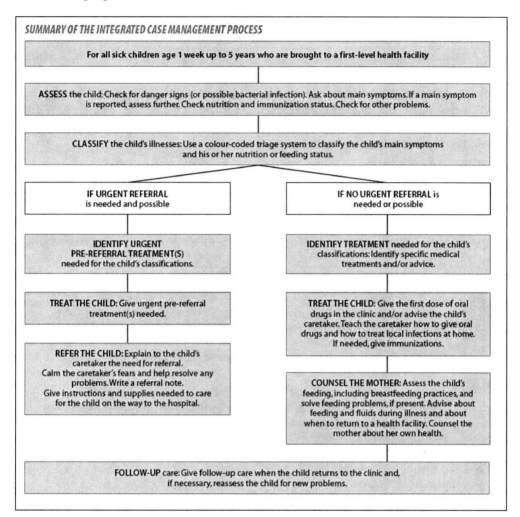

Look at the boxes in the above diagram—it's a set of medical rules.
(Source, World Health Organisation, `http://whqlibdoc.who.int/`
`publications/2005/9241546441.pdf`.) Using these rules a health care worker
can quickly come to the following conclusions:

- When the child is under two years of age, then refer to doctor immediately

- When the child's skin does not bounce back when pinched, then the child
  is dehydrated

- When the child is dehydrated then give rehydration salts

This is a real life example of business rules. Although it is paper-based and useful to the medical profession, it's a good example of business rules all the same.

- Rules are 'when something is present, then do this'. And not just single rules, but many of them. Together, loads of simple rules allow you to come up with quite a sophisticated diagnosis.

- Ruleflow and Workflow allow you to group your rules and decide which should fire first. If you're a health worker with a sick child, you want to do the most important checks first. Depending on the outcome, you then apply the next set of medical rules.

Everybody, including the doctors, is happy that his or her knowledge has been translated into rules. The doctors are happy because they can (guiltlessly) move to better-paying jobs. The medical workers using the system are happy because they can help the sick children that they see every day. The children gain because the better availability of medical knowledge is literally the difference between life and death.

> If you've used a computer language before, you might find the above example strange. 'Traditional' computer languages are more like a set of instructions: Do step 1, do step 2, repeat 5 times, and so on. Rules are different; they allow you to make many individual statements of what you know to be true and then let the computer decide if these rules apply (or not) to the current situation. This is similar to the way in which the human mind works.
>
> Look again at the example. We don't specify any order for our rules. All of them, one of them, or none of them might apply in a given situation. A child under two who was dehydrated potentially could be referred to a doctor and given rehydration salts on the way in. This could be the outcome we want, or we may wish to rewrite our rules to be more precise—but always in the "when (something is true) then (do this)" format.

For more information on this real life example, read *The Economist* magazine's online article at: `http://www.economist.com/research/articlesBySubject/PrinterFriendly.cfm?story_id=9440765`.

Business rules in your organization

You're going to be hearing a lot about 'business rules' over the next couple of pages, so it might be helpful to clarify what they are. We use the term 'business rule' to show that rules are non-technical. They could also be called 'medical rules', 'financial rules', 'insurance rules', 'benefit payment rules', and so forth. It all depends on the organization you work for, and the particular niche that it finds itself in.

A business rule is any bit of knowledge that can be expressed in the following format:

When 'something' is true, **Then** do 'this'.

Er, that's it. Nothing more complicated than that.

You do have knowledge like that in your organization, don't you? All companies and organizations have business rules, even if they are implied (that's, unwritten) or buried (as code) in existing systems (for example the ones with black screens and green text that you see in Hollywood movies).

Examples of these rules are:

- When a football team wins a game, jump up and down and shout loudly
- When a staff member gets promoted, give them a pay rise of 10%
- When a person's salary is less than 30,000 dollars, apply a tax rate of 20%
- When somebody leaves the office before 4 pm, make sarcastic comment about 'taking a half-day vacation'

> This book uses the "when...then" format for business rules. In practical terms, these are very similar to "if...then" statements you may have seen in any computer language.
>
> The key reason for using 'when' is to underline that business rules will 'fire' whenever the condition is true. Traditional 'if' statements will only fire if we happen to be at that step in the process at the time.

Business rules themselves tend to be simple. Their power comes from the fact that there are many of them (tens, hundreds, or even thousands). Just as you have many rules in your head (when you see a bear, run away), the trick is knowing when to apply them (what happens when you see a bear in the zoo?). Later we'll look at writing rules clearly and testing them to ensure that they do what you want.

Business rules should be written as clearly as possible (in English, or your human language of choice). While this makes your life easier when writing the rules, more importantly, it allows other people to review your rules in the future. Various estimates are that 95% of all work on a computer system is in this 'review and update' phase long after the original team has left. So clarity is one of the biggest advantages of using rule engines.

Exercise — rules in your organization

As a simple exercise, take 10 minutes to list some of the business rules in your organization. Don't worry if they are simple or difficult. Just write them out in the "when...then" format.

Here's one I did earlier.

The chocolate factory

The following figure shows sample business rules for a chocolate factory:

	A	B	C	D
1	**Department**	**Product / Area**	**Details**	**Take the following action**
2	Finance	Chocolate Crunchie	Sales more than 30,000 units	Order more chocolate
3	Finance	Chocolate Crunchie	Sales more than 30,000 units	Start planning new factory
4	Finance	Total Sales	Total Sales are less than $500,000	Ask the bank for some more money
5	Manufacturing	Mint Surprise	Sales more than 30,000 units	Order more mint essence
6	Manufacturing	Mint Surprise	Less than 100 boxes left in stock	make some more
7	Manufacturing	Chocolate Crunchie	Less than 100 boxes left in stock	make some more
8	Manufacturing	Chocolate Crunchie	Sales less than 1000 units	Give everybody an extra weeks vacation
9	Manufacturing	Chocolate Crunchie	Sales more than 30,000 units	Ask people to do overtime
10	Product Testing	Mint Surprise	Sales less than 1000 units	Come up with a new chocolate bar
11	Product Testing	Chocolate Crunchie	Sales more than 30,000 units	Get some more tasters in to help
12	Sales	Mint Surprise	Sales more than 30,000 units	Take clients on golf holiday
13	Shipping	Mint Surprise	Sales more than 30,000 units	Buy a new truck

Since I was a child, I've always wanted to work in a chocolate factory, and here's my chance. The figure shows the sample rules that I came up with. The first three columns are the 'when' part of our business rule or the Left-Hand Side (LHS). The last (fourth column) is the 'then' part, also known as the Right-Hand Side (RHS).

For example, the first record in the table says:

When the **Finance** department sees that we've sold more than **30,000 Chocolate Crunchie** bars, then they should **Order more chocolate**.

You'll notice that there are a couple of departments other than **Finance** (**Manufacturing, Product Testing, Sales,** and **Shipping**). Although I made these rules up, often the rules that get deployed are a combination of rules from various teams.

> When I'm reading books such as this, I wonder how I take this concept or theory and actually use these in a 'real system'. Well, I don't want to spoil the surprise, but the actual business rules we will be writing and deploying are very similar to the 'clear English' examples discussed earlier.
>
> There's a lot of clever stuff happening under the covers to keep our business rules simple, but that's how it should be ,with the machines, rather than people, doing the hardwork.

Build your own rule engine in Excel

You are probably wondering why some of the rules in the figure are highlighted. These are the rules that will 'fire' whenever we sell more than **30,000 Chocolate Crunchie** bars. You could imagine another set of rules highlighting whenever we have less than 100 boxes of **Mint Surprise** left in stock.

That's all a rule engine does. It selects the rules that are correct for the current situation and then carries out whatever they say. If you're good at Excel, you could probably mimic this behavior using auto filters or conditional formatting so that the colors would change automatically.

> Sometimes things can be as simple as they seem. If you're coming from a business department, it makes sense that all the rules should be applied, often all at once. Why shouldn't the manufacturing and finance people carry out their actions simultaneously?
>
> Technical people (like me, for the first couple of months) might miss this point. We're used to telling computers to do things one at a time and have to 'unlearn' our years of experience that says that computers must do things exactly one step at a time.
>
> We did say that this book is for everybody. Items like this just help level the playing field.

Speaking of technical people…

Why can't the tech guys write the rules for me?

If you're a good business manager, you've probably been taught to delegate. Until now, for anything technical (such as computer systems) you've probably been delegating to those 'techie guys'. So why don't the tech guys write the business rules for you?

The answer is that the tech guys can write the rules on your behalf, but it's a bit like booking a flight through a travel agent rather than over the Internet. Sometimes it's a much better idea to do it yourself.

- Have you ever turned up at the airport and found that the travel agent got it wrong? Doing it yourself means that there is one less link in the chain that can go wrong. Booking your own flight (and writing your own rules) is quicker and easier.

- Have you understood what all the hieroglyphic codes on the paper ticket meant? (I'm showing my age—most airlines phased out paper tickets years ago). The chances are that if you give a technical person the rules to write, he or she is probably going to do it in a computer language such as C#, Java, or VB. There is nothing wrong with that; it's just that they might as well write it in Egyptian hieroglyphics for all that you will able to understand it—there is no way you will be able to check if they got it right. Business rules solve this problem.

For simple flights (for example, Dublin-London return), booking online (that is, doing it yourself) is fine. For multi-stop round-the-world tickets, getting advice from a travel agent is often a good idea. Likewise for rules: write most of the simple ones yourself and then get some help with writing the complex ones.

Why existing solutions don't cut it

Computers have been around for a long time and we're not the first people to use them to solve these kinds of problems for business people. In general, these business systems do three things:

1. Capture information, for example, via a web interface (presentation layer).

2. Apply business knowledge to this information (business layer).

3. Store or forward this information (service or data layer).

It is the business layer that we are most concerned with. The presentation and service layers, while not trivial, are known problems that lend themselves to some degree of standardization. In contrast, the business layer will be unique to each organization, as it reflects the processes and knowledge of the organization.

In some ways, the business layer is the 'learned memory of the organization'. Despite (or perhaps because of) years of implementing **EIS** (**Executive Information Systems**), many of them suffer from the following problems:

- All three layers tend to be tightly interlinked, so it is not easy to extract the business logic and use it elsewhere.
- Business knowledge and rules are often hidden in code. This is difficult to audit and can lead to discrepancies between the documentation and the actual implementation.
- It is hard for the domain experts (the guys with the business knowledge) and the technical experts to collaborate as they (literally) speak different languages.
- The business layer can be difficult to update, both in implementation and for fear of undesirable side effects.

Although theory states that these functions should be separated, the fact that the business tier is often expressed in a programming language like Java means that other functions (for example, database access) often creep in over time. Even worse, there is no clearly delineated place to put the business logic, which is why it can become scattered throughout the system, making it hard to reuse.

Given that we've had these problems for many years, how can we do any better?

Rule engines to the rescue

A rule engine can solve these problems—at least to some extent. Instead of having technical, spaghetti code, it allows us to keep our business rules as simple as possible, just like the examples we saw earlier. A rule engine allows us to 'run' these business rules into the rest of our bigger computer system so that we can get our values from a web page, save the results into a database, or anything else we need to do with our information. At the same time, our business rules stay in a 'clear English' format so that we are able to review them later.

So, what is a **rule engine**? Very simply, it is a place in which we can evaluate our business rules. Without it, our rules would be stuck 'on paper' and we'd have no way of feeding them into our system.

Here are a couple of points that explain why rule engines are better than most computer systems:

- Rule engines allow you to say "what to do", not "how to do it". This means that you can focus on what you know to be true, and allow the machine do the heavy lifting of figuring out the consequences of all of these combined truths'.

- Logic and data separation: You probably already have a database to store information. It's a good place for data, but a bad home for your business rules. Having a rule engine gives your rules a natural home where you can manage your (entire) business knowledge properly.

- Speed and scalability: The way rule engines work (based on the Rete algorithm, if you're interested) has been mathematically proven to be faster and more scalable than most traditional handcoded 'if...then' solutions.

- Powerful tools: For developers, as well as for business analysts, tools provide easy ways to edit and manage rules. More importantly, they give immediate feedback—no more slogging through 10 web screens to reproduce a 'bug' in the business logic.

- Auditing: Rule systems provide an explanation facility allowing you to audit how and why a particular decision was made.

Other rules (Microsoft Outlook)

If you're a power user of Microsoft Outlook, then you probably have mail filters set up that say something like:

- **When** a mail comes in that looks like spam, **then** put it into the trash can
- **When** a mail comes in saying 'Jboss Rules', **then** put it in the folder marked 'rules'

The figure shows business rules hiding in your mailbox. In this figure can you recognize the 'when...then' format? You've already been using a rule engine without even knowing it! But the rule engine in Outlook is limited to email sorting and we need something more powerful to meet our business problem. Enter JBoss Rules.

Meet JBoss Rules

Your boss or somebody from the IT department or a consultant has mentioned Drools as part of the solution. After having a good laugh at the name (it's a long story) you want to find out more. We'll look at this in two parts—Who is JBoss, and what is the Drools/JBoss Rules team.

JBoss is a division of Red Hat (NYSE:RHT). This means that Drools is backed by an industry-leading company. The support from this company is available whenever you need it.

Even better, a key part of JBoss and Drools is open source. To put this in quality terms, both the JBoss and Drools teams are confident enough about their product to let you poke inside it. It's a bit like getting a tour of the Mercedes car factory.

Open source also shows the confidence that the team has in the quality of the product and of their support, If you don't think the support is good enough, you are free (and able!) to get third parties to do the job to your satisfaction. Because the bulk of how JBoss/Red Hat makes their money is service related, they're pretty confident that that option won't be needed.

You may be confused by the naming of the project. Is it **Drools** or **JBoss Rules**? Officially it is now the latter, although it started out as 'Drools' and the name is still in common usage. This book tends to use 'Drools' as it is shorter to type and read. Both terms refer to the same thing—the business rules product from Red Hat and JBoss.

Drools is an advanced rule engine (and a lot more besides, as we shall see later). It allows you to state things that you know to be correct (for example, if the expenses claim is above $5000, then a senior manager needs to sign it off). As somebody who has knowledge of business rules, you'll be able to feed the rule engine with what you know.

A bit more on open source

A few years ago, if you searched for the words 'open source business' on the internet, you would have found people describing it as a little bit 'hippy', or maybe old style communists resurfacing in another form. Those critics (including Microsoft—for example, `http://port25.technet.com/`) have now happily embraced open source as a part of their business model.

Imagine buying a car with the bonnet welded shut so that only the car's manufacturers could service it. Would you be happy with that? (Audi almost did this with their smaller A2 model). Most closed source traditional software are like that—you are at the mercy of the one supplier for bug fixes and improvements. What happens if that supplier goes bust?

Now, I know next to nothing about car engineering, but I still find it comforting that I could choose almost any mechanic to fix my car. Likewise, with open source software you're unlikely to change the software yourself, but it's comforting to know that you could hire somebody to do it for you if required.

All of JBoss Rules is available as open source under the Apache open source license. That's Apache, the web server that powers most of the web sites you read every day.

The Apache license is particularly business-friendly, and you can take the code and use it in pretty much any way you want, as long as you acknowledge that your product was 'built using Drools'. You don't have to publish your changes or additions (as another famous open source license, the GPL, requires you to do). Nor do you have to pay any license fee for using their product, even as part of a commercial deployment.

Of course, you'd want to confirm the exact details with your lawyer. But the chances are that he or she will tell you the same thing and charge you a lot more for doing so.

The next question is where do Red Hat and JBoss make their money if they're not selling a product? The answer is through a combination of training and consulting services, as well as selling cross-tested 'stable' versions guaranteed to work with most standard server configurations.

All of the software we use in the book is available for free from the JBoss community web sites. And it's also available as an enterprise product with full Red Hat support, if that's important to your organization.

The JBoss Rules community

As JBoss develops its rules' code 'in the open', it's easy to get in touch with the developers to get help.

Where to get help

Check around the sites listed as follows before firing off your 'please help me' email.

- The **Product home page** is the official home page, tailored more to a business audience. If you're trying to sell a Drools **BRMS (Business Rules Management System)** to your boss, this is the place to go.

  ```
  http://www.jboss.com/products/rules
  ```

- The **Community home page** is a slightly more detailed resource. This provides links to a lot of useful resources, including the Drools technical documentation. The information on this page tends to be more 'bleeding edge', including stuff that may not yet have made it into the official enterprise versions.

  ```
  http://www.jboss.org/drools/
  ```

- The **Wiki** is a much more rough-and-ready resource. It has guides of varying quality, dealing with specific issues (for example, deploying the rules engine on non-JBoss web/application servers). Wikis are writable as well as readable, so if you're doing something that doesn't appear to be documented here, think about adding it. The chances are that the solution is technical and generic enough to be sharable.

  ```
  http://wiki.jboss.org/wiki/JBossRules
  ```

- The **mailing lists** are where you can see previous questions asked by Drools users and developers. This is where you can ask for help. But read the next section on how to ask for help, or I can guarantee that your pleas for assistance will go unanswered.

  ```
  http://www.jboss.org/drools/lists.html
  ```

- The **Bugs and feature requests** page shows you what the Drools development team is currently working on. Yes, when we said the project was open, we meant it. You may get far too much information, but better that than too little. If you feel something is missing from the current version, checking here might show that it's on its way. And if you talk to the guys on the mailing lists (they really appreciate end-user feedback), you might be able to persuade them to add your feature here.

  ```
  http://jira.jboss.com/jira/browse/JBRULES
  ```

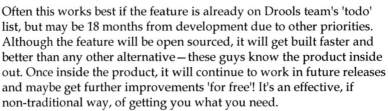

If there is a bug that you need fixing or feature that you need implementing as soon as possible, one way of getting it done quickly might be to offer to sponsor development. That is, pay for the JBoss Rules team to add it on your behalf.

Often this works best if the feature is already on Drools team's 'todo' list, but may be 18 months from development due to other priorities. Although the feature will be open sourced, it will get built faster and better than any other alternative—these guys know the product inside out. Once inside the product, it will continue to work in future releases and maybe get further improvements 'for free'! It's an effective, if non-traditional way, of getting you what you need.

How to ask for help

If you got locked out of your house, how would you ask your neighbor for help? Would you be arrogant, and demand the he/she helps you straight away (ignoring that he might be doing something important themselves), or would you ask nicely, explaining your problem, what you've done to try and sort it out, and then ask him or her if they can help you? Which approach is most likely to succeed?

Asking for help in an open source project is somewhat similar. Any open source team is busy—the core guys also have bosses and deadlines to meet. So if you've got a problem with Drools, you can increase the chances of getting help from the JBoss Rules guys by doing the following:

1. To start out, assume that the problem is due to a mistake that you've made. I'd consider myself experienced with computers, but you'd be amazed at some of the 'duh!' errors that I still make. Check spellings. Check the instructions. Check that you're connected to the network. Then check again.

2. Read the manual or search the Web. Then read it again. Unless you're pushing the boundaries of what Drools does, the chances are that somebody has seen this problem before. Google is great for this. Put in the error message that you're getting and you'll get back plenty suggestions of areas to investigate.

3. When you search the Web/mailing lists, look at problems that are similar but not exactly the same as your own. Often, the solution will be similar (if not exactly the same).

4. Ask a colleague for a sanity check, even if he or she may not be familiar with the product. Two pairs of eyes are better than one. Often, while you're walking through the sample, you'll see the basic mistake you've made.

Have you done all of this once, twice, thrice? Now you're ready to ask a question from the mailing lists. If your question is clear, has enough (relevant) detail, and you have put in lot of effort to solve the challenging problem yourself, the greater are your chances of getting a quick reply. Before you type your email, read the classic article *How To Ask Questions The Smart Way* at `http://catb.org/~esr/faqs/smart-questions.html`

This section might make the Drools team appear unfriendly, but they're not. They're very approachable and down-to-earth guys. You also have a direct line to them, unlike most commercial software projects. But, like all open source projects, they are asked a lot of lazy I-can't-be-bothered-to-read-the-manual type of questions. So spend an extra 10 minutes to compose your email and you'll be rewarded with support worth hundreds of dollars. If you want to know what really irks the Drools guys, read this blog post: `http://blog.athico.com/2007/11/drools-user-mailing-list-growth.html`.

After all that preparation, send your email to the user mailing list at `http://www.jboss.org/drools/lists.html`. Then wait. Do not re-send it. Remember that Drools is an open source project and you may never get your question answered, or get it answered only after a couple of days' delay. If you need guaranteed support, consider buying a subscription from Red Hat.

Don't be surprised that the answer, if and when you get one, is along the lines of 'have you considered trying X, Y, or Z?' Don't expect a complete solution, but just good suggestions as to areas that you can try to resolve the problem.

When you do find the solution, post the answer to the mailing lists. Keep it technical, with nothing confidential to your organization. Drools users who will follow in your footsteps will be eternally grateful. It will also earn you major kudos with the team, which will benefit you when you ask another question in the future.

The bigger picture

You're unlikely to go through the trouble of putting your knowledge into a rules system and leave it at that. You've a problem that you're trying to solve. For that, you're going to use rules as part of a bigger system.

Here's the five-minute guide to almost any computer system. It takes information from users (these days, mainly via a web page), does something with it, and then stores it somewhere (normally in a database). You may recognize some database brand names such as Oracle, SQL Server, or MySql. Think of the database as a very big version of Excel. Sometimes the flow of information goes the other way—access information in the database, and then show it on the web page. That's it! So what are you paying all these IT consultants for?

Drools helps you with the middle 'do something with the information' bit. Here you apply the business knowledge (the stuff that's currently in your head) to the information that is passing through.

We recommend Drools, as one of the other options is to put your brain into a glass jar (think of a mad scientist lab with rows of brains suspended in bubbling liquid) and somehow wire it in to the system. Drools is a much less painful option.

Members of your team

Unless you're a business user by day and techie by night, we don't expect you to build the entire web system by yourself. In general, as a business user, you'll supply two bits of information to the IT team. The rest should be considered 'plumbing'—stuff that should be done according to industry standards and best practices, but that otherwise will be hidden from you (the user) and should 'just work' (like water coming out of the tap).

The two sorts of information you'll generally need to provide are:

- The user's interactions with the completed system. For example, the web page that the user uses to log in, the first screen they see after they log in, and what the various buttons on this screen do. Entire books have been written on this subject and so we won't get into those details.

- The actual business rules. Unlike the screens, this is 'behind the scenes' stuff. This is your knowledge applied to the data that's being captured on the web pages. Even if you don't use Drools or any another rule engine, you'll still need to do this step. Otherwise, how will the system know to pay for prescriptions for Viagra,and not for aspirin? (or whatever your business rules actually are).

How do I write the rules

So, you want to get right in and start wiring up the rules. You've got four choices of editors for rule-writing:

- You can use the **Business Rules Management System (BRMS)** from Drools, which is called **Guvnor**. This is a web-based application that's aimed at people like you. Not only is it easy to use, but it can be set up once for the entire team to use via Internet Explorer, Firefox, or your favorite web browser. In general, this is the editor that we recommend, unless you need a feature that is only available in one of the other editors. The following screenshot gives an idea of what a business rule looks like in Guvnor— there is more information on this in Chapter 4.

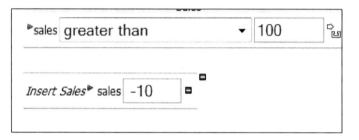

- You could write the rules via a simple text editor such as Notepad. This a bit masochistic and dull, staring at black and white text with no help as to what is expected. We mention it here only to show that there is nothing special about the rules format; it's just a plain text file.

- You can write rules in Microsoft Excel or any spreadsheet that can output Excel-like spreadsheets (for example, Sun's Open Office). You have to follow a certain template (it's not that difficult once you see it). The Excel format lends itself to rules that repeat themselves a lot (the sample Drools for Decision Tables has lots of different categories of car insurance claims).

- Use the Drools IDE, which is based on Eclipse. **IDE** stands for **Integrated Development Environment**, so Eclipse is a bit like 'Microsoft Office for Techies'. The chances are that your technical team is using it anyway (to write in a language called Java, although it can be used with other computer languages). The Drools IDE bit adds plug-ins to Eclipse to allow rule editing and debugging.

The IDE is more powerful, but also more complex. We'll talk about its extra features later, but most of the commonly used ones are already in the BRMS (and over time, the remainder will be implemented). It's possible to easily switch between IDE and BRMS.

Whichever way you choose, the rules that get fed into the rule engine are pretty much the same. In fact, the BRMS allows you to import and manage rules written as text/Decision Tables via the IDE. So, for now, following the BRMS is a good choice.

Introducing the BRMS (Guvnor)

The BRMS is a web page that you open in Internet Explorer, Firefox, or your favorite Internet browser. You've seen web pages before, right? The BRMS allows you to enter your knowledge as business rules via a web page.

> BRMS or Guvnor? The web-based rule editor that we will talk about in this section started out as the Business Rules Management System or BRMS. Unfortunately, other rule engine vendors use the term BRMS to refer to something completely different (not just the editor, but the core rule engine as well). Hence the renaming of the Drools BRMS to Guvnor, which also reflects that this web-based application can also be used to manage other things such as deployment, testing, and processes.

At the start you can enter rules via the guided editor (a similar idea to the helpful 'wizards' that you might have come across in Windows). Later, as you get more used to the rules syntax, you might want to edit the rules directly in the text editor.

There are a couple of other things that the BRMS gives you over and above basic 'rules editing', such as:

- Team editing
- Version management of rules and related assets
- Asset management
- A deployment mechanism
- Security (Login)
- Import and export of data

Parts of the solution

By now you should have understood the basic concept that a rule engine allows you to capture your knowledge and integrate it into an enterprise web system. However, a rule engine isn't just a black box. There are a couple of parts to it that are useful to know about. (I don't know much about car mechanics, but I can check the oil and tyre pressure. We'll keep the Drools technical bits at that level.)

Rules editor

This is the choice of BRMS, IDE, Decision Table, or plain text file. All produce a similar underlying rule language. The mechanism for deploying these rules (RuleAgent or some other equivalent) is similar.

Rules compiler

Something needs to translate the near-English rules language into something the rules engine can understand—this is what the compiler does. Your main awareness of the compiler (as a BRMS user) is when it complains that it does not understand the way that you are phrasing your rules.

Runtime

As the information flows through your system, something has to be applied to the (compiled) rules. This is where the Drools runtime comes in. In general, you don't worry about the technical aspects of this. You just care that there is something applying the business rules that you have written in the live/production system.

Fact model

So we have a working system with information flowing from the Web, modified by the rules, and then saved in the database. Obviously, when writing our rules, we need to know the form that this information will be in. (Will we ask the user for salary before or after tax? Will we ask the user what country he or she lives in or just the post/zip code?) The information has to be in a certain format. (Think of an Excel spreadsheet. We need to know which column the salary information is stored in, and if this is before or after tax.) The description of the information we need and the format it is stored in is known as the fact model.

Java

Rather than writing the fact model in Excel, it's mostly written in Java. Don't worry, at the level we're working (specifying the names of the information that we're collecting and if it's a number, piece of text, and so on), it's not that complicated. Remember that if you can handle Excel, you can do this. We've two approaches to building the fact model:

- For most of this guide, we'll assume that somebody else has done the analysis and that all the information you need when writing the rules will magically be there. Realistically, you're going to find things that are missing when you start writing your rules. The Drools technical guide has more information on how to build the fact model using Java.

- It's probably not beyond your ability to modify the fact model (just follow the recipe even if you don't fully understand the low-level details). The main reason you won't update it is that other parts of the system, such as the web screens and the database, also use the fact model as it's a key part of how the system is linked together. So, change a bit here without talking to the other guys and you risk breaking things for them.

An important note is that the BRMS helps you edit the rules, and typically does not form a part of the production system that the end users will see. That task is left to the core rules engine.

Rule repository

Rules are important and you're going to spend a substantial amount of time writing them. While you can store them on your PC's hard disk, can you guarantee that they're not going to get corrupted? If you store them on a shared network drive (with backups) how to you manage the different versions (for example, you want to see the business rules as of July 4th last year)? How do you allow collaborative editing and track changes made by different people?

A rule repository solves these problems for us. Luckily, there is one built into the BRMS/Guvnor. But we've a couple of other options (for example, Subversion) should be wish to tie into the rest of the system.

Rest of the system

Remember that a rule engine will not run in isolation, but be embedded in a wider system. What the 'rest of the system' will be will depend on your project, but the rules will pass data back and forward to it by means of the fact classes.

When not to use a rule engine

This may seem strange for a book about (JBoss) business rules, but there are times when you should not use a rule engine, even if it initially appears to be a good idea. A couple of things you should consider before using a rule engine, are:

- Don't use a rule engine if your application doesn't have much complexity. A lot of applications are just web pages that save information in a database. Even if there are a couple of checks for business logic, is there enough to justify the complexity of a rule engine? However, applications tend to increase in complexity over time. So keep this in mind when you're making your decision.

- Don't use a rule engine for the first time on a project that has strict deadlines or is high-profile. Like all new technologies (to your organization), either prototype the solution or gain the skills on a smaller project first.

- Don't use a rule engine when it's the wrong technology. What you may be looking for is workflow, or doing things in a strict sequence. Or you may just need a web page management solution such as Spring Webflow.

There are many places where you can use a rule engine. This is especially true when:

- The business logic changes often

- There are people who understand the business problem in great detail, but may not have the technical IT skills

- The problem may be too fiddly or complex for other solutions

- You need an agile solution—rule engines allow you to easily change the business logic in an iterative manner

Summary

This chapter has given us a good platform for understanding business rules and JBoss Rules. We saw the problems that you might have. We looked at what business rule engines are, and how they can evaluate business rules that appear very simple, yet when multiple rules are combined are extremely powerful.

In the next chapter, we'll use this platform to dive into hands-on business rules. We'll start with learning more about the Business Rules Management System (Guvnor).

2
Getting the software

The previous chapter showed you all of the wonderful things that we can do with Drools. But we will not get very far if we don't install the software first. So, in this chapter we will see how to install the software.

What are we going to install?

We will be installing four pieces of software. All of these are open source (that is, free), can be downloaded easily from the Internet, and are available under a business-friendly license.

- Java: This is the core computer language upon which all of the other tools are built.

- BRMS/Guvnor and JBoss App Server: This is a web-based rules editor aimed at business users. We install JBoss App Server as the easiest place to run this editor.

- Maven, a build tool that takes the various Java scripts (source) and transforms them into a package that we can deploy on a web server. Using Maven makes our examples easier to understand, as Maven automatically downloads all the other software required.

- Eclipse and the Drools plug-in: Eclipse allows us to edit the Java files that we will use for transporting information around the system. The Drools plug-in gives us a more technical editor for rules, and the ability to see what is going on inside the rules engine.

- Drools examples for this book— hands-on samples so that you get to know Drools inside out.

Who should install it?

Broadly speaking, there are two types of people reading this book.

- Technical people, who are already familiar with Java, but who want to understand business rule technology
- Business people who have the domain knowledge, but to whom the technology (and Java) may be new territory

Although the setup guide here is suitable for both groups, don't be afraid to ask for help. The reason why all of the setup instructions are here in one place is that you can ask your nice, friendly, technical support person to 'set up everything in Chapter 2', and then return to Chapter 3 knowing that everything is in place. Indeed, many companies have their desktops locked so that regardless of your knowledge, you're going to have to request this technical assistance.

Why are the instructions in this guide only for Windows? What about the Mac and Linux users?

As a complement to the Linux users, we'll assume that you know enough about a computer to translate the instructions for your platform. Mac users are in a trickier position. I am sorry that we had to concentrate on the most popular platform. The software here will work on the Mac (it is Java, after all), but you may need to follow up the links at the end of the chapter to get Mac-specific instructions.

If you're technically adept, allow about one to two hours to install all of the software, assuming you have a fast Internet connection so that you're not waiting too long for downloads. Many of these instructions may be obvious (or you've done them before). So feel free to plough on, but quickly check through to ensure that you've got things set up correctly.

Installing Java

Java is the computer language in which Drools and all other products used in this book are written. So it's pretty important that we install it. Fortunately, it's an open source product from Sun that will run on almost every computer platform.

It's important to note that there are different versions of Java, such as:

- The **JRE (Java Runtime Engine)** is intended for end users. The **JDK (Java Development Kit)** contains this runtime, plus tools for the people developing using Java (that's us!).

- **Standard Edition (SE)** is what we'll be using. There is also an **Enterprise Edition (EE)** that takes the SE and adds a few more powerful services. While it is likely that your business rules will be deployed in an enterprise system, the SE is enough for the topics that we will cover in this book.

- Some versions of Java come bundled with the Netbeans IDE (a Java editor). This is optional, as we use the Eclipse Java editor instead (because we can get a Drools plug-ins for Eclipse, but not Netbeans).

When downloading Java, remember that the version we use is the JDK (developers' edition) of Java SE. To start, go to the web site `http://java.sun.com/javase/downloads/index.jsp`.

Download the latest version (at least 6 or 6.1) of Java, selecting the correct language and operating system for your computer. On the next screen, select the download method that you want to use. If you're not sure, click the link **Windows Offline Installation** and save the file in a place that you'll remember.

Once the download is complete, open this file. Click on **Run**, and then **Accept** the license agreement, (but only if you don't intend to export it to North Korea, as per the licence!). Unless you've specific reasons for doing otherwise, accept the defaults of features and location by clicking **Next**. But be sure to make a note of the **Install to** folder first (for example **C:\Program Files\Java\jre1.6.0_06**).

The install should chug away for a couple of minutes. You'll also be asked to install the runtime. Again, unless you've any specific reasons for doing otherwise, accept the default features and locations by clicking **Next**.

Let the install chug away for another couple of minutes. Amuse yourself by looking at the advertisement for OpenOffice that appears. (By the way, OO is a very good, and free, replacement for Microsoft Word, and is being used to write this book. So if you have (ahem) a less-than-legal copy of Word, consider using OpenOffice as a 'drop in' replacement/upgrade available from www.OpenOffice.org.)

After another couple of minutes, you should see the 'Install complete' screen. Click on **Finish**.

The installer may open a web browser asking you to register. This is an optional step. Feel free to provide your personal details to Sun if you wish. It's a reputable company, but I prefer to keep my private details, well, private.

Congratulations, you now have the Java development tools installed!

Installing JBoss

The BRMS/Guvnor is a web-based business rules editor. So we need a web server to install it on. If you don't happen to have a web server that can run Java to hand (although many companies do), then it's easy enough to install one. We're using JBoss App server as it has the fewest steps to get the BRMS up and running.

 Even though we're installing JBoss here, it is possible to run the BRMS/ Guvnor on other Java-based App/Web servers such as Websphere, Weblogic, Tomcat, or Oracle Application server. See the wiki on www. jboss.org/drools for more details.

Before we start the process, we need to tell JBoss where to find the version of Java that we just installed. We do that by carrying out the following steps:

1. First, right-click on the **My Computer** icon on your computer desktop.

2. Then, from the pop-up menu, select **Properties,** and the following screen should appear. (A quicker way to carry out these two steps is to press the *Windows + Pause* keys at the same time.)

```
┌────────────────────────────────────────────────────────────┐
│ System Properties                                      ? X   │
├────────────────────────────────────────────────────────────┤
│   │ System Restore │ Automatic Updates │   Remote    │       │
│   │ General │ Computer Name │ Hardware │   Advanced   │      │
│                                                              │
│   You must be logged on as an Administrator to make most     │
│   of these changes.                                          │
│   ┌─ Performance ────────────────────────────────────────┐   │
│   │ Visual effects, processor scheduling, memory usage,  │   │
│   │ and virtual memory                                   │   │
│   │                                        ┌──────────┐  │   │
│   │                                        │ Settings │  │   │
│   │                                        └──────────┘  │   │
│   └──────────────────────────────────────────────────────┘   │
│   ┌─ User Profiles ──────────────────────────────────────┐   │
│   │ Desktop settings related to your logon               │   │
│   │                                        ┌──────────┐  │   │
│   │                                        │ Settings │  │   │
│   │                                        └──────────┘  │   │
│   └──────────────────────────────────────────────────────┘   │
│   ┌─ Startup and Recovery ───────────────────────────────┐   │
│   │ System startup, system failure, and debugging        │   │
│   │ information                                          │   │
│   │                                        ┌──────────┐  │   │
│   │                                        │ Settings │  │   │
│   │                                        └──────────┘  │   │
│   └──────────────────────────────────────────────────────┘   │
│        ┌──────────────────────┐  ┌──────────────────┐        │
│        │ Environment Variables │  │ Error Reporting  │        │
│        └──────────────────────┘  └──────────────────┘        │
│            ┌──────┐  ┌────────┐  ┌───────┐                    │
│            │  OK  │  │ Cancel │  │ Apply │                    │
│            └──────┘  └────────┘  └───────┘                    │
└────────────────────────────────────────────────────────────┘
```

3. Click on the **Advanced** tab in the window that appears.

4. Then click on the **Environment Variables** button.

```
┌─────────────────────────────────────────────────────┐
│ Environment Variables                          ? │ × │
├─────────────────────────────────────────────────────┤
│ ┌─User variables for Paul─────────────────────────┐  │
│ │  Variable        Value                          │  │
│ │  TEMP            C:\Documents and Settings\Paul\Local S...│
│ │  TMP             C:\Documents and Settings\Paul\Local S...│
│ │                                                 │  │
│ │          [  New  ]  [  Edit  ]  [ Delete ]      │  │
│ └─────────────────────────────────────────────────┘  │
│ ┌─System variables────────────────────────────────┐  │
│ │  Variable        Value                       ▲  │  │
│ │  CLASSPATH       .;C:\Program Files\Java\jre1.5.0_10\lib...│
│ │  ComSpec         C:\WINDOWS\system32\cmd.exe    │  │
│ │  FP_NO_HOST_C... NO                             │  │
│ │  NUMBER_OF_P...  2                              │  │
│ │  OS              Windows_NT                  ▼  │  │
│ │          [  New  ]  [  Edit  ]  [ Delete ]      │  │
│ └─────────────────────────────────────────────────┘  │
│                           [  OK  ]   [ Cancel ]       │
└─────────────────────────────────────────────────────┘
```

5. Click on the **New** button in this window. In the **New User Variable** window, enter the variable name **JAVA_HOME** and the location at which you installed Java on the previous step. On my machine this is **C:\Program Files\Java\jdk1.6.0_06**, but it may be different on yours.

```
┌─────────────────────────────────────────────────────┐
│ New User Variable                              ? │ × │
├─────────────────────────────────────────────────────┤
│  Variable name:    JAVA_HOME                         │
│                                                      │
│  Variable value:   C:\Program Files\Java\jdk1.6.0_06 │
│                                                      │
│                        [  OK  ]   [ Cancel ]         │
└─────────────────────────────────────────────────────┘
```

6. Click on **OK** (multiple times) to close the windows that have been opened during the preceding steps.

Actual install

Now you're ready to download JBoss from `http://www.jboss.org/jbossas/downloads/`. Click on the download link on this page (take the latest stable version). At the time of writing it's 4.2.2.GA, although 5 should be stable by the time you read this. You'll be taken to the SourceForge download page. Select the filename ending in `.zip` (and no other letters). Your download should begin. Save this file in a place that you'll remember.

 At the time of writing, there is an issue between JBoss 5 and the (in progress) Guvnor. While this is likely to be resolved by the time you read this, if you do encounter any problems (Error setting attribute SecurityManagement) please try the 4.2.3 version

When the download has finished, unzip (that is, extract) the files to a folder of your choice. By default, I use `c:\software\JBoss`. It might be helpful to follow this convention on your machine so that all path names given in the book will be exactly that same as on your PC.

If you don't already have a ZIP program (such as WinZip) installed on your machine (that is, if you double-click on the ZIP file and nothing happens, or Windows asks you which program you want to use), then install a ZIP utility. (There are several. I tend to use the open source 7-zip utility, which is available from `http://www.7-zip.org/`.)

That's it! We now have the JBoss App Server installed (which was painless!). Now, to run it, open the folder we just created (using Windows Explorer). Double-click on the bin folder and you'll see a set of files. To start JBoss, click on `run.bat`.

After a couple of seconds, you'll see a new window with white text on a black background. Look for the words **Starting Jboss (Microcontainer)**, which indicate that JBoss has found Java on your machine.

You may get a security question from Windows (or whichever firewall software that you use). This is normal, so click on **OK** or **Unblock**.

After a few seconds churn away, the text whizzing past should stop and you should get a message that JBoss has started successfully (this message has been highlighted for emphasis in the following screenshot).

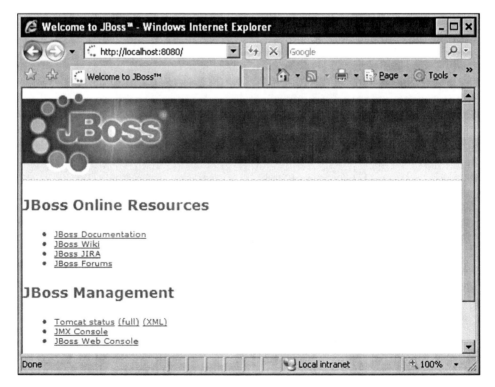

As a final step to confirm that everything is working OK, open the following address in your web browser:

```
http://localhost:8080
```

Congratulations, you now have the JBoss Web/App Server running on your PC!

Installing the BRMS/Guvnor

Open `http://www.jboss.org/drools/downloads.html` in your web browser and look for the 'Drools BRMS' download section). This may have been renamed to Guvnor/version 5 by the time that you read this. In general, take the latest available version.

Download this file to a place that you will remember. Once the download has completed, extract (unzip) these files to a temporary folder—it should contain at least one file, with the name `drools-jbrms.war` or `guvnor.war`.

Copy this `.war` file to the JBoss deploy directory. If you followed the same directory name as I did when installing JBoss, this should be `C:\software\jboss\jboss-5.0.0.Beta4\server\default\deploy` (that is, [wherever-you-installed-jboss]\server\default\deploy).

Make sure that JBoss is running. (If it isn't, start it as per the previous step by clicking on `run.bat`.)

You should see the following line (highlighted) appear in the console telling you that the application has been successfully deployed.

```
Select C:\WINDOWS\system32\cmd.exe                               _ □ ×
11:32:04,578 INFO  [testDurableTopic] Bound to JNDI name: topic/testDurableTopic
11:32:04,578 INFO  [testQueue] Bound to JNDI name: queue/testQueue
11:32:04,609 INFO  [UILServerILService] JBossMQ UIL service available at : /127.
0.0.1:8093
11:32:04,640 INFO  [DLQ] Bound to JNDI name: queue/DLQ
11:32:04,796 INFO  [ConnectionFactoryBindingService] Bound ConnectionManager 'jb
oss.jca:service=ConnectionFactoryBinding,name=JmsXA' to JNDI name 'java:JmsXA'
11:32:24,765 INFO  [TomcatDeployer] deploy, ctxPath=/drools-jbrms, warUrl=.../tm
p/deploy/tmp36355drools-jbrms-exp.war/
```

To check this, open Internet Explorer (or your browser of choice) and go to the web page `http://localhost:8080/drools-jbrms/`.

 This web link will change depending on the name of the war file you copied. If the name changes to `guvnor.war`, then the web page that you need is `http://localhost:8080/guvnor/`.

After a couple of seconds you should see more activity in the console (make sure that you have no text highlighted there, as this will block JBoss). Eventually, you should see the **BRMS login** screen in the browser, which look somewhat similar to the following screenshot:

```
JBoss Guvnor - Microsoft Internet Explorer

File   Edit   View   Favorites   Tools   Help

Back  ·           Search   Favorites

Address   http://localhost:8080/drools-jbrms/org.drools.brms.JBRMS/JBRMS.html      Go

BRMS login                                                          [x]

BRMS login

User name:

Password:

OK

Local intranet
```

Congratulations, you now have the BRMS/Guvnor successfully installed! If you're tempted, just click on **OK** (using a blank **User name** and **Password**) to log in and have a look around.

> By default, BRMS/Guvnor doesn't have security enabled. However, it's easy to switch it on and use the same password security that you use to log into Windows (via LDAP). See the Drools documentation for more details.

Installing Eclipse

We use Eclipse to edit the Java files that transport data to and from Drools. It's also the basis for the Drools plug-ins, including the advanced rule editor. To get started, download Eclipse from http://www.eclipse.org/downloads/. The version that we want is the Eclipse IDE for Java EE developers, as this version pre-packages a lot of additional tools and features.

On the following screen, select your nearest mirror, and the Eclipse download should start. Save the downloaded file in a place that you will remember (probably the same place where you downloaded Java and JBoss). When the download is complete, unzip the file to a folder of your choice. (I use `c:\software\eclipse`.)

Opening this folder in Eclipse shows a set of files including `eclipse.exe`. This is the Eclipse IDE file. Congratulations, you now have Eclipse installed! (This was too easy.)

Clicking on the `eclipse.exe` starts Eclipse. You should see the splash screen, and then a request for where Eclipse should save its internal files. Normally I just accept the default, making sure that the checkbox is selected (on the bottom left) so that I am not asked the question again.

After that, a 'quick start screen' will appear with several useful links (feel free to click around). When you are ready to go to the workbench, click on the curved arrow icon on the far right of the screen.

A blank Eclipse workspace should be displayed, as shown in the following screenshot:

That's it. Not only have you installed Eclipse, but you have it up and running.

Installing the Drools plug-in

Eclipse is not just a Java editor, but also a platform. This means that we can extend it with any tool that we require. In this case, we're going to add the Drools plug-ins, making it easier to edit and debug business rules.

The easiest way to install a plug-in is via the Eclipse update manager. This can find plug-ins on the Internet and then download them, so it will need to know your connection details. If you have a direct connection to the Internet (dial-up or broadband) you won't need to change these.

However, in most corporate situations you will need to tweak the Eclipse settings. The good news is that the Internet connection details you need will probably be exactly the same as the connection details in Internet Explorer (and other web browsers).

To find your Internet connection details, open Internet Explorer. From the toolbar at the top of the screen, select menu option **Tools | Internet Options**. In the dialog box that appears, click on the **Connections** tab and then on the **LAN Settings**. Make a note of the details that appear in the pop-up box.

To copy these settings to Eclipse, open the Eclipse IDE. From the Eclipse toolbar (which is at the top of the screen), select menu option **Preferences | General | Network Connections**. You should see a window similar to the following, in which you can enter in your connection details:

If you are unsure of what to enter here (or if you need to change anything in the first place) ask your colleagues — the answer will vary from organization to organization.

Finding the plug-in

To find out the latest Drools Eclipse update site, open Internet Explorer and go to `http://www.jboss.org/drools/downloads.html`. Look for the text 'Eclipse Workbench update site' — the update site link will be shown next to this. You'll probably want the most recent version (unless you specifically downloaded an older version of Eclipse).

Right-click on the **Update** site link and go **Copy shortcut** — the text will be similar to `http://downloads.jboss.com/drools/updatesite3.3/`. We'll need this address in a minute.

Back in Eclipse, open the update site wizard from the main Eclipse toolbar (via menu option **Help | Software Updates | Find | Install**). On the screen that appears, select **Search for new features to install,** and then click on **Next**. Now we're shown a list of already-installed features. As we want to add a new one, we click on **New Remote Site**.

In the pop up dialog box, give the new remote site a name (for example `drools-ide`), and the URL of the update site that we searched for and copied earlier.

New Update Site

Name: drools-ide

URL: http://downloads.jboss.com/drools/updatesite3.3/

OK   Cancel

Click on **OK** to return to the previous **Update Sites** dialog box (the **New Update Site** should now have been added to the list, with a tick mark against it) and then click on **Finish**. Eclipse should then contact the update site to see which (new) plug-ins are available. A new screen will appear showing the plug-ins that Eclipse has found. Make sure that the checkbox next to the Drools IDE is selected, and then click on **Next**.

On the next screen, accept the terms in the license agreement (by selecting the checkbox), and then click on **Next**.

Unless you've any particular reason for doing otherwise, accept the default install directory and click on **Finish**. Eclipse should now take several minutes to download the Drools IDE software. After all of the features have been downloaded, you'll get a message displaying the jars that have not been digitally signed. This is OK (most Eclipse plug-ins don't have signatures). Click on **Install All** to proceed with the installation.

Verification

Feature Verification

⚠ Warning: You are about to install an unsigned feature.
You may choose to install the feature or cancel its installation.

This feature has not been digitally signed.
The provider of this feature cannot be verified.

Feature name: **JBoss Drools Workbench**

Feature Identifier: **org.drools.eclipse.feature_4.0.7**

File Identifier: **org.drools.eclipse.feature_4.0.7**

Install   Install All   Cancel

Everything going well, you should (after a moment or two) get the **Restart Eclipse** message. Click on **Yes** to complete the installation. You'll know that the install of the Drools tools went smoothly if you can see the Drools icon toolbar as part of your Eclipse screen when Eclipse re-opens.

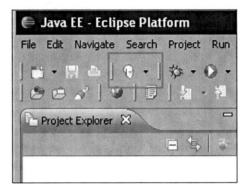

Congratulations, you now have the Drools IDE running on your PC!

Installing Maven

Maven is a Java Build system from Apache (the same people who built the popular web server). It takes Java source files and converts them into a format that we actually deploy and use. We use Maven for two things: to build our samples (makes the samples much easier to download and use), and later to build some of our own Java code. More Maven documentation is available from the Maven site at `http://maven.apache.org/`.

To get Maven, download it from `http://maven.apache.org/download.html`. Select the ZIP file (all versions are the same, but compacted for download in different ways). It's normally best to take the latest stable version. You'll then be asked to select a mirror. Pick the one nearest to you; it should normally be OK.

Save the file to an easily-remembered place, and then unzip the file to a folder of your choice. Following the same convention as before, I use a folder such as `C:\software\maven\`.

Open the folder that you just created in Windows Explorer, and there should be one more folder inside it (named **apache-maven-x.x-.x**). Copy the folder name in the address bar. In this case it's `C:\software\maven\apache-maven-2.0.9`, but it is likely to be different on your computer. We'll use this address to tell Maven which directory it is located in.

> If you can't see the address bar, select menu option View | Toolbars | Address Bar from the very top of the screen in Windows Explorer.

Open the environment variables as we did for setting the **JAVA_HOME** earlier (right-click on **My Computer** and go to **Properties | Advanced | Environment variables**). This time, click on the **New** button on the screen to create a new environment variable.

New User Variable ? X

Variable name: | M2_HOME
Variable value: | C:\software\maven\apache-maven-2.0.9

OK | Cancel

Add an entry for **Variable name (M2_HOME)**, and a **variable value** of the folder (for example, **C:\software\maven\apache-maven-2.0.9** that we copied earlier. This value could be different on your machine; make sure that you use the correct path!). Make sure there is no trailing '\' character.

Click **OK**, and then highlight the **Path** entry in the **Environment Variables** dialog box (this is the dialog box that you returned to when you clicked **OK**). Now click on **Edit**, as shown in the following screenshot:

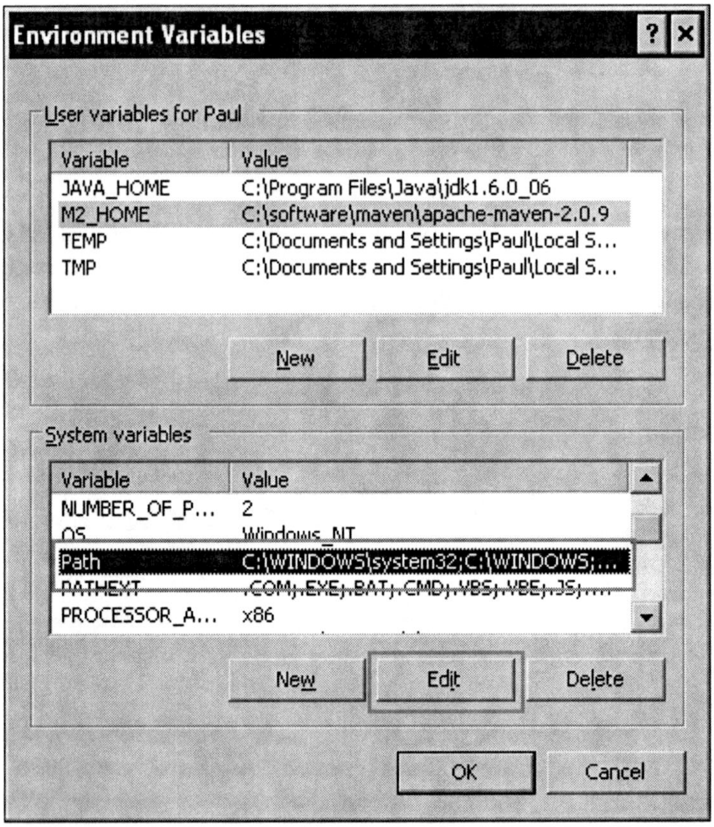

Add the value to end of the variable value as shown. This tells Windows where to find Maven, no matter where we try to start it from.

;%M2_HOME%\bin

> Warning! Paths can be temperamental at times, so play around with this setting a bit if you have any problems with installing Maven..

Edit System Variable ? ✕

Variable name: Path

Variable value: QuickTime\QTSystem\" %M2_HOME%\bin

OK   Cancel

Click on **OK** a number of times to close all of the open dialog boxes.

Now, to check that we have installed Maven correctly, open a command window (you may remember this as being called the DOS prompt). We'll be doing it a couple of times, so it's worth remembering how to do it.

1. In Windows, press *Windows* + *R* and a dialog box similar to one shown below should appear. (The windows key is the one with the windows logo on it, often found on the bottom left of your keyboard next to the *Alt* key.

2. In this box, type **cmd** then click **OK.**

Run ? ✕

Type the name of a program, folder, document, or Internet resource, and Windows will open it for you.

Open: cmd

OK   Cancel   Browse...

3. This will open a command window with white text on a black background. If you're older than 30, you might remember all computers as looking like this!

Another way to open a command window is to find it from the Windows start menu. This will vary depending on your version of Windows, but in Windows XP, it is found under, **Start | All Programs | Accessories | Command Prompt**. Just look for the following icon on the menu.

 Command Prompt

4. In the command window, type:

```
mvn -version
```

5. Then press *Enter*. If your Maven installation has been successful you should see something like the following screenshot:

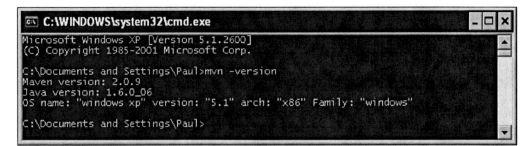

If you need to change the details of your Internet connection in Eclipse, then you will need to do something similar for Maven too. This allows Maven to automatically find and download all the libraries required. The details of your Internet connection will be same as the ones we used before. To pass these details to Maven, carry out the following steps:

1. Find the Maven configuration file (which is named `settings.xml`) and open it in an editor such as Microsoft Notepad.

2. Find the section beginning with `<proxies>` and edit it so that it is similar to the following example. Of course, the values will be different for your system.

```
<proxies>
  <proxy>
    <id>optional</id>
    <active>true</active>
    <protocol>http</protocol>
    <username>user-name-if-required-or-delete-line</username>
    <password>password-if-required-or-delete-line</password>
    <host>url-of-proxy-host</host>
    <port>80</port>
  </proxy>
</proxies>
```

Note that we've removed the lines beginning with `<!--` , |, and `-->` as these are comments. We've also deleted the line beginning with `<nonProxyHost>`. For more information on configuring proxies in Maven, refer to the guide found at `http://maven.apache.org/guides/mini/guide-proxies.html`.

Installing sample projects for this book

All of the samples in this book follow the same format. So, a good time to download one of the samples is when you have technical people around. Our first downloadable example is from Chapter 6, which can be downloaded from the sample site at `http://code.google.com/p/red-piranha/`. Unzip the file to `c:\projects\drools-book-examples`. Open a command window (using the *Windows +R* key as we used earlier). Move to the directory that we just created by typing the following line:

`cd C:\projects\drools-book-examples`

Now we can use Maven to build the samples project by typing the following command and pressing the *Enter* key:

`mvn clean package`

Maven will automatically download all of the required software and libraries. This can take a couple of minutes. If the download is successful, you should see output similar to the following:

```
C:\WINDOWS\system32\cmd.exe                                      _ □ ×
[INFO] [source:jar {execution: default}]
[INFO] Building jar: C:\projects\drools-book-examples\target\rules-poc-4.0.7-sou
rces.jar
[INFO] Preparing source:test-jar
[WARNING] Removing: jar from forked lifecycle, to prevent recursive invocation.
[WARNING] Removing: test-jar from forked lifecycle, to prevent recursive invocat
ion.
[INFO] No goals needed for project - skipping
[INFO] [source:test-jar {execution: default}]
[INFO] Building jar: C:\projects\drools-book-examples\target\rules-poc-4.0.7-tes
t-sources.jar
[INFO] [jar:test-jar {execution: default}]
[WARNING] JAR will be empty - no content was marked for inclusion!
[INFO] Building jar: C:\projects\drools-book-examples\target\rules-poc-4.0.7-tes
ts.jar
[INFO] ------------------------------------------------------------------------
[INFO] BUILD SUCCESSFUL
[INFO] ------------------------------------------------------------------------
[INFO] Total time: 21 seconds
[INFO] Finished at: Tue Jun 17 08:09:10 BST 2008
[INFO] Final Memory: 8M/254M
[INFO] ------------------------------------------------------------------------
C:\projects\drools-book-examples>_
```

Congratulations! You have now successfully downloaded the samples for this book, and all of the required software. Now we're going to set up the samples in Eclipse to make it easier to look around them.

Setting up the sample project in Eclipse

Maven can automatically set up the Eclipse project for us. In the same command window as the one shown earlier, type the command:

```
mvn eclipse:clean eclipse:eclipse
```

This is much quicker and should only take a couple of seconds to run.

Now open Eclipse (using the previous steps, double-click on `eclipse.exe`). When Eclipse opens (and you've selected the workspace), select **File | New Project** from the menu (on the top left) and the following dialog box will appear:

Select **Java Project** under the **Java** folder, and then click on **Next**. In the dialog box that appears next:

- Give the project a name (I've used **drools-book-examples**, as I find it easier to keep the project name the same as the folder name)
- Uncheck the **use default location** checkbox

- For the location, enter the folder to which we unzipped the sample files (for example, **C:\projects\drools-book-examples**)
- Leave all of the other values as they are
- Click on **Next**

Eclipse will find the project files that Maven created for us at this location, so all our libraries and source paths are already set up for us on the next screen.

We can safely click on **Finish**. Eclipse will ask if you wish to switch to the Java Perspective. Click on **Yes**.

If you see a screen without a red cross next to the project name (unlike the following screenshot) then rejoice, as this means that the samples for this book are set up successfully and you're ready to go to Chapter 3.

Getting Maven and Eclipse to work together

If you see a red cross next to the project name or if you see the following errors in the **Problem** tab, then you need to tell Eclipse where Maven stores its files.

In Eclipse, select **Windows | Preferences** from the toolbar at the top of the screen.

In the dialog box that appears, select menu option **Java | BuildPath | Classpath Variables.** You will see a screen similar to the following:

Click on the **New** tab on the righthand side of the dialog box. In the dialog box that appears next, enter the **Name (M2_REPO)** and the **Path** where Maven stores its files.

On Windows XP machines, this is likely to be in the format:

C:\Documents and Settings\Administrator\.m2\repository

Replace **Administrator** with your username.

On Windows Vista machines, this is likely to be in the format:

C:\Users\Administrator\.m2\repository

Again, replace **Administrator** with your username.

If there is any doubt, open Windows Explorer and try to navigate to the files. Alternatively, use the search facility in Windows Explorer to find the .m2 folder on your machine. It's best to search all of the files under the C drive. This takes longer, but there's a better chance of finding the file.

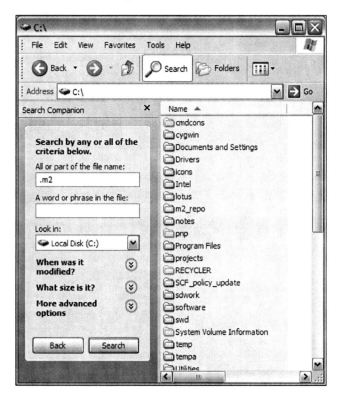

Back in Eclipse, when you've finished entering the variable name and value, click on **OK**. You will be asked if you want to do a full build. Click on **Yes**.

After a few seconds, the red crosses should disappear and you should see the project set up as per the screenshot in the previous step.

Troubleshooting

Here is a list of things for you to check if anything goes wrong:

1. Ensure that you have the developer version of Java installed, and not just the runtime.

2. Check the proxy settings for Eclipse and Maven. If your download stops or hangs half way through, try running the command again.

3. Check that you don't have two copies of JBoss or Eclipse running at the same time.

4. Check the versions of JBoss and BRMS/Guvnor that you have installed. If BRMS/Guvnor is not working, try dropping back to an older version (of both JBoss/BRMS) and repeat the steps again.

5. If you have any problems with setting up the Eclipse project for the samples (or even if you're seeing strange Eclipse errors later), remember that Maven is the master build, and Eclipse (in this case) is just a glorified text editor. So try these steps; Close Eclipse, Delete the `.classpath` and `.eclipse` files in the root of the folder and the `.settings` folder, then run the Run the command mvn eclipse:eclipse again. Then follow the instructions to setup the eclipse project again

6. If you get a specific error message, try searching that term in Google.

7. Double-check the instructions on the Java, JBoss, Maven, or Eclipse web site (as appropriate).

8. If everything else fails, read *How to ask for help* from the previous chapter.

Summary

Whew! We have covered a lot. If you've just re-joined us (because somebody has kindly set up the technical items for you), then this is what we did:

1. Set up Java.

2. Set up BRMS/Guvnor running on the JBoss App Server.

3. Set up Eclipse and installed the Drools plug-in.

4. Installed the Drools examples for this book and the Maven to build them.

We'll be using all of these tools in the next couple of chapters, starting with the BRMS/Guvnor to edit our business rules.

3
Meet the Guvnor

By now, you're probably keen to see if rule engines can live up to the hype. In the previous chapter, we set up all of the tools that we need. Now we're going to dive right in and write our first business rule.

Although we have a couple of choices of business rule editor, we will start writing our rules using the Guvnor editor (formerly known as the BRMS). This is a user-friendly web editor that's powerful enough to test our rules as we write them. Along the way, we'll explain some of these concepts:

- A quick tour of Guvnor
- Loading the samples
- Our first business rule—Hello world

Taking a tour with the Guvnor

If you've ever been in London, most of the taxi drivers will call you Guv'nor. We'll avoid all play with words (and cockney rhyming slang) about 'taking a tour' and 'taxis' in this chapter, and just get on and see what the Guvnor screens can do.

Getting started

When we set up Guvnor in the previous chapter, we tested it by going to a web address similar to:

```
http://someServerName:8080/drools-guvnor
```

```
http://localhost:8080/drools-guvnor
```

Open up the address in a web browser. The following screenshot uses Internet Explorer (even if it only shows the web page), but Guvnor will also work with Firefox, Safari, Opera, and most other browsers. You will see a screen similar to the following one:

The screenshot shows the Guvnor login screen. By default, any username and password will be accepted, unless the version has been configured with extra security (for example, to use your Windows account details-ask whoever did the setup). Click on **OK**, and you'll be shown the welcome screen.

General navigation

The first screen you will see is the search screen. This screen, like most screens in Guvnor, has the following components:

- The Drools logo on the upper-left of the screen.
- Details of who you are logged in as on the upper-right (this will be blank if you logged in using a blank username). This area also gives you the option to log out.
- The Guvnor Navigation sidebar (**Navigate Guvnor**) allows you to access all of the Guvnor functionality. In the search screen **Rules | Find** portion is shown.
- On the main, rightmost part of the screen is the functionality that we happen to have open (in this case the search screen). This part of the screen will change depending on what we are doing.

Navigating in Guvnor is fairly intuitive. Just click on the links (that's anything with a '+' sign next to it) on the lefthand side of the screen within the navigation toolbar to make them expand. Click on the displayed items to open them in the righthand side of the screen. Note that after you open a few screens in this way, you'll have a row of tabs across the top of the screen (similar to Excel). These allow you to switch easily between the most commonly used Guvnor screens. The following figure shows the tab bar in Guvnor:

Find	Category Ma...	Backup Manager	Category: Dis...

The search screen

If you opened any other tab, you can return to the default search screen by clicking on the **Find** tab of the Guvnor tab bar. You will see something similar to the following screenshot:

The search screen (**Find**) works just like Google, allowing you to search for rules and other assets that you use within your rules. But what's the **Include archived items in list** option for? Remember we said that the Guvnor gave you version management? Nothing is ever deleted, just shuffled into an archive in case you need it again in the future—a bit like the 'Undo' feature in word, only much more powerful. Selecting the **Include archived items in list** checkbox allows you to search for older or deleted versions of rules and other assets.

> What's this about assets? I thought this was a book about rules.
>
> Rules can't work in isolation. They need a support team. Assets provide this support—things such as a data model (to get information to and from rules), packages (to organize the rules into folders), and more. Remember that all rules are assets, but not all assets are rules.

Administration

If you did a search on the previous screen, the chances are that no results were returned. By default, there is nothing to search for (unless samples or other rules are hanging around on your machine from a previous version). This is good when we write our rules (as we have a clean sheet), but not so good for our quick tour. To make this clearer, let's load some sample rules.

Loading the samples

The Guvnor samples, which provide the business rules for an extremely shady car insurance company, are available from the Book Samples web site `http://code.google.com/p/red-piranha/`.

Download the `droolsbook_chapter3_sample.zip` file and extract it to a temporary folder. Find the `repository_export.xml` file. We'll need this in a minute.

Within Guvnor, click on the **Admin** tab, then click on **Import/Export**. (You may need to expand the **Admin** tab by clicking on the '+' sign next to it.) You will see the **Backup Manager** tab, as per the following screenshot:

Click on the **Browse** button and select the `repository_export.xml` file that we found earlier. Then click on **Import** (the button with the up arrow next to it).

After clicking on **OK** to confirm that you want to import the file (remember, this will wipe out anything that you have done up to this date), the system will churn away for a few minutes. Then it will display a message indicating that the import is successful.

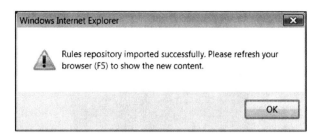

Now go back to the search screen (click on the **Find** tab, or on the left sidebar click on the **Rules tab,** and then select **Rules | Find**) and look for items with the word 'insurance'. You will now get plenty of search results.

 Go ahead, and play around with Guvnor. You can always clear everything by redeploying Guvnor. To do this, first stop JBoss (you may need to press *Ctrl+C*). Then, in the folder that you installed JBoss into (for example, C:\software\JBoss), there will be a folder called repository—this is where Guvnor stores all of the rules. If you delete the folder and restart JBoss, you have a new, clean, version of Drools Guvnor. Be careful though, as this will wipe everything (Rules and other assests) that you've created in this version of Guvnor!

What did we just do?

In short, you saved yourself a lot of typing.

By now, you will be getting the feeling that the Guvnor is more than just a web page. It is an industry-standard repository for your rules. A repository is useless without being able to import and export information. We just imported the standard Drools insurance sample into the Guvnor. It makes the web pages that we're going to view a lot clearer when we see some real life examples.

 The Drools repository is based on Apache Jackrabbit. This has its own storage, but can be configured to use an industry-standard database such as Oracle, Microsoft SQL Server, or MySQL. No matter how good the database is, it's still reassuring if we can import to it and export from it. For this, Guvnor uses and XML-based format. If you're curious, open repository_export.xml in your favorite text editor and have a look at it.

More on the admin page

The administration page can do more than just import rules. This page gives you functionality not directly related to rules editing, but vital for managing the system—for example archiving items, managing rule categories, and so on.

To see what else the **Admin** tab can do, open it (if you haven't already done so) by clicking on **Administration | Admin | Categories**. On the lefthand side you'll see the following options:

Let's run through these:

1. **Categories**: Every rule lives in a folder (or package) similar to what you might find on your computer's hard disk. But we can also 'tag' the rule or asset with a category name (such as 'sales' or 'accounts'). This screen gives the ability to change these categories and tags.

2. **Archived Items**: Archiving is like deleting (except that nothing really gets lost). If we archive a rule or asset, it normally 'disappears' from that screen. Otherwise the screens would get cluttered with older rules. This option lets us find archived items if we need them again.

3. **Statuses**: Rules and assets don't get written in one sitting. Often they pass through various states such as 'draft', '2nd draft', 'review' and 'production'. The various states will differ depending on the process your organization follows. Luckily, this screen allows us to set various asset states (the default ones being draft and production).

4. **Import/Export**: We've already seen how to import rules into a system. Export is the process in reverse (extracting rules from our system so that we can import them on another computer and/or back into our own system at a later date). Note that the file exported is a compressed ZIP file. The `repository_export.xml` file needed for importing it later is stored inside it.

5. **Error log**: What happens when something goes wrong? The error log gives you more details (over and above the usual error message that you will see on the screen).

> What's the difference between a category and a status? Although both are used to describe a rule, they do different things. A status may change over the lifetime of a rule (for example, moving from draft to production), while a rule will normally stay in the same category (for example, sales) during its lifetime. In addition, a rule can have only one status, but can have many categories assigned to it.

Categories are important—every rule and every asset must have a least one of them. So let's take a minute to look at the following **Edit categories** screen. The screen shows the insurance categories that we imported in the previous step. If you want, you can add, rename, or delete category names here. We can even nest categories inside categories. But don't get carried away, as often the complexity isn't needed!

Rules

Now that we understand categories, we're ready to look at the rules pages. We already saw the search/find rules screen as soon as we opened Guvnor. To see the other rules pages, click on the **Rules** tab, then expand both the **States** and **Categories** submenus (by clicking on the '**+**' sign). Double-clicking on the **Production** state will allow you to see the insurance rules, as shown in the following screenshot.

If you're clicking through **States** and **Categories**, you'll see that many of the rules/ assets are repeated. That's OK—a rule will have a state and one or more categories. Think of it as many different ways of finding the same thing.

There are a lot of entries here (on the righthand side), but they all belong to a few simple types.

Process

You are probably familiar with workflow diagrams. JBoss Rules allows you to draw workflow diagrams in the Eclipse IDE (but not yet in Guvnor). This allows you to have more control over the order in which groups of rules fire. The **insuranceProcess** item in the above screenshot is an example of a process.

The model

We mentioned earlier that rules are deployed as a part of a larger system. So we need a way of getting information into and out of the rule engine. The model lets us do this.

To explain this in more detail, think of how you might email sales information around our imaginary chocolate company from the previous chapter. You'd probably send the information in a spreadsheet similar to one that follows, showing customer sales for the month of February.

The **insuranceModel** item in the above screenshot is an example of this.

In the above screenshot, we have four columns showing **Customer Name**, **Sales**, **Date of Sale**, and an indication of whether we've sold items other than chocolate to the customer. Imagine the spreadsheet for March—the customer details might change, but the structure of the spreadsheet (including the columns) remains the same. The structure of the spreadsheet (but not the contents) is the model. For JBoss Rules, it's written in Java.

Clicking on a model item (in the case of the rules in our Guvnor example, the **insuranceModel** item) is a shortcut to the screen to upload or download the model files that we created in Java.

Guided rules

The aim of the Guvnor is to allow the easy editing of business rules. The guided rules screen (available by double-clicking on the **Quick approval - safe driver, any policy type** rule in the previous screen) allows you to do this. This is a guided editor that makes intelligent suggestions to help you write your rules. With this editor you won't be typing any text, but using dropdowns and clicking on icons to create business rules.

The following screenshot is the guided rule editor for the **Quick approval** rule:

The key features of the lefthand side of this screen are:

- Buttons at the top left to **Save changes**, **Copy**, and **Archive** the rule
- The **When** and **Then** sections of the business rules on the upper-left and middle left
- Three green '+' icons next to the **When**, **Then**, and **Options** sections to add more constraints or consequences
- Multiple '-' icons (next to the textboxes) allowing you to delete existing constraints or consequences
- Options that describe the rule; for example, is it part of a process flow, is it enabled, and the date that it is effective from
- Buttons (near the bottom), used to view the source (**View source**) and validate the rule (**Validate**)
- A space (at the bottom of the screen) to allow (optional) information about the rule to be specified

On the righthand side of the screen, you will find the following features:

- Options on the upper-right,used to change the **Status** and **Categories**
- Notes on the package to which the rule belongs
- **Version** history and other metadata about the rule, such as who created it and when

Everything that you do on this screen actually creates the technical rule behind the scenes (and hides the complexity from you). The **View Source** button allows you to see (but not edit) the rule that is created for you. If you want the additional power of editing technical rules, you can always use the technical rules screen.

Technical rules

Most of the assets in the insurance sample are actually technical rules (for example, the **Quick approval** rule. If you open the **Driver Glass Coverage** rule (by double-clicking on it in the list of rules) you'll see a similar screen, but with text instead of the guided editor.

Note that this text-based rule follows the same "when…then" format.

```
when
        $driver : Driver ( driverID : id )
        $supple : SupplementalInfo ( driverId == driverID,
        glassCoverage  == true)
then
        $driver.updateInsuranceFactor( 1.05 );
        System.out.println("Driver wants glass coverage: " +
        $driver.getInsuranceFactor());
```

Or, in plain English:

```
When
        There is a Driver
        And that Driver has requested glass coverage
Then
        Update the driver's insurance factor
        Print a message saying that the driver wants coverage
```

The technical rules follow a predictable pattern, so it gets easier to understand and even to write. We've to leave something for the next few chapters!

Creating a new rule

Clicking on the **Create New** button just underneath the **Rules** section on the navigation bar brings up the following menu. This menu allows you to create new technical and business rules (like the one's we've just seen). It also allows you to create DSL-based rules (a way of writing near-English business rules), Decision Tables (an Excel-like format for business rules), and test scenarios (to make sure that your rules work the way you intend them to).

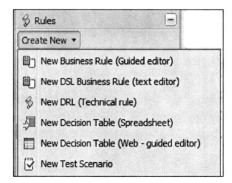

Packages

Packages are like folders. They are a way of organising rules and assets. The difference between packages and directories comes at deployment time, when everything in one package gets deployed at the same time. Opening the package (**org | acme | insurance | base**) shows you all of the assets available in the package.

Most of these concepts (business rules, technical rules, DSL, models, rule flows, and test scenarios) are familiar, but there are two new items: **Functions** and **Enumerations**. We might want to call **Functions**, which are useful for calculations and the like, from the rules. **Enumerations** are lists of values that we can use in our rules.

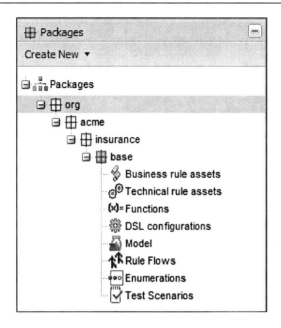

The **Create New** button (just below the **Packages** tab) allows you to create new ones of each of these items.

If you select the main package (**base**), you will be able to see a summary of the package details.

Java recommends a standard notation for packages names (that's where the name `org.acme.insurance.base` comes from). Although you don't have to follow this convention, there is no harm in doing so (especially when we start talking about the Java-based rule model later). The package name looks a little bit like an Internet web address (although it doesn't actually link to anything). The format is:

`companyurl.projecturl.subproject.`
`anyotherdivisionsrequired.`

Most of the packages that you create will only need three or four levels. However, there can be as many subdivisions as you need. You will see more of these subdivisions when we talk about Java code (Fact models).

Some of the features on the package details screen (from top to bottom) are:

- The buttons **Copy**, **Rename**, and **Archive** at the top of the screen, used to to copy, rename, and archive (delete but save a copy) respectively.
- Next, just below the **Configuration** heading are the statements that import the fact model into the package. These are normally generated automatically when we add the (Java) fact model.
- An optional **Description** of the package.
- A **Save and validate configuration** button, used to to save (and validate) the configuration.
- A **Build package** button, used to to build the package and put it into a deployable condition (or let you know of any problems).
- A **Show package source** button, used to show the package source (for example, the technical rules language that has been written by Guvnor on your behalf). This shows the entire package (including imports and functions), and not just single rules.

The button used to build the package is important, as building the package is the step before deployment (that is, using our rules in a real-life production system).

Deployment

To open the deployment screen, click on the **Deployment** bar in the lefthand navigation section (available on all screens). This screen plays a very important role. It gets your rules and assets from the Guvnor editor and puts them into the production systems.

When you edit your rules, they don't get deployed (to the live or real world system) immediately. Can you imagine being in the middle of writing the second of three new rules and having the incomplete rule set deployed? The **Deployment** tab allows you to control when your rules are released to the end users. It also allows you to view previous deployments.

Clicking on the **Deployment** tab displays the following screenshot. The list of available snapshots comes from the packages built by the **Build package** button under the **Package** tab.

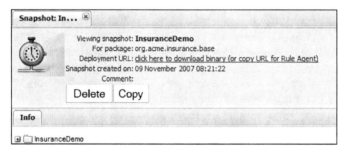

In addition to the **Delete** and **Copy** buttons, there is a web link (URL). You can use this in two ways. You can click on it here to download the package (if you wish to copy and deploy it manually to the target system). Or you can right-click on the link and copy the URL. Drools provides a component (called the RuleAgent) that we can deploy into our production system. The RuleAgent can check for updates to the package (via the URL) and deploy them to production automatically.

The architects of your target system will probably have a specific deployment plan (generally it's not a good idea to deploy rules directly to production). Guvnor gives you a couple of options, but this default one will help you to get your system up and running quickly.

QA—Quality Analysis

Here's a problem: You write rules and you check them to make sure they do what you intend them to do. They work OK. Then you change a rule. So you have to test them again. Still OK this time. What if it's the 60th time you've made a tiny change? Are you tempted to skip the testing yet? Or maybe you'll test, but not as well as you should. What if you've 600 rules? Do you test all of them?

Automating testing in Guvnor

The solution: You automate the testing. This is what the Guvnor Quality Analysis page allows you to do.

This page is pretty simple. You know the inputs to your rules (for example, the insurance application form for your typical first-time 21-year old driver) and the outputs from the rules (the insurance premium that they should pay). The inputs and outputs should be the same every time, which makes them ripe for automation.

The testing framework alerts you if the test results differ from what you expect. That way, you spend less time testing and more time playing golf (or whatever it is that you do). And you end up with better quality tests.

We'll create a simple test scenario when we'll write our 'Hello World' sample in the next section. But as you can see from the following screenshot, this screen allows you to run all of the tests.

Many people (me included) recommend **Test-Driven Development** or **TDD** that is, you write your test **before** you write your business rule (write test, write rule, verify test, write test, and so on). The reason for testing first is that, as a human, you may be tempted to "forget" to write your test if the business rule appears to work OK.

Over time, these single tests build up to give you a 'safety net' that dramatically reduces the cost of things going wrong. It's much easier and cheaper to fix something that you've just written (when your tests fail) rather than three months later when you go live and your airline is giving away free transatlantic flights by accident on it's web site.

The test scenario screen allows us to run all of the tests in our package simultaneously, which is a useful sanity check for our rules, before deploying them.

The analysis page

The power of business rules comes from writing many simple rules that cover most business scenarios. For example, insurance rates for drivers under 20 years of age, insurance for the people above 40 years, insurance for the people above 60 years. But what if we leave a gap (in this example, insurance for drivers in the age range of 20-40 years)?

The analysis page carries attempts to catch these gaps. It's not perfect (especially for more complicated scenarios), but for the items that it catches, you'll be glad that you used it.

Hello World example

It's traditional to show the simplest possible example—a rule that just says 'Hello World' when it is fired during a test scenario.

Writing the rule

The easiest way to do this is to create a new technical rule. In Guvnor, select the **Rules** tab, click on the **Create new** dropdown, and then select **New DRL** (technical rule). A new screen will appear.

We enter a name (**HelloWorldRule**), a category (that can be created using the **Admin** tab we saw earlier), and use the **defaultPackage** and (optionally) enter a description of the rule.

Clicking on **OK** will take us to the (technical) rule editor, similar to the one we saw on our tour of the Guvnor (although at this point the rule is blank). In the main part of the screen (the blank part) enter the following text:

```
rule "Hello World"
when
    eval(true)
then
    System.out.println("Hello world");
end
```

The important thing about this rule is the when... `eval(true)` statement. This means that the rule will always try to fire and carry out the `then` part— that is, print the 'Hello World' message.

Normally, our business rules would be much more choosy about 'when they fire' (and have a lot more conditions in the 'when' part). But for our simple sample, this suits us fine.

Next, save the changes by clicking on the **Save changes** button. You should be asked for an optional 'check in' comment after clicking this button. Congratulations, you've written your first business rule!

Firing the rule

Now we've a problem. Unlike most computer languages (for example, Java or C#), we can't 'run' a set of business rules—after all they have no single start point!

So how do we test our shiny new 'Hello World' rule? The answer is that we contrive a scenario that we know should cause our rule to fire. In Guvnor, this is relatively easy to do using the QA screen that we saw above. We'll use the QA screen to create a new test scenario where we can exercise our business rule.

This point about not being able to run rules is important and may be a major change from what you are used to. Remember that with rules, you say 'do this when this is true' and leave the rule engine to carry out that instruction when it finds itself in that scenario.

Let's create a new test scenario in Guvnor. A little bit strangely, this is done via the **Packages** tab. Select **Packages | Create new | New test scenario**, and a screen similar to the one shown in the following screenshot will be displayed:

Similar to what you did for creating a new business rule, enter a **Name**, **Package**, **Initial description** and then press **OK**. The scenario-editing screen will then be displayed.

This screen has three green '**+**' signs that we use to set up our scenario. From top to bottom these are:

- **GIVEN** — allows us to set our inputs (that is, create a scenario in which we know a business rule will fire)
- **EXPECT** — allows us to inspect the output after the rule has fired, to make sure that it has worked correctly
- **globals** — allows us to pass in environmental variables that the rule may need

Fortunately for us, as our rule is set to fire every time, we don't need to set these up. All we have to do is click the **Run scenario** button. When we do this, two things will happen:

1. We will see a message appear on the web page—**1 rules fired in 0ms**. Pressing the **Show rules fired** next to this message shows that the 'Hello World' rule was activated.

2. We will see a 'Hello World' message in the web server (JBoss) log, similar to the following:

```
JBoss
20:39:36,838 INFO  [STDOUT] INFO  06-07 20:39:36,838 (ServiceImplementation.java:checkinVersion:422)
IN asset: [HelloWorldTestScenario] UUID: [30d954f5-b106-4a58-b89a-1e57bf93fe2a]  ARCHIVED [false]
20:38:58,196 INFO  [STDOUT] Hello world
```

What just happened?

In the first part we created a rule that essentially said:

```
rule "Hello World"
when
    Anytime the rules are run
then
    Print a message to the console ("Hello world");
end
```

The next step (firing the rules) was to contrive a situation where the preconditions in the when part were met so that the rule would fire. For such a simple rule, this was easy. In fact, we had nothing to add in this case.

Finally, when we ran this scenario, the rule was activated, and the **Hello world** message was successfully printed to the console.

Summary

In this chapter we did three things. We loaded the Drools insurance sample into the Guvnor editing tool to give us some very good examples. Then we looked at the various Guvnor screens and saw that Guvnor can not only write rules (using both guided and advanced editors), but can also organize them and other assets into packages. The Guvnor screens also allow us to test and deploy these rules. Finally, we wrote our very first business rule—the traditional 'Hello World' message, announcing to everyone that we are now business rule authors.

We will use all of these skills in the next chapter. In that chapter, we will start on more sophisticated business rules, using both Guvnor and more advanced editing options.

4
Guided Rules with the Guvnor

In the last chapter we took a tour with the Guvnor and used it to write our first business rule, and printed out a traditional 'Hello World' message. Although this rule is a major step forward for us, we're not really using the full power of the Drools rule engine. In this chapter, we're going to stay with the Guvnor rule editor, and use it to write some more sophisticated rules. In particular, we're going to:

- Show how to put information into and out of our rules
- Build a fact model to hold this information
- Import our newly built model into Guvnor
- Create guided rules using this fact model
- Run and test our new fact-based rules

Passing information in and out

The main reason for the simplicity of our Hello World example was that it neither took in any information, nor passed any information out—the rule always fired, and said the same thing. In real life, we need to pass information between our rules and the rest of the system. You may remember that in our tour of the Guvnor, we came across models that solved this problem of 'How do we get information into and out of the rules?'.

 If you're familiar with Java, models are just normal JavaBeans deployed into Guvnor/JBoss rules in a JAR (ZIP-like) file; nothing more, nothing less. In fact, a lot of the time you can use the JavaBeans that already exist in your system.

Here's a quick reminder of the spreadsheet that we used as an example in the last chapter:

	A	B	C	D
1	Customer Name	Sales	Date of Sale	Chocolate Only Customer
2	Acme Corp	$100,000	01-Feb	Y
3	Breakfast Roll Inc	$250,000	01-Mar	N
4	Chocolate Creams Co.	$30,000	01-Apr	Y
5	Dunkin Dreams	$200,000	01-May	Y
6	Easy Eating	$150,000	01-Jun	N

If we want to duplicate this in our model/JavaBean, we would need places to hold four key bits of sales-related information.

- Customer Name: String (that is, a bit of text)
- Sales: Number
- Date of Sale: Date
- Chocolate Only Customer: Boolean (that is, a Y/N type field)

We also need a description for this group of information that is useful when we have many spreadsheets/models in our system (similar to the way this spreadsheet tab is called **Sales**)

> Note that one JavaBean (model) is equal to one line in the spreadsheet. Because we can have multiple copies of JavaBeans in memory, we are able to represent the many lines of information that we have in a spreadsheet.
>
> Later, we'll loop and add 10, 100, or 1000 lines (that is, JavaBeans) of information into Drools (for as many lines as we need). As we loop, adding them one at a time, the various rules will fire as a match is made.

Building the fact model

We will now build this model in Java using the Eclipse editor we installed in Chapter 2. Don't worry if this is your first bit of Java; we're going to do it step-by-step.

1. Open the Eclipse/JBoss IDE editor that you installed earlier. If prompted, use the default workspace. (Unless you've a good reason to put it somewhere else.)

2. From the menu bar at the top the screen, select **File | New Project**. Then choose **Java Project** from the dialog box that appears. You can either select this by starting to type "Java Project" into the wizard, or by finding it by expanding the various menus.

3. In the **Create a new Java Project** dialog that appears, give the project a name in the upper box. For our example, we'll call it **SalesModel** (one word, no spaces).

4. Accept the other defaults (unless you have any other reason to change them). Our screen will now look something like this:

When you've finished entering the details, click on **Finish**. You will be redirected to the main screen, with a new project (**SalesModel**) created. If you can't see the project, try opening either the **Package** or the **Navigator** tab.

When you can see the project name, right-click on it. From the menu, choose **New | Package**. The **New Java Package** dialog will be displayed, as shown below. Enter the details as per the screenshot to create a new package called **org.sample**, and then click on **Finish**.

If you are doing this via the navigator (or you can take a peek via Windows Explorer), you'll see that this creates a new folder **org**, and within it a subfolder called **sample**. Now that we've created a set of folders to organize our JavaBeans, let's create the JavaBean itself by creating a class.

Did you play with Lego blocks as a kid—multicolored plastic blocks that you could pull apart and stick together again and again? JavaBeans are like those Lego blocks—instead of building toy houses, we can build entire computer systems with them.

Often, while playing Lego, you'd run out of blocks (often red roof tiles) just when you were about to finish. Luckily, in Java, we can create as many blocks as we want. The class that we're about to put together is our mould to let us do this.

To create a new Java class, expand/select the `org.sample` package (folder) that we created in the previous step. Right-click on it and select **New Class**. Fill in the dialog as shown in the following screenshot, and then click on **Finish**:

We will now be back in the main editor, with a newly created class called `Sales.java` (below). For the moment, there isn't much there—it's akin to two nested folders (a `sample` folder within one called `org`) and a new (but almost empty) file / spreadsheet called `Sales`.

```
package org.sample;
public class Sales {
}
```

By itself, this is not of much use. We need to tell Java about the information that we want our class (and hence the beans that it creates) to hold. This is similar to adding new columns to a spreadsheet.

Edit the Java class until it looks something like the code that follows (and take a quick look of the notes information box further down the page if you want to save a bit of typing). If you do it correctly, you should have no red marks on the editor (the red marks look a little like the spell checking in Microsoft Word).

```
package org.sample;

import java.util.Date;

public class Sales {

private String name;
private long sales;
private Date dateOfSale;
private boolean chocolateOnlyCustomer;

public String getName() {
return name;
}

public void setName(String name) {
this.name = name;
}

public long getSales() {
return sales;
}

public void setSales(long sales) {
this.sales = sales;
}

public Date getDateOfSale() {
return dateOfSale;
}

public void setDateOfSale(Date dateOfSale) {
this.dateOfSale = dateOfSale;
```

```
}
public boolean isChocolateOnlyCustomer() {
return chocolateOnlyCustomer;
}
public void setChocolateOnlyCustomer(boolean choclateOnlyCustomer) {
this.chocolateOnlyCustomer = chocolateOnlyCustomer;
}
}
```

Believe it or not, this piece of Java code is almost the same as the Excel Spreadsheet we saw at the beginning of the chapter. If you want the exact details, let's go through what it means line by line.

- The braces ({ and }) are a bit like tabs. We use them to organize our code.
- `package` — This data holder will live in the subdirectory `sample` within the directory `org`.
- `import` — List of any other data formats that we need (for example, dates). Text and number data formats are automatically imported.
- `Public class Sales` — This is the mould that we'll use to create a JavaBean. It's equivalent to a spreadsheet with a **Sales** tab.
- `Private String name` — create a text (string) field and give it a column heading of 'name'. The private bit means 'keep it hidden for the moment'.
- The next three lines do the same thing, but for sales (as a number/long), `dateOfSale` (as a date) and `chocolateOnlyCustomer` (a Boolean or Y/N field).
- The rest of the lines (for example, `getName` and `setName`) are how we control access to our private hidden fields. If you look closely, they follow a similar naming pattern.

> The `get` and `set` lines (in the previous code) are known as **accessor methods**. They control access to hidden or private fields. They're more complicated than may seem necessary for our simple example, as Java has a lot more power than we're using at the moment.
>
> Luckily, Eclipse can auto-generate these for us. (Right-click on the word **Sales** in the editor, then select **Source | Generate Getters and Setters** from the context menu. You should be prompted for the Accessor methods that you wish to create.)

Once you have the text edited like the sample above, check again that there are no spelling mistakes. A quick way to do this is to check the **Problems** tab in Eclipse (which is normally at the bottom of the screen).

 If you do have any problems, you may be able to use the Eclipse quick-fix feature (highlight the problem, then press *Ctrl+1*). If that doesn't work, check again and ensure that the spelling is exactly the same as shown earlier. If that doesn't work, follow the steps in the *How to ask for help* section near the beginning of this book.

Now that we've created our model in Java, we need to export it so that we can use in the Guvnor.

JAR Export

JAR File Specification

Define which resources should be exported into the JAR.

Select the resources to export:

☑ 🖿 SalesModel   ☑ ⊠ .classpath
☑ ⊠ .project

☑ Export generated class files and resources
☐ Export all output folders for checked projects
☐ Export java source files and resources
☐ Export refactorings for checked projects. Select refactorings...

Select the export destination:

JAR file: c:\temp\SalesModel.jar ▾   Browse...

Options:
☑ Compress the contents of the JAR file
☐ Add directory entries
☐ Overwrite existing files without warning

⑦   < Back   Next >   Finish   Cancel

1. In Eclipse, right-click on the project name (**SalesModel**) and select **Export**.

2. From the pop-up menu, select **jar** (this may be under Java; you might need to type **jar** to bring it up). Click on **Next**. The screen shown above will be displayed.

3. Fill out this screen. Accept the defaults, but give the JAR file a name (**SalesModel.jar**) and a location (in our case **C:\temp\SalesModel.jar**). Remember these settings as we'll need them shortly.

4. All being well, you should get an 'export successful' message when you click on the **Finish** button, and you will be able to use Windows Explorer to find the JAR file that you just created.

What is a JAR file? JAR stands for Java Archive and is just another name for a ZIP compressed file (you may be familiar with the WinZip utility). Although our model is pretty small (only one file), compressing the files and putting them in one place (the JAR) saves a huge amount of time when deploying larger systems.

Congratulations! You have not only built your first Java file (possibly), but also successfully exported it elsewhere for use. But now that we've built this, how do we use it in the Guvnor?

Importing the fact model into Guvnor

Switching back to the Guvnor, we're now going to create a package to hold our brand new model that we created in the previous steps.

If you want, you can clear out the samples of Hello World from the last chapter. Remember that you can't actually delete the items, but you can archive them. Either way, none of the older samples will get in the way of what we're doing in this chapter.

1. From the lefthand side menu, select the **Packages** tab.

2. Go to **Package | Create New Package (org.sample) | Create Package**.

3. From just below the **Packages** tab, highlight **Create New** and then select the **New model (jar) of fact classes**.

4. Fill out the dialog box that is displayed, as follows. The **Name (SalesModel)** and **Package (org.sample)** should be the same as the ones we created in Eclipse. Click on the **OK** button.

5. Back in the main Guvnor screen, check that everything is in place.

In addition to the **upload** button (that we're going to use in a minute), this screen also has a **Download** button (to retrieve JAR files that you may have uploaded earlier). It also has the usual **Save**, **Copy**, **Archive**, and **Delete** options.

To upload our fact model JAR into Guvnor , follow the steps shown below:

1. Click on the **Browse** button, and then navigate to and select the JAR file that we exported earlier. Click on **OK.**

2. After returning to the screen above, click on the **upload** button (actually, the 'up' arrow icon to the right of **upload**).

3. If everything goes well, you will get the message **File was uploaded successfully**. Click on **OK** to return to the **SalesModel/Package** tab.

4. Save the updated package (by clicking on the **Save Changes** button). As with other saves/check-ins you'll be asked for an optional **checkin** comment.

5. We can check whether Guvnor has successfully picked up the new package information by expanding the **org.package** that was created.

You can see from this example that in the **Configuration** section, under **Imported types,** our class (`org.sample.Sales`) is listed. This means that Guvnor has not only uploaded our class file, but will also allow us to write rules that use this class. Now that Guvnor knows the format of the information that we want to pass in and out, we can start writing rules using Guvnor.

Guided rules using the fact model

Back at the chocolate factory, we've decided to implement a customer loyalty scheme. When any customer has sales of greater than 100 dollars, we want to give them a flat rate discount of 10 dollars. To put it in a slightly more 'rules-like' format, our new business rule will look something like this:

```
when
      we have a sale greater than 100
then
      Give a discount (by adding a 'negative' sale)
```

Yes, as a business rule it's slightly clunky, but it keeps things simple. In real life we'd just update our sales object with the new balance after the discount (and keep a note of what discount was given).

Of course, we're going to write this rule using the Guvnor. Or rather, you're going to try to write the rule in Guvnor based on the last chapter's tour of the guided editor. I'll show you the full step-by-step answer soon, but the end result will look something similar to the following:

Some key notes and buttons to use in the Guvnor are:

1. You're going to create a new rule using the guided editor in Guvnor.
2. Click the '+' next to WHEN and THEN to add new conditions/consequences (such as **greater than 100** and **Insert Sales -10**).
3. The 'green arrow' icon allows you to refine these further.
4. Guvnor will pick up the sales model that we imported earlier and offer it as choice to you on a menu.
5. If you make a mistake, the '-' icon allows you to delete a line.

The step-by-step answer

Before we write a rule we must make sure that we have a category assigned to it. We can use any existing category or we can create a new one (under the **Admin** tab, expand **Categories | New Category**). For this step-by-step example, we've created a new **SalesCategory**. But categories are just descriptive tags, so it will work with pretty much any name.

After you've chosen a category, follow these steps:

1. Create a new business rule by selecting menu option **rules | create new | New business rule (guided editor)**.

2. Enter the following values in the screen that is displayed. We will give the new rule a name (**SalesDiscount**—although anything descriptive is OK). We will assign a category (the **SalesCategory** that we created earlier). Then we will pick the package (**org.sample**) from the drop-down list. After entering a description (optional) we need to click on **OK**.

3. We'll then be taken to the guided business rule editor that we saw earlier on our quick tour. In the main section, click on the '**+**' sign next to the **WHEN** label, to add a condition (that is, to restrict the circumstances under which our rule will fire).

4. The **Add a condition to the rule** dialog will be displayed. We're going to choose a fact type of **Sales**. (Actually, this will be the only fact type in the drop-down list.) This means that our rule will fire only when a sales fact is present. To put it another way, our rule only applies to the rules spreadsheet.

5. After choosing this, we'll automatically be taken back to the guided rule-editing screen.

6. Back on the main screen, we'll see that **Sales** has been added as a condition. Currently, this rule will fire for all sales, so we want to restrict it to only those sales of more than 100 dollars.

7. Because we want to elaborate on the **WHEN** condition, we need to click on the green 'arrow' icon immediately next to the **Sales** condition. We'll be shown the **Modify constraints for Sales** dialog box, shown as follows:

8. The first dropdown field contains a list of all of the fields (columns) available for the **Sales** object. We'll choose **sales** (that is, the dollar value or amount) from the drop-down list.

9. Back in the guided editor, another line will have been added. The default value is **please choose**. Change this to **greater than or equal to,** as shown in the following diagram.

10. Now we need a value to compare this field to (as part of the filter). Click on the pencil icon to set this. In the **Field value** dialog box that is displayed, click on **Literal value**. Literal values are numbers we can enter directly.

11. Back in the guided editor, a new text box will have appeared. Enter **100** (the value we want to use in our rule) in this text box.

That's it—the WHEN part of the rule is done and should look like the objective picture that we saw at the very start of this sample). Now would be a good time to save the rule (and enter a comment if you see fit).

The THEN part is somewhat easier, in that there are fewer steps to create it.

1. Click on the green plus sign next to the **Then** section. The **Add a new action** dialog box will be displayed:

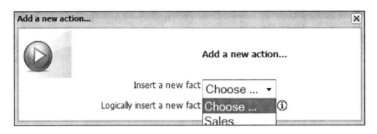

2. We choose to insert a new fact (in the first dropdown). **Sales** will be the only option in this menu. Inserting a new fact is like adding a new row to the Excel Spreadsheet (that is another line of information into the memory).

>
> **Logically insert a new fact** does the same thing as inserting a new fact, but automatically removes the row/fact/object as soon as the condition stops being true. For this example, this wouldn't change anything as the **Sales** won't stop being more than 100, but it would make a difference to more dynamic rules (for example, if another rule reduced the price, and we wanted to withdraw the discount in this circumstance).

3. Back in the guided editor, the text **Insert Sales** will now be displayed. Click on the green arrow next to this to begin setting to values for our new sales object (this is similar to saying: once we insert a new line into the Excel Spreadsheet, here are the values that I want to use in the newly created cells).

4. First we're going to add a **name** field. This will appear in the main guided editor. Click on the pencil next to the **name** field to add a value. Enter the value **Discount** (so that the purpose of the new line/new fact is clear).

5. Now that we've created our first field, we can repeat the process for the second one—**Sales**. Add a field (click the green icon next to **Insert sales**) and choose **sales**. Back in the guided editor, click on the pencil next to the new line, and enter a value of **-10**.

6. By now, the screen will look like the screenshot back at the start of this section. Now is a good time to save your rule. Validate the rule by clicking on the **Validate** button. All being well, you will see a dialog box similar to the following example. To close the dialog box, click on the 'x' in the upper-right corner of the dialog box.

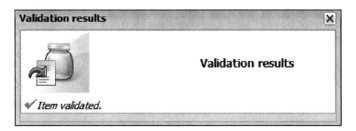

Validation results

Validation results

✔ *Item validated.*

Remember that validation is only a check to catch the most obvious errors. It's still possible to get warning messages when we run and test our rule in the next section.

To confirm that the guided editor has written the rule for us, click on the **View source** button. The meaning (give a discount for sales of 100) is pretty much as we'd expect. We've converted the rule into plain English.

Viewing source for: SalesDiscount

Viewing source for: SalesDiscount

```
rule "SalesDiscount"
        dialect "mvel"
        when
                Sales( sales > "100" )
        then
                Sales fact0 = new Sales();
                fact0.setName( " discount" );
                fact0.setSales(  -10 );
                insert( fact0 );
end
```

```
Rule "SalesDiscount"
//name of the rule
// use the slightly more readable mvel
when
    we can find a fact / line of more than 100 sales
then
    create a new line / fact
    set the name to "discount"
    set the sales to -10
    add the line back to the model
end
// end of rule
```

You'll notice that this text is read-only. In the next chapter, we'll show you how to create your rule directly in the text (technical rule) editor. For the moment we've a more pressing problem — how do we try this rule out?

Running this scenario

The solution is similar to the one we used for running the Hello World example in the previous chapter. The rule we want to exercise is a little bit more complicated, so the scenario that we need to construct is also a little more complicated.

To start, expand the **Package** tab and then create a new test scenario. Give it a name (for example **TestSales**), and select the same package for our rule (**org.sample**). You will be presented (again) with the blank scenario test screen. The scenario that we're going to create is similar to the following screenshot:

The steps for building this screen are similar to those we used before. We use the '**+**' sign to insert a new **GIVEN/EXPECT**, the small green arrow to refine the scenario, and the '**-**' sign to remove.

1. Click on the plus sign next to **GIVEN** and choose to insert a new **sales** fact (under any name). Click on **Add**.

2. Click on the **Add a field** button that appears. In the dialog box, select the **name** field.

3. Click on the green arrow next to **sales** to add another field (column in our new row). In this case, use **Sales** and give it a value of **200** (that is, greater than 100!).

4. Click on the green '**+**' next to **EXPECT**. In the **New Expectation** dialog box that is displayed, click on **show list** and then choose the **Sales Discount** rule.

5. Change the default (that we expect this rule to fire at least once) to **Expect Rules,** to fire this many times, and then enter '**1**' in the new text box that appears.

6. Save this test scenario using the button at the top of the screen.

All being well, if you now click the **Run Scenario** button, you will get a green bar at the top of the screen saying **Results 100%**, along with some additional text: **Rule [SalesDiscount] was activated 1 times**, which indicates that our rule is running as expected.

What just happened?

The test scenario that we created was equivalent to passing in a spreadsheet with one row (that is, one **Sales Java** object with sales of **200** and a name of **Acme Corp**). We'd expect our sales discount rule to fire under these circumstances and we tell our test scenario to look out for this. When we run the scenario, our rule behaves as expected and fires, giving **Acme Corp** a discount of **–10** Sales for their order.

Summary

In this chapter we have covered five main areas. We saw how to get information in and out of our rules, and created the fact model in Java needed to do this. We imported our new fact model into the Guvnor and then built a guided rule around it. Finally, we tested our rule to make sure that it ran correctly.

Using our fact model in a guided rule is a good foundation for the next chapter. In the next chapter, we start writing more powerful text-based rules, starting by using the Guvnor editor, and then moving on to the desktop-based JBoss IDE.

5
From Guvnor to JBoss IDE

In the previous chapter, we wrote our first real rule using the guided editor in Guvnor. Although the guided editor is very useful, the rule that we wrote could do with a few enhancements. We also had a glimpse of the behind-the-scenes text rules, but they were for read-only purposes. As a part of our enhancements, it would be good to use the additional power of these text rules. We'll look at using variables in our rules by using rule attributes to provide extra information about our rules, and editing text-based rules using Guvnor and the JBoss IDE.

A more powerful rule

Our business rule from the last chapter was a bit silly. In real life there is no such thing as 'negative sales'. It would confuse not only our customers, but also our own company. (How would the Oompa Loompas in the shipping department put 10 boxes of chocolate into an empty truck?) Instead, we're more likely to modify the price of our sales and update this price with the discount, to give the actual price to be paid.

Applying this concept to our business rule, we'd end up with something like this:

```
when
        We have a sale greater than 100 Dollars
then
        Discount the sales cost by 10%
```

The following screenshot shows the same rule, expressed in the Guvnor's guided editor:

WHEN		
	[mySales] Sales➤	
[salesValue]sales	greater than or equal to ▾	100
	Sales➤	
➤name sounds like	▾	acme
	Sales➤	
➤name matches	▾	acme corp

The screenshot above shows a business rule that applies a discount to the sales price.

> We're not going to get very far without understanding variables (such as **mySales** and **salesValue**). You may be familiar with Variables from other programming languages.
>
> Variables are placeholders for things that we want to refer later. They are a bit like cells in Excel, but instead of names such as 'a1' or 'b15', we give them easy-to-remember names. Here, any value put in **mySales** or **salesValue** will be saved until we need it again.

Taking into consideration the knowledge that we have about variables, this rule is more subtle than our plain-English version. What it actually says is:

- When you find a line of sales (in Java or on our spreadsheet) greater than 100, make a note of that line (and store it in a box called **mySales**).

  Make a note of the actual sales figure in that line (and store it in a box called **salesValue**).

- Then modify our line of sales (**mySales**) so that the new sales figure is now the previous figure minus 10.

Have a go

That's the easy bit. Now you're going to build it, in order to try it out! Try it yourself before skipping on to the step-by-step guide below.

Updating the rule—step by step

Our new or updated rule uses the same Java fact model as the previous chapter, so it's going to be a lot easier to build. In fact, the step process is very similar, as it uses '+' signs to add When (conditions) and Then (consequences). We'll concentrate on the changes.

The When part

1. Create a new rule and add a condition using a sales fact, exactly as before.

2. When adding the first constraint, enter a variable name (**mySales**), as shown in the following dialog box.

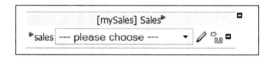

3. This brings you back to the main guided editor, which will now show a rule similar to the following:

4. As before, select **equal or greater** in the drop-down box (**please choose,** in the previous diagram), and use the 'pencil' icon to enter the value (**100**) that we are filtering on.

5. On the second line of the newly updated rule, click on the green arrow above **sales**. An option to bind the actual sales total to a variable is shown. In this dialog box, assign it to **salesValue**.

Remember that our **mySales** variable is akin to one line in a spreadsheet. The **salesValue** is the sales column from within that line.

6. In the guided editor, the **Add a new action** dialog box now has additional options. Click on the green '+' sign, which is next to **Then**, to make these options appear.

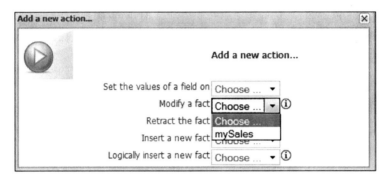

7. In this dialog box we choose to modify the **mySales** fact.

 The other options on this screen include retract (deleting the fact from memory) and inserting, or logically inserting a new fact, which work in the same way as before.

Back in the guided editor, we can click on the 'pencil' icon and enter the formula (**=salesValues-10**) to make our rule look like the one in the screenshot back at the start of this chapter.

Looking behind the curtain—a text-based rule

Before we jump in and run our new rule, let's catch our breath and take a look at the source. Remember that when we were working through and building the above rule, we were actually building up a text-based rule behind the scenes. Clicking on the 'view source' button might make our rule a little bit clearer.

```
rule "SalesDiscount"
    dialect "mvel"
    when
            mySales : Sales( salesValue : sales >= "100" )
    then
            mySales.setSales( salesValue-10 );
            update( mySales );
end
```

We can guess most of what this means, but running through it allows us to see what is going on.

- Name the rule (`SalesDiscount`)
- Use the `Mvel` style for writing our rule (slightly clearer than the Java dialect)
- When

  We can find a row `Sales` of greater than `100`, keep a handle to it called `mySales`, and put the actual sales value into `salesValue`

- Then

  Reduce the sales by `10`

  Notify (`update`) all of the other rules that the sales has changed, so that they may fire (or not)

- End of rule

A small problem...

Now that we know what's going on, we go back to our test scenario that we created using Guvnor in the previous chapter—the one called **TestSales**. We would expect that when we click on the **Run Scenario** button (making no changes), we would get the same **results 100%** message. But that doesn't happen.

What happens is that the scenario fails with the message **Rule [SalesDiscount] activated 11 times. Expected 1 times.** What happened? How can our rule have fired 11 times if we only have one test scenario?

What actually happened when we ran the test scenario is this:

1. We put our sales object into the working memory (that is, passed it to JBoss Rules), with a total sales of 200.
2. Our discount sales rule kicks in.
3. The sales value is now updated by this rule to 190 dollars.
4. Drools detects that our sales object has been modified, and sees if any rule can be applied.
5. The same discount sales rule is found (as the sales value is still greater than 100).
6. The sales value is discounted by a further 10 dollars.
7. Repeat the last two steps until the sales value finally drops below 100 dollars.
8. No more rules fire and JBoss Rules exits.

So the rule is doing exactly what we asked it to do—applying a discount to orders with a sales value greater than 100 dollars. There are many instances in which we want this recursive behavior. In fact, it's one of the advantages of using a rule engine: It matches the business rule to the situation that it finds itself in, and then it fires.

> What exactly is this working memory? Working memory is like a scratchpad. All of the information that we pass to Drools is stored here. When rules fire, the information in the working memory gets updated. And when Drools is finished, a copy of the working memory is passed to the rest of the program.
>
> The important thing to remember is that Drools only knows about and fires its rules according the information that we explicitly place in the working memory.

Rule attributes

However, what we want the rule to do is fire once and then stop. To be more precise, we do not want to have a rule that fires recursively in a tight loop. How do we express this intention in a rule?

Luckily, Drools has a feature called rule attributes. This allows us to state more information about our rule. The rule engine can use this extra information to modify its behavior.

In our example, we want to switch on the **no-loop** attribute—meaning that the rule will fire again only if some other rule has modified the working memory in the meantime. To express this in our rule using the guided editor in Guvnor, follow these steps:

1. At the bottom of our rule click on the '+' sign next to the options.
2. Choose **no-loop** from the drop-down menu.

3. Save and run the rule (via the test scenario). It now behaves as we expect. The test passes it correctly saying that the rule has fired only once.

> The **no-loop** attribute will stop the rule from being called; or rather it will stop a rule from changing a fact in working memory, which could otherwise cause the same rule to fire again.
>
> What **no-loop** will not prevent is the looping of two (or more) rules; for example, Rule A causing Rule B to fire, which then causes Rule A to fire, and so on. Well-written business rules with appropriate restrictions (in the When part) will avoid this situation. For example, we can add a 'discount amount' column in our fact model. Our rule will check that this column was empty before firing and update the column when it fires. That way, we would avoid any chance of looping.

Congratulations, you've not only written a much more sensible business rule, but you've also touched upon your first bit of rule engine theory!

More on the guided editor

When we were writing our rule using the guided editor, we came across a lot of options that we didn't use. Some of these are obvious, but it's worth running through what they are.

Possible comparisons

When we added a fact comparison, we chose the option of testing to see if our sales value was greater than 100. This comparison can also be a less than, equal to, not equal to, equal to or greater than, or equal to or less than test. For text fields (String), Guvnor will also give you the option of using **matches** and **sounds like**.

Condition types

When previously we added our first condition (using the '+' icon next to the **WHEN** statement), we chose the **Sales** fact from the **Add a condition to a rule** dialog that appeared. Not specifying a condition type means that the rule will fire every time a fact is in memory.

We have a few other options in the second drop-down box (**Condition type**) in this dialog:

- **This is no**: This option is a simple negative value. The rule will fire only if the fact does not exist at all in the working memory.

- **There exists**: The rule will fire once, no matter how many times the fact exists in working memory.

- **Any of**: The rule will fire, no matter how many times the facts exist in working memory. It differs from **There exists** because it can be applied to multiple types of facts at the same time.

Once we add one of these condition types, we have the option in the main guided editor to specify (as before) the **Fact** (for example, **Sales**) that the condition applies to.

Add more options

On each part of the rule you'll see the **Add more options** icon (it looks like this). This allows you to add additional conditions to the same line, based on the same value. You'll see the full list in the dropdown once you click on this icon, but it allows us to write more sophisticated conditions, such as:

- If **salesValue** is greater than 100 and less than 200, then give discount level 1

- If **salesValue** is less than 100 or greater than 100, then give discount level 2

Note the following differences between using the ' ⬚ ' (add more options) icon and the large green '+' icon that we've been using until now:

1. The '+' icon only allows us to add **And** conditions (that is, all parts of the rule have be true before the rule fires). The **Add more options** allows **And** conditions as well as Or conditions. **Or** conditions are used when only one of the conditions needs to be true for the rule to fire.

2. The '+' icon allows comparisons based on multiple facts (for example, Sales and Existing customers). The **Add more options** only allows comparisons based on the same fact (for example, only Sales).

Multiple field constraints

When we clicked on the 'green arrow' icon next to **Sales**, we modified the constraints for the **Sales** object via the dialog box that appeared. At the time, we chose to add restrictions on a field (**salesValue**), but we have a few other options in this dialog.

We can add a multiple field constraint, which will allow us to combine one or more conditions. This can be done as **All of** (and) or **Any of** (or). If you choose this option in the editor, you can see that these can be nested to build up sophisticated (but easy to get lost in) rules.

We also have the option to add a formula according to our condition. We won't go into the details of this here, as we will come across a similar formula in our text rules, before this chapter ends.

The following screenshot shows our rule once it has been updated with a multiple field constraint. In this case, our rule will fire only when the sales value is **greater than or equal to 100** and the name either **sounds like acme** or **matches acme corp**.

So what's the difference between multiple field constraints and just simply adding constraints using the '+' icon in the editor? Take a look at the same rule using the '+' icon to add the additional conditions in the following screenshot. When do you think this rule will fire?

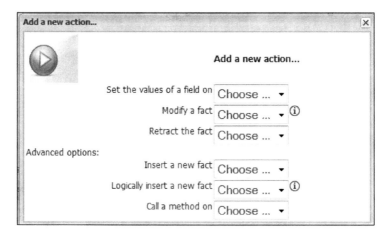

WHEN

[mySales] Sales

[salesValue]sales greater than or equal to ▾ 100

Sales

▸name sounds like ▾ acme

Sales

▸name matches ▾ acme corp

The answer is: never. What this rule is saying is that it should fire only when our **Sales** are **greater than or equal to 100** and the customer **name sounds like acme** and the customer **name matches acme corp**. The last two conditions are contradictory— our name must match **acme corp**, but if it does it won't sound like **acme**.

So, just by changing the icon that we clicked on, we've changed our rule from 'or' to 'and', thus giving a very different behaviour. Beware of subtleties such as these when building your rules, and test your rules using scenarios, to ensure that they behave as you expect.

The Then part

There are also a few options that in the Then part of the guided editor we skipped over. These are context-sensitive, so they may or may not appear, depending on what you have in the When part of the rule.

Add a new action...   ✕

Add a new action...

Set the values of a field on Choose ... ▾

Modify a fact Choose ... ▾ ⓘ

Retract the fact Choose ... ▾

Advanced options:

Insert a new fact Choose ... ▾

Logically insert a new fact Choose ... ▾ ⓘ

Call a method on Choose ... ▾

The options are:

- **Set the values of a field on**: If we set a variable in the When part, we can update that value here.

- **Modify a fact**: This is the same as setting the values, except that we notify the rule engine that the values have changed (which may cause another set of rules to fire, as in the last example).

- **Retract a fact**: Remove an item from working memory (which is akin to deleting a line from our spreadsheet). This may cause other rules to fire.

- **Insert a new fact**: This will create a new line on our spreadsheet (and may cause other rules to fire). This is the option that we used in the last chapter, in our first sales discount rule.

- **Logically insert a new fact**: This is the same as **Insert a new fact**, but the fact is removed again, as soon as this rule stops being true.

- **Call a method on**: This allows you to call a Java method (advanced). In this way, you can pretty much use the full power of Java to send messages, link to other systems, and so on, from your rules.

All of the options have dropdowns, which will provide appropriate selections from our fact model and will update the main editor, allowing you to build your rule step by step.

More rule options and attributes

In our last version of the sales discount rule, we added a rule option called **no-loop**, to ensure that the rule did not recursively cause itself to fire. You may have noticed that there were several other options in that dropdown, and you may be wondering what they are used for.

- **date effective** and **date expires** allow us to switch our rules on or off, depending on the current date.

- **dialect:** Rule can be written in different dialects — currently Java and MVEL, with more to come. Both of the currently-supported dialects follow the same 'when...then' format, although MVEL is slightly easier to read (unless, or sometimes even if, you are familiar with Java). **dialect** should not be confused with **DSL** (**Domain Specific Language**), which is a templating mechanism that allows near-English language rules. We'll look at DSL shortly.

- **duration** forces the rule to remain true for the specified duration before it fires. This can be useful for a commodity-trading application, where the price (of chocolate beans, for example) must remain high for a specified period of time before we'd fire a rule to sell it.

- **salience**: In general, you can't control the order in which multiple rules will be fired; either something is true, or it isn't. (Remember that this in one of the big differences from traditional programming languages.) However, we can give hints to the rule engine as to which rule we consider should be fired first. All other things being equal, the higher the salience for a rule, the more likely it is that this rule will be fired first.

- **agenda-group**, **auto-focus**, and **activation-group** are all used by Ruleflow, which we will cover in more detail in a later chapter. For the impatient, Ruleflow is a means by which you can group rules so that they are only available to be fired at specific stages in a business process.

- **no-loop**, as we already know, stops rule recursion.

- **lock-on-active** is a stronger version of **no-loop**, for use with Ruleflow.

Text editing

We looked behind the scenes earlier, and viewed the text rule that Guvnor automatically builds up for us. That view was read-only, but it is possible to write text rules directly using the Guvnor editor — that's how we wrote our first 'Hello World' rule. Even better, it is possible to start writing our rule using the guided editor, and then switch to the text editor for the trickier parts. To do this, carry out the steps shown below:

1. View the source of the rule that we created in the guided editor. For this example, open the sales discount rule and then select **View Source**.

2. Copy the text of the rule from **rule** to **end**, inclusive.

3. In the side bar of Guvnor, create a new technical rule (**Rules | Create New | New DRL**). You'll be presented with a New DRL dialog box that looks familiar. Enter the values as shown in the screenshot below these steps, and then click on **OK**.

4. We will be shown the technical rule editor. This is similar to the guided rule editor except that in place of all the dropdowns, you have space for editing text.

5. Into the text editor, paste the text of the rule that you copied in step 2 earlier. We can then save the rule and run it as before.

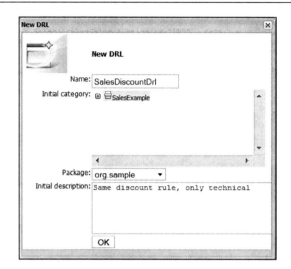

That's it. You've written (and run) your first text-based rule. But what is this DRL thing? A DRL file (often with the extension `.drl`) is the file where Drools stores its rules, in much the same way that a file with the extension .doc is a Word file, and a file with the extension `.xls` is an Excel file. Inside, it's a DRL file just a text file, which we can open in Notepad, or one of the other text editors, such as the JBoss IDE.

Introduction to the JBoss IDE

The text editor in Guvnor is useful, but for the moment, it is not as powerful as some of the other editors that are available. For example, it doesn't have syntax highlighting (coloring that makes the business rules easier to read) or the inline highlighting of errors. Compare the plain grey text in Guvnor with the following screenshot of the JBossIDE, where the rules are much easier to read.

So what is the JBoss IDE? There are a few ways to answer this question:

- An **IDE** is an **Integrated Development Environment**. This is a fancy way of saying 'you can edit all of your files in one place'.
- The JBoss IDE is based on the Eclipse open source platform. If you look at the applications on your desktop, you'll see that a lot of them have common functionality (open file, save file, and so on.). Eclipse provides this functionality not only for Java, but also for editors for other languages. There are even Eclipse-based financial applications.
- The whole aim of Eclipse is a platform for extensions, so basically the JBoss IDE = Eclipse + extensions. The extensions provided are not only for rules editing, but also for things such as workflow, storing information in databases (Hibernate), faster web development, and distributed applications (Seam).

Think of the IDE as a text editor that can edit multiple files at a time. Yes, it can do a lot more powerful things, such as allowing us to test and run our text-based rules, but we'll get to that later. Now, does a text editor seem quite as daunting?

We came across the JBoss IDE in Chapter 3, when we used it to edit our Java-based fact model. In this chapter we're going to concentrate on the rules-editing extensions.

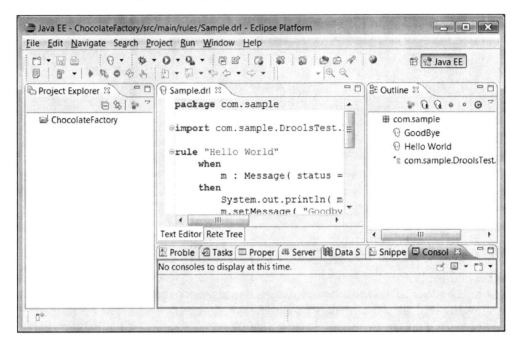

Previously, we only looked at the IDE in passing (as we were using it to create just enough Java to get by). This time it is worth taking a more detailed look around, as we'll be using the IDE quite a bit in the next few chapters. The parts of interest in the above screenshot are:

- Main menu bar: This is at the top of screen, and contains commands such as **File**, **Edit**, **Search**, **Window**, and **Help**. A lot of these commands (such as **File**, **Save**, and **Edit**) will be familiar to you.

- Menu icons: There is a set of icons just below the menu bar. Just like Word or Excel, these are shortcuts to the functionality provided by the main menu bar.

- Main editor: In the centre of the screen is the main editing space. In the screenshot above, this is showing a rule (**Sample.drl**) being edited. If we have more than one file open at a time, multiple tabs will appear (in the same line as **Sample.drl**) which allow us to switch between the open files. There is an '**X**' on each tab, which allows you to close it. (You will be prompted if you want to keep any unsaved work.)

- The lefthand panel, by default, shows the project explorer (that is, a way to view all of the files of the project). Like most things in Eclipse, this panel is configurable. For example, selecting **Window | Show View | Other | General | Navigator** will cause a Windows Explorer type view to appear in the lefthand panel. The project explorer will remain open, and tabs are available to allow you to switch between these two views of the same project.

- The righthand panel, by default, shows an outline of the currently open file—in this case, the rule we are editing. This is also configurable. For example, dragging the **Outline** tab and dropping it onto the lefthand panel will cause it to be displayed there.

- Right-clicking will cause a context-sensitive menu to pop up, just like in other Windows applications. For example, right-clicking on the **Outline** tab and selecting **Fast view** will minimise the view to an icon in the bottom left of the screen, to save screen space. Don't worry; you can click on this icon to see its contents again (or right-click on it to restore it to the way it was previously).

- The Status Bar at the bottom of the screen is where the fast view icons migrate to. It also shows messages from Eclipse, such as if Eclipse is working on a background task (for example, validating a rule).

- The bottom set of tabs are also configurable (that is, we can drag and drop, or fast-view just like the left- and righthand panels). The two tabs shown in the screenshot that we're most interested in are **Console**, where anything we print out from our rules is displayed, and **Problems**, which shows any problem (for example, incorrect spelling) that we may have.

Now that you're interested in using the JBoss IDE to edit your rules, lets get started. This is similar to creating a new Java project (which we did in Chapter 3), that is:

1. Choose **File | New | Project** from the main toolbar, but this time choose **New Drools Project** as the next step.

2. Give the project a name (for example, **ChocolateFactory**), but click on **Next** (and not **Finish**). The dialog that is displayed is shown in the screenshot that follows.

3. Take the existing samples. (Actually, the only samples we need right now are the first two, but selecting them now will save you having to recreate the project later.)

Next, click on **Finish**. Your JBoss IDE will look similar to the one we walked through.

Hello World in the JBoss IDE editor

When we started with the Guvnor IDE editor, our first rule was 'Hello World'. It would be a pity to break a fine tradition, so let's write our first rule in the JBoss IDE in the same way. Even better, the steps that we just followed (to set up samples as part of a new Drools project) means that all the hard work of typing is done for us. All we need to do is poke around and understand what is going on.

Looking at the project explorer (on the lefthand side) and expanding the folders (using the small arrow icons) shows that quite a few folders and files have been added to our project. These follow a standard format, so once you understand them for this project, you'll be at home in bigger, more complex projects.

- **src/main/java**: this folder contains the text files holding the Java code (*.java). We saw these in Chapter 3 when we were building our Fact Model to transport information into and out of the Rules Engine. Of course, Java is a lot more powerful than that. **DroolsTest**, a Java-based test, is highlighted in this folder. We will run it shortly.

- **src/main/rules**: This folder contains the text files containing the source for the rules.

- **JRE System Library**: This is a shortcut to the Java toolkit. Without the Java toolkit, the Java code wouldn't mean anything to the computer.

- **Drools Library**: This is a shortcut to the Drools toolkit. If the Drools toolkit is missing, the computer will not know how to convert the rules into code that it can understand.

- **bin**: Before we can run our rules, we must convert them from text that we understand to a format the computer understands. This step is called compilation, and the computer-format output is stored in the bin folder. In Guvnor this step is performed behind the scenes, but we are still notified of any errors in compilation (for example, spelling mistakes).

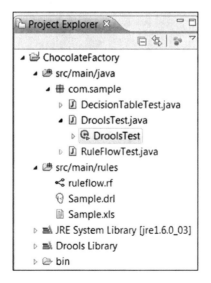

I promised that we were going to have a look at the HelloWorld rule. Let's run it first. Right-click on the DroolsTest.java file and, from the pop-up menu that appears, select **Run As | Java Application**. After a second or two, the following message will appear in the **Console**. (Remember the Console? It will be in the bottom set of tabs on your screen.)

```
Console ☒
Hello World
Goodbye cruel world
```

What just happened?

In summary: we loaded some rules and passed them some information; the rules fired; and words were printed to the Console.

The business explanation

A longer explanation will gloss over what is happening in the Java file (**DroolsTest**), except to say that it loads the rule file (Sample.Drl), passes in a fact object (Message) with a status of 'Hello' and message text of 'Hello World', and then fires the rules.

So what happens when the rules fire? That's the bit we're interested in. So, open Sample.Drl and let's have a look. We'll see that one file contains two rules: Hello World and GoodBye. The first two lines of the file are a package statement (saying what folder it lives in) and an import statement.

What's this import statement? Our Java code passes to the rules the Message fact object, which contains important information. Drools needs to know more about what sort of fact it is. The import statement (standard in Java) tells Drools about the folder and file where it can find more information. Previously, Guvnor automatically generated the import statement for us.

```
package com.sample

import com.sample.DroolsTest.Message;

rule "Hello World"
    when
        m : Message( status == Message.HELLO, message : message )
    then
        System.out.println( message );
        m.setMessage( "Goodbye cruel world" );
        m.setStatus( Message.GOODBYE );
        update( m );
end

rule "GoodBye"
    no-loop true
    when
        m : Message( status == Message.GOODBYE, message : message )
    then
        System.out.println( message );
        m.setMessage( message );
end
```

The intention of the business rules is fairly clear. Let's work through them line by line:

```
rule "Hello World"
    when
        We find a message fact, and its status is 'Hello' , put the fact
        in a box called 'm' and put our message text in a box called
        'message'
    then
        Print the contents of the 'message' box
        Set our message text to 'Goodbye Cruel World'
        Set our message status to 'GoodBye'
        Notify the Rule engine that our message fact has changed
end

rule "GoodBye"
no-loop true
    when
        We find a message fact, and its status is 'Goodbye', put it in
        a box called 'm' and put our message text in a box called
        'message'
    then
        Print the contents of the 'message' box
end
```

So, this is what happens when the rules are called:

1. When Drools gets called, it starts with a message fact that has a status `Hello`. It also looks for rules that match this fact.

2. The first rule (`Hello World`) matches. It prints the message, updates its status to `GoodBye`, changes the message, and notifies Drools of the change in the fact status.

3. On hearing that facts have changed, Drools searches for rules that match this newly-updated fact and finds the `Goodbye` rule that applies to the new situation.

4. The contents of the message (`GoodBye Cruel World`) are printed.

5. There are no more matching rules to fire, so Drools finishes and returns the updated fact objects to the program that called it.

Easy when you know how, eh?

The technical explanation

Normally, as a business rule writer, you don't care about the system that calls your rules. You let somebody else worry about all that stuff. But if you're the 'somebody else' (for example, if you're a Java programmer wanting to know how the magic is done and how to deploy rules as part of a web application), read on. If you're not a 'techie', there's nothing going on 'behind the scenes' that Guvnor doesn't do for us automatically; so it may still be worth a peek.

Not surprisingly, the bit that you're interested in as a (Java) programmer is in the (Java) file `DroolsTest`. Open it in Eclipse. (Pressing *Ctrl+Shift+R*, and then typing **DroolsTest** is a quick way of opening it.) The key lines to watch out for are as follows:

*   The `public static final void main(String[] args)` method is a Java convention. When we run **DroolsTest**, the starting point is in this method.

*   The first line, `try`, and the `catch` line towards the end mean 'stop if you encounter a problem and do something'. In this case, the 'something' is to print out the details of the problem.

*   The `readRule()` method contains the lines of code that we use to find (and load) our `Sample.drl` file, and convert it into a RuleBase (that is, a set of rules that are ready to fire). It may look complicated, but the steps that we take here are pretty much the same as if we had loaded the rules from a file or directly from Guvnor. We'll go into these steps in more detail later, when we cover other rule deployment options.

- The following two lines call the `readRule()` method and use it to get a working memory — a stateless or goldfish-type memory that remembers the results of our rules firing, and then forgets it as soon as we want it to forget:

```
RuleBase ruleBase = readRule();
WorkingMemory workingMemory = ruleBase.newStatefulSession();
```

- At the end of our file is the fact object `message` (`public static class Message`). It's the same idea as our `sales` object from the previous chapter (a placeholder for carrying information into and out of the rules), except that this time it shares the file with the rest of the code, instead of having a `.java` file all to itself.

- Using this message template, the following lines create an actual object (a bit like making a cookie using a cookie-cutter template), and then add the information that we want to pass:

```
Message message = new Message();
message.setMessage(  "Hello World" );
message.setStatus( Message.HELLO );
```

- Finally, the following lines pass our message to the rules and tell Drools to start firing the rules as is appropriate (that is, the bit that we discussed in the previous section):

```
workingMemory.insert( message );
workingMemory.fireAllRules();
```

Try it yourself

Although the business and technical explanations of our rules may appear daunting, the fact is that the same lines appear again and again — familiarity may not breed contempt, but hopefully, confidence! In fact, to prove the point, you're going to use the IDE to change the above rules. Change the rules so that instead of printing Goodbye Cruel World, it prints Goodbye (whatever your name is). For the really advanced readers (those who have a taste for playing around with the .java files), do the same for the Hello message: change it to Hello (insert name here).

Why should we use the JBoss IDE instead of Guvnor? It's your choice, but many people find that the text editor is more powerful. And if you're interested in the way we call rules (that is, you going to be the poor soul writing the Enterprise Java code as well), then this chapter has shown you that we need to load and call our rules; and you're probably already familiar with the Eclipse environment anyway.

So the IDE isn't that big and scary; it's just another way of wiring the same rules. Go ahead and play with it. If the worst happens, you can delete and start again.

Summary

This chapter pushed the boundaries of what we can do with the Guvnor rules editor, and then brought in the JBoss IDE as an even more powerful tool for writing rules.

We started by using variables in our existing sales discount rules, to get around the problem of having negative sales. Then we came across rule attributes (for example, salience) to stop our rules from making changes that cause them to fire again and again. After testing this successfully, we looked at text-based rules — both in Guvnor and the JBoss IDE — that run the Hello World example in the new environment.

Now that we've written more complicated rules, in the next chapter we'll look at ways to make sure that our rules don't break — both now, and in the future.

6
More rules in the JBoss IDE

In the previous chapter we moved away from the Guvnor editor and started using JBoss IDE to edit our rules. Our Hello World example was a useful start, but we know that rules can do much more. For example, consider the poor Ooompa Loompas that are shipping the chocolate bars out of the factory door. Wouldn't it be nice if we drew up a shipping schedule for them? Before we do that we'll look again at the structure of a rule file. Towards the end of this chapter, we'll look at some more advanced rules that we can write and run in the IDE.

Rule syntax

We bumped into our first rule (`.drl`) file in the previous chapter. We will see a lot more of it here, so it's worth going over it again. Our rule file can contain the following elements:

1. package: Package-name is the name of the folder in which a rule file lives. This is useful for organising our rules (especially when you build up hundreds of them).

2. import: This pulls in any Java class files (including fact models) that we use in our rules.

3. global: This defines the global variables that we use. Remember variables (boxes that hold values)? Earlier, they were emptied as soon as our rule had fired and only changes to the facts lived on. Compared to 'normal' variables, global variables live longer, and allow us to pass information into and out of our rules.

Passing information into and out of our rules via a global variable is almost the same as passing a fact into the rules. The difference is that the rule engine does not match (or fire) against global variables. This makes the rule engine more suitable for passing in items that change slowly, such as the current date, counter, and so on, and giving rules access to external resources (such as log files).

4. function: Sometimes you may need to perform the same calculation in many rules. Defining a function allows you to perform the same calculation again and again. Note that it's often easier to call a normal Java function to carry out the same task.

5. rule: This is the 'when…then' structure that we've spent most of this book talking about.

6. comments: These are pieces of text ignored by the rule engine, which explain what is going on with us. They can be on a single line (anything after '//' until the end of the line) or split over multiple lines (everything between the /* and */ Comments split over many lines).

In the Hello World example, our rule (the 'when…then') was fairly simple. We matched `Message.STATUS` (when), updated that status and printed a message (then). Let's look at the other options available to us. We'll start with the When part of the rule.

Patterns for the When part

Remember our rule from Chapter 4 that calculated the discount on the chocolate sales? Using the fact model from that example (`sales.java`), the following are all valid 'when' conditions. The following code extract shows most of the simple conditions that we can use in our rules. Note that it would be impossible for this rule to fire, given that all of the contradictory conditions cannot be met at the same time. Drools would also complain that we use same variable name ($mySales) twice in one rule.

 Drools recommends the convention $variableName; dollar sign, first letter small, and capital letter for each of the following words in the variable name. But it's only a convention. Note that variable names are also case sensitive, that is, $variableName is not the same as $VARIABLENAME.

Note the use of the "//" single-line comments to explain what each line does.

```
rule "show various conditions"

when

//Simple match on all sales, no assignment of variable
Sales()

// matches all sales lines, one by one, assigns to local var MySales
$mySales : Sales()

//additional filter on customer name. Corrpesponds to getName() on
sales JavaBean
$mySales : Sales (name=="acme corp")

//'or' - both lines do the same thing
$mySales : Sales (name=="acme corp" or name=="beta corp")
$mySales : Sales (name=="acme corp" name=="beta corp")

//and - three lines do the same thing
$mySales : Sales (name=="acme corp" and sales>100)
$mySales : Sales (name=="acme corp" , sales>100)
$mySales : Sales (name=="acme corp" && sales>100)

//Number comparison
$mySales : Sales (sales==100) //equals 100
$mySales : Sales (sales<100) //less than 100
$mySales : Sales (sales>100) //greater than 100
$mySales : Sales (sales!=100) //not equal to 100
$mySales : Sales (sales>=100) //greater than or equals 100
$mySales : Sales (sales<=100) //less than or equals 100

//Use of bracket reorder the evaluation of the condition
//The 'and' condition is performed first, then the 'or' condition
$mySales : Sales (name=="acme corp",(sales>100 && sales<200))

then
    //do something
end
```

In the above example, we could also test for customers with empty names by using a condition similar to:

```
$mySales : Sales (name== null)
```

`null` is another of those words with a special meaning; think of it as void or completely empty. Note that this is different from `name== ""`, which means it does have a name, but that name is blank. `""` is like a blank sheet of paper, whereas null means no piece of paper at all. Still confused? Then you can test for both as follows:

```
$mySales: Sales (name== null or name=="")
```

Sometimes when you're running rules, do you get an error related to `null` called `nullPointerException`? OK, make that you will frequently get a `nullPointerException`.

This error means that we are trying to do something like `sales.getName()`, except that sales are `null`. Drools and Java do not know how to handle this. So it stops, tells you what went wrong, and waits for your next move.

Patterns for the Then part

In the Then part of the rule we can use just about any Java code, plus the Drools constructs given as follows. The following consequences are all valid, as long as we have a variable called `$mySales` defined in the When part (like we defined in the previous example):

- Any valid Java code, such as the `System.out.println("HelloWorld")` from the previous examples.
- The insert statement tells Drools that we have created a new fact that it should be aware of. This can be done using a variable (for example, `insert ($mySales)`) or creating a new fact on the spot (for example, `insert (new Sales())`).
- The update statement is similar to insert, but is used where the fact existed before the rule started (for example, `update($mySales)`).

In the next example, we'll use a variant of `update()`, called `modify()`. This is a useful shortcut when we need to change several items in a fact at once (for example, Sales number, date, and name).

Shipping chocolate bars

Armed with the latest business rule information, we can now go about helping our Ooompa Loompas. They work hard at loading all of the chocolate bars that we are making onto trucks, to ship to the customers who are busy sending us orders. In fact, we are getting so many orders that we are limiting each customer to one box of 210 chocolate bars a week.

Now, if you've ever worked in a packing or a shipping department, you know that your hands are always busy. You just want to be told what and when to pack, and you don't have to calculate your next step. So, using Drools, we're going to write a list of what to ship and when to ship to each customer.

Because we are nice people, we give our overworked Ooompa Loompas a holiday now and then. We don't work on holidays, so we ship our chocolate bars the next working day.

How do we write this in a way a computer can understand?

The problem (and remind me why I need business rules)

If we were writing this in a normal computer language, we'd have something like the following:

```
Start Loop
Have we shipped all the chocolate bars yet?
Yes - go to end of loop
Is today a holiday
No - Ship 210 bars and update totals
Is tomorrow a holiday?
No - Ship 210 bars and update totals
. . . .
Have we shipped all the chocolate bars yet?
Yes - go to end of loop
End Loop
```

This code will (almost) work, but we've got the following problems:

- Even though it's written in plain English, can you identify the six business rules that are embedded in it? Take a peek down to our business rule solution to find them all.

- Most code is not written in English, but in Java or C#. Would you be able to find the business rules hidden in a technical language like Java?

- This example will break if we have more than two holidays in a row, but it's not immediately obvious from the text.

- What if we want to change our business rules (for example, to have time off on the weekends)? If we do this on a separate line (to keep our sample clear) and have two days off per weekend, the code becomes 40% (four lines) longer.

Why rules scale better—a reminder

Imagine that each additional business rule in the above example adds 40% to our sample function's length. Adding 10 business rules would take about 500 lines to write (and the size increases exponentially). For the mathematically inclined, that is 10 lines times our 40% extra complexity per rule times our 10 extra business rules or 10*1.4^10. A fault in any of these lines could break the entire function.

By contrast, our Drools business rules are independent. Adding another means that we add only 10 extra lines each time (not including whitespaces or comments). See the business rules example below and count the lines yourself! That's 10 lines extra for the first rule and 10 lines extra for the 16th rule, as each rule does not make the previous rules more complex to write.

Rules may give a slightly longer solution at the beginning, but increase in efficiency as the project grows for all but the most trivial solutions.

Getting and building the sample

You could type in the entire example that we will describe in the next couple of pages. Or you could download the Chapter 6 example from `http://code.google.com/p/red-piranha/`, unzip it into a directory of your choice, and then review it at your leisure. We recommend downloading, as it's a much more pleasant option.

Once you've downloaded and unzipped the Chapter 6 example, you're ready to open the JBoss IDE. The sample includes the necessary Eclipse settings. Create a new Eclipse project (as we've done for the previous samples) and in the wizard that appears, open the folder where you have unzipped the Chapter 6 example. Eclipse should automatically pick up the project settings.

When you've created the Eclipse project, you will notice that the supporting libraries (such as the Drools core) are missing. This is deliberate, as it reduces the size of the example file that you have to download. Fortunately, the sample also contains a Maven project file (`pom.xml`). We set up Maven in Chapter 2, so you can build the project (and download the required libraries) as follows:

1. Open a command window (DOS prompt).
2. Go to the folder containing the project, for example,
   `cd \some-project-folder`.
3. Type `mvn eclipse:eclipse`. This will generate the Eclipse project. Then, download all of the dependencies.

At this point (once you see the **build successful** message) when you refresh the project (right-click on the project name in Eclipse and select **Refresh**), all of the required libraries will be available.

Downloading the libraries using Maven is a lot faster than downloading them as part of the ZIP file. After the first download, Maven keeps a local copy, and as long as the version number is up to date, it will use that file for future examples. You'll notice the speed difference in future chapters.

For information, if you wanted to go one step further and build the project from the command line you can also run the command `mvn clean package`. This will give you a deployable JAR file. For the rest of this chapter, we'll concentrate on running the examples through Eclipse.

Rules

Let's take a quick look at our rule file, `shipping-rules.drl`. The first part of the rule file contains the usual package and import information. At the bottom of the extract, we can see the declarations for two global variables.

```
package net.firstpartners.chap6;

import java.util.Date;

import org.apache.commons.logging.Log;

import net.firstpartners.chap6.domain.CustomerOrder;
import net.firstpartners.chap6.domain.ChocolateShipment;
import net.firstpartners.chap6.domain.OoompaLoompaDate;

global OoompaLoompaDate nextAvailableShipmentDate;
global Log log;
```

In this case we import the following: handles to Date; where to get information on the Apache log (a smarter way of printing to the console); three facts that we use to organize our data; and two global variables.

The three other facts that we import to organize our data are `OoompaLoompaDate`, `CustomerOrder`, and `ChocolateShipment`. A customer order is the total amount of chocolate that the customer wants, and will contain many `chocolateShipments` as we send them one box a week to meet their order.

Our global variables (the `nextAvailableShipmentDate` and the handle to the external log) are placeholders for items that we pass in when we call our rules.

Our first rule confirms the holidays when the Ooompa Loompas will not work. Whenever we find a date, we print out a message to the console. If we don't want to see this message, we could safely remove this rule.

```
rule "confirm holidays"

    when
            $holiday : OoompaLoompaDate()

    then
            //Logging message
            log.info("Remember - Ooompa Loompas don't work on:"+$holiday);

end
```

This rule actually matches against all OoompaLoompaDates in working memory. This works in this particular example, as the only OoompaLoompa dates directly in working memory will be holidays. In real life, our rule would need to be a bit more particular, that is, it should check whether the date is a holiday using something similar to the following:

```
When
$holiday : OoompaLoompaDate(holiday==true)
```

The next rule is one of the key ones in the example. When we find a customer order for which we haven't shipped all of the chocolate, then we add a new chocolate shipment to the order.

```
rule "Chocolate Shipment"
    when
        $CustomerOrder : CustomerOrder(currentBalance>0)
    then
        //Add a new shipment into the CustomerOrder
        ChocolateShipment ChocolateShipment = new
        ChocolateShipment(210);
          modify($CustomerOrder){
          addShipment(ChocolateShipment)
        }
        //notify the working memory of the new shipment
        insert( ChocolateShipment );

        //Logging message
        log.info("Fired Customer Shipment rule - customer is still
        waiting for "+$CustomerOrder.getCurrentBalance()+"
        chocolate bars");
    end
```

The next rule looks for any shipments (like the ones created in the previous rule) that have no shipment date set yet. When it matches, it sets the shipment date to the next available date (as retrieved from the `nextAvailableShipmentDate` global variable), and then rolls forward the `next available shipment date` by a week.

```
rule "Add Next Available Shipment Date"
    when
        $ChocolateShipment : ChocolateShipment(shipmentDate ==null)
    then

        modify($ChocolateShipment){
          setShipmentDate(nextAvailableShipmentDate.getCopy())
        }

        nextAvailableShipmentDate.rollForward(7);

        //Logging message
        log.info("Add Next Available Shipment Date:"+$ChocolateShipment
        .getShipmentDate());
end
```

Our holidays are passed in as facts, so rules can match against them. Whenever a shipment date lands on a holiday, our next rule will fire and move the shipment forward one day. If that date also happens to be a holiday, this rule will automatically fire again. We don't need to write any specific code to handle the 'holidays in a row' situation. We just state what we know to be true, and let the rule engine manage the complexity.

```
rule "modify due to holidays"
    when
        $holiday : OoompaLoompaDate()
        $ChocolateShipment : ChocolateShipment(shipmentDate==$holiday)
    then

        modify($ChocolateShipment){
        getShipmentDate().rollForward(1)
        }

        //Logging message
        log.info("Reschedule Shipment Date to:"+$ChocolateShipment.
        getShipmentDate()+" due to holiday on:"+$holiday);
end
```

When we are shipping our boxes of chocolate, it is likely that the last box won't be full. For example, an order for 500 fudge chocolate bars will be made up of two boxes of 210, and one smaller box of 80. Our next rule covers this situation by ensuring that the last box we ship does not leave us with items still to ship of less than 0. It does this by matching any customer order with a negative items still to ship and adjusting the numbers accordingly.

```
rule "Don't ship more than the customer order"
    when
        $CustomerOrder : CustomerOrder(currentBalance<0)
        $ChocolateShipment : ChocolateShipment(itemsStillToShip<0)
    then
        long $newShipment = $ChocolateShipment.getShipmentAmount()+$
        ChocolateShipment.getItemsStillToShip();

        modify($ChocolateShipment){
        setShipmentAmount($newShipment),
        setItemsStillToShip(0)
        }

        modify($CustomerOrder){
        setCurrentBalance(0)
        }

        //Logging message
        log.info("Removed CustomerOrder Overshipping - new shipment:"+
        $newShipment);
    end
```

ChocolateShipment.java

Our rules depend on three Java-based facts that we saw earlier when we imported them into our business rules. The first of these is the **ChocolateShipment**—a note to the Ooompa Loompas in the shipping department to put a box onto a truck. You can inspect the code if you want, but given that it is a simple JavaBean (that is, a placeholder for carrying information into and out of our rules) we can see a better overview using the outline view in Eclipse / the JBoss IDE.

Reading from the bottom up, we can see that our bean allows us to get (and set) the following values: the number of items still to ship; the amount in this shipment; and the date that we are shipping on. The **toString** method is a Java convention that makes it easier to print the information that we hold in this Java class to the log. The two **ChocolateShipment** methods give us information on how we can create new shipments.

All of these are referenced in the rules. In fact, if the spelling used in the rules doesn't match the one we have here, we get an error.

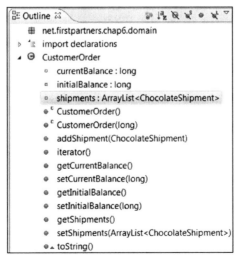

CustomerOrder.java

We also saw the **CustomerOrder** JavaBean imported into our **ChocolateShipment** JavaBean. In this sample, we can have one overall customer order containing many customer shipments to fulfill the order. The outline of the `CustomerOrder.java` file (image below) reflects this.

The **toString** (logging) method, and the get or set methods for **shipments**, **InitialBalance**, and **currentBalance** follow the normal JavaBean style (remember that JavaBeans are still just a means of passing information around). The two **CustomerOrder** methods give us different options for how we create this bean. (For information, **CustomerOrder()** means that we can create the bean with no parameters, which is perhaps the easiest way of all.)

Note the subtle difference in three similar methods that we use to deal with shipments:

- The addShipment method allows us to add another customer shipment to the existing list.
- The getShipments method returns the current list of customerShipments.
- The setShipments method allows us to pass in an entirely new list of customerShipments.

There is also an iterator method to make it easier for us to loop over the list of shipments.

> More information on the full power of Java collections (a more powerful form of the lists we're dealing with here) is available on the Java web site, http://java.sun.com. We are able to write rules using this power.
>
> For example, the following condition would match customerOrders with a first shipment to a customer of less than 100.
>
> CustomerOrder (shipments[0].shipmentAmount <100)
>
> Note the use of [0] to refer to the first shipment in the CustomerOrder. For those interested in how this works, the shipmentAmount matches to the getShipmentAmount() method on our CustomerShipment class.

OompaLoompaDate

Dealing with dates in Java can sometimes be nasty. For example, Java counts the days in the month from 1 (as you'd expect), but months in the year start from 0 (January). For this reason we have wrapped the Java Date in **OoompaLoopaDate** to hide some of the ugliness and make dates behave as you'd expect.

There's a second, even better, reason for the having OoompaLoompaDate.java in this sample. Remember that we talked about functions in our rule (.drl) file and said you'd be better off using normal Java code? The rollForward() method is an example of this, as it allows us to move to a date 'x' days in the future. In our rules, we don't care how this is done, just that it works!

Although business logic works great in rules, calculating dates isn't business logic. Calculating dates in Java makes it easier to unit test. There is more on unit tests in the next chapter. If you can't wait until then, it's a method of quality assurance—when we ask to move 10 days on, we know that it will do exactly that.

The outline of the `OompaLoompaDate.java` file can be seen in the following screenshot:

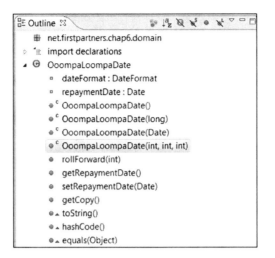

The other new methods to note are `hashCode()` and `equals()`. These are standard JavaBean conventions that allow us to match one date against another more easily.

The RuleRunner file

We saw some code in the HelloWorld example in the previous chapters that loaded our rule (`.drl` file) and called the rule engine. For convenience, we have put it into one file called `RuleRunner.java`.

The main starting point in this file is the second `runRules()` method. The steps to follow for this method are:

1. Load the rule file(s) from disk. We pass in the names of the files when calling the methods.
2. Create a RuleBase and a session (our scratchpad) using these rules.
3. Pass any global variables (name, value) into our rule session.
4. Pass any facts.

This code is fairly generic and could easily be reused in your own rule projects. We will look at the content of the `RuleRunner` file in more detail in Chapter 11. For the moment, we'll concentrate on the actual business rules.

MultipleRulesExample

By now you must be itching to run this sample; don't worry, we are almost there. We will run the `MultipleRulesExample.java` file soon. It's the starting point for the example. Reading through the file, the main points are:

- The package and import statements tell Java what directory this file lives in and the files from other directories that we need

- `NEXT_AVAILABLE_SHIPMENT_DATE` is a constant value that matches the global variable of the same name in our rules file

- `RULES_FILES` is a constant value of the name where we find our rules file

- The main method, like our previous sample, is where we start when we click the **Run** button

```
public static void main(String[] args) throws Exception
```

The step-by-step procedure for running the `MultipleRulesExample.java` class is given as follows:

1. We create our customer order.

   ```
   //Initial order
   CustomerOrder candyBarOrder = new CustomerOrder(2000);
   ```

2. We create a placeholder for the starting date for a first shipment. We add it under the `NEXT_AVAILABLE_SHIPMENT_DATE`, so that we can pass it into the rules as a global variable.

   ```
   HashMap<String,Object> startDate = new
                                   HashMap<String,Object>();
   startDate.put(NEXT_AVAILABLE_SHIPMENT_DATE, new
                                   OoompaLoompaDate(2009,02,03));
   ```

3. We create the two Oompa Loompa holidays that we will pass to the rules later.

   ```
   //Holidays
   OoompaLoompaDate holiday2= new OoompaLoompaDate(2009,2,10);
   OoompaLoompaDate holiday1= new OoompaLoompaDate(2009,3,17);
   ```

4. We print out our starting point before we fire the rules.

   ```
   log.info("===== Setup =====");
   log.info(candyBarOrder);
   ```

5. We put our facts into an array (a type of collection) so that we can pass them all at once.

   ```
   //Call the rule engine
   ```

```
    log.info("========= Calling Rule Runner =========");
Object[] facts = new Object[3];
facts[0]=candyBarOrder;
facts[1]=holiday1;
facts[2]=holiday2;
```

6. We call the rules via the `RuleRunner` class that we looked at earlier.

```
// A lot of the running rules uses the same code. The
// RuleRunner (code in this project)
// keeps this code in one place. It needs to know
// - the name(s) of the files containing our rules
// - the fact object(s) containing the
//    information to be passed in and out of our rules
// - a list of global values

new RuleRunner().runRules( RULES_FILES, facts,startDate );
```

7. Finally, we print out our results.

```
//Look at the results
log.info("======= Results - shipping schedule =======");
log.info(candyBarOrder);
```

Running the sample

Let's run the sample. Right-click on the `MultipleRulesExample.java` file in either the navigator view or the package view (just as we did for `DroolsTest` in the previous chapter). From the pop-up menu that appears, select **Run As | Java Application**. After a second or two the output should appear on the console.

Console

1. In the output we can see the starting customer order (date and time removed for clarity).

    INFO: ===== Setup =====

    INFO: Initial Chocolate Order:2000 itemsStillToShip:2000 shipments:none-listed

2. We can see the rules file being loaded.

    INFO: =========== Calling Rule Runner ==============

    INFO: Loading file: src/main/java/net/firstpartners/chap6/shipping-rules.drl

    INFO: found file:src/main/java/net/firstpartners/chap6/shipping-rules.drl

3. We can see the globals being passed into the rules session.

   INFO: Inserting global name: nextAvailableShipmentDate value:03/02/2009

   INFO: Inserting handle to logger (via global)

4. The next step we see is that the rule engine is called (we pass the facts as we call the rule engine).

   INFO: ========= Calling Rule Engine ===========

5. The first rule fires twice, confirming the facts/dates that Ooompa Loompas take a holiday.

   INFO: Remember - Ooompa Loompas don't work on:10/02/2009

   INFO: Remember - Ooompa Loompas don't work on:17/03/2009

6. The shipment and the shipment date rules fire (several times) in turns.

   INFO: Fired Customer Shipment rule - customer is still waiting for 1790 chocolate bars

   INFO: Add Next Available Shipment Date:03/02/2009

   INFO: Fired Customer Shipment rule - customer is still waiting for 1580 chocolate bars

   INFO: Add Next Available Shipment Date:10/02/2009

7. Because **10/02/2009** is a holiday, our holiday rule fires.

   INFO: Reschedule Shipment Date to:11/02/2009 due to holiday on:10/02/2009

8. The shipment and the shipment date rules fire in turns again, with our holiday rule firing again as we don't work on March 17.

   INFO: Fired Customer Shipment rule - customer is still waiting for 1790 chocolate bars

   INFO: Add Next Available Shipment Date:03/02/2009

   INFO: Fired Customer Shipment rule - customer is still waiting for 1370 chocolate bars

   INFO: Add Next Available Shipment Date:17/02/2009

   INFO: Fired Customer Shipment rule - customer is still waiting for 1160 chocolate bars

   INFO: Add Next Available Shipment Date:24/02/2009

   INFO: Fired Customer Shipment rule - customer is still waiting for 950 chocolate bars

   INFO: Add Next Available Shipment Date:03/03/2009

   INFO: Fired Customer Shipment rule - customer is still waiting for 740 chocolate bars

   INFO: Add Next Available Shipment Date:10/03/2009

   INFO: Fired Customer Shipment rule - customer is still waiting for 530 chocolate bars

   INFO: Add Next Available Shipment Date:17/03/2009

   INFO: Reschedule Shipment Date to:18/03/2009 due to holiday on:17/03/2009

9. The rules continue firing in this manner until we reach the final shipment, which should contain only 110 bars. However, our normal shipping rules put too many in the box, 210, leaving us with a negative number. At this point, our Overshipping rule steps in and corrects the number.

   INFO: Fired Customer Shipment rule - customer is still waiting for 110 chocolate bars

   INFO: Add Next Available Shipment Date:31/03/2009

   INFO: Fired Customer Shipment rule - customer is still waiting for -100 chocolate bars

   INFO: Removed CustomerOrder Overshipping - new shipment:110

   INFO: Add Next Available Shipment Date:07/04/2009

10. At this point, our `CustomerOrder` object has been completely populated, and there are no more rules waiting to fire. Control returns to our Java code, which prints out our completed shipping schedule.

    INFO: ======= Results - shipping schedule =======

    INFO: Initial Chocolate Order:2000 itemsStillToShip:0 shipments:

    Shipment:210 date:03/02/2009 chocolate bars left in order:1790

    Shipment:210 date:11/02/2009 chocolate bars left in order:1580

    Shipment:210 date:17/02/2009 chocolate bars left in order:1370

    Shipment:210 date:24/02/2009 chocolate bars left in order:1160

    Shipment:210 date:03/03/2009 chocolate bars left in order:950

    Shipment:210 date:10/03/2009 chocolate bars left in order:740

    Shipment:210 date:18/03/2009 chocolate bars left in order:530

    Shipment:210 date:24/03/2009 chocolate bars left in order:320

    Shipment:210 date:31/03/2009 chocolate bars left in order:110

    Shipment:110 date:07/04/2009 chocolate bars left in order:0

That's it. The example has now finished running.

More powerful rule syntax

Some of the rules in the previous section hinted at more powerful key words than we have used in our rules to date. Let us go through the remaining key words in our rules and explain what they mean. You're unlikely to use all of these, although it is good to know that they are there for some of the weird and wonderful rules that you'll be asked to write (or review). More information on the rules syntax can be found in the Drools documentation, if you're into that kind of thing.

Lefthand side

not

We came across `not` at the start of the chapter, where we used it within an expression to select lines where **Sales** were not equal (!=) to 100. We can also use it at the top level of a rule. For example, if we add `not` to our last shipping rule we completely change its meaning. In this case, it fires only if we do not have any customer orders left to fulfil.

```
rule
    when
        not (
        $CustomerOrder : CustomerOrder(currentBalance<0)
        $ChocolateShipment : ChocolateShipment(itemsStillToShip<0)
        )
    then
```

Note the use of brackets after `not` — they make clear to Drools the order in which we want to read the conditions.

Contains and memberOf

If we wanted to check whether a customer order had shipments, we could use the `contains` keyword. `contains` allows us to examine a list or collection (in this case, our shipments) and act accordingly. The following rule will fire when a particular shipment (if we previously assigned a value to `$mySpecialShipment`) is actually a part of a customer order.

```
rule
    when
        CustomerOrder(shipments contains $mySpecialShipment)
        )
    then
```

The `not contains` keyword would have the opposite effect.

`memberOf` is a similar test, but in the reverse order. We have a handle to a fact, and we want to check if it is contained within a wider collection (for example, `$shipmentsToAcmeCorp`).

```
rule
    when
        Shipment(shipment memberOf $shipmentsToAcmeCorp)
        )
    then
```

Similarly, `not memberOf` is the reverse of this.

matches and Soundslike

Both `matches` and `soundslike` allow powerful text comparisons. Previously, we compared `text1 == text2` using the standard equals operator. `Soundslike` uses the well-documented Soundex algorithm (`http://en.wikipedia.org/wiki/Soundex`) to gauge if two pieces of text sound similar when spoken—for example, to match all `Sales` where the customer name sounds like `acme`.

```
Sales (name soundslike "acme")
```

`matches` is even more powerful, but requires an understanding of the industry standard regexp (regular expressions). For example, the following condition will match all customer names that begin with `a`:

```
Sales (name matches "a*")
```

We can also use `not matches` and `not soundsLike`, if required.

in

`in` allows Drools to check if a single value is a part of a collection. For example, if we want our rule to fire only for our three favourite customers (`Acme Corp`, `Breakfast Roll Inc` and `Chocolate Creams Co`), we could add the following condition:

```
Sales (name in ("Acme Corp","Breakfast Roll Inc","Chocolate Creams
Co"))
```

exists

Another way of saying `exists` is 'at least one'. So the following rule will fire when we have pushed at least one customer shipment out the door:

```
rule
    when
        exists (ChocolateShipment())
    then
        log.info("Hurray! We made a shipment!");
end
```

forall

Normally, when we write a rule, it will match against any of the facts in memory and fire against the matched facts. But what if we want our rule to fire only if all of the facts match our condition? Something like 'fire only if all our customer shipments have dates' could be written as follows:

```
rule
    when
        forall( Shipment( shipmentDate !=null ) )
    then
```

`forall()` can also take multiple conditions, all of which have to be true for all facts matched, before the rule fires.

collect/accumulate

collect allows us to check how many facts in memory match a given rule, and then test the results. For example, if we had more than one customer order, we'd have no easy way of counting the total number of shipments that we made on a particular date. (We can get shipments for single customer using `getShipments()`, but this approach won't scale.)

The following rule will display the total number of shipments (for all customers) on 1st January, 2009:

```
rule
    when
        $numberofShipmentsOnDay : collect (
                ChocolateShipment(
                        new OoomplaLoompaDate(1,1,2009)
            )
    )
    then
        log.info("Boxes shipped today:"+$numberofShipmentsOnDay);
end
```

`accumulate` is a more powerful form of `collect`. It can do everything that `collect` can do, along with additional things such as firing custom code as it works it's way through the collection. (The Drools documentation has more details on how to use this power.)

eval

Sometimes, after looking at all of those expressions, you still can't find one that fits. `eval` allows any expression or formula that returns a Boolean value (that is, a true or false answer) to be used in evaluating a rule. For example, if we want to get the names of customers that are longer than 10 letters, we could use the following:

```
rule
    when
        $s : Sales()
        eval ($s.getName().length >10)
    then
```

`eval` is also useful when calling functions. For example, if we had a function, 'name too long', which returned a Boolean, we could call it using `eval(nameTooLongFunction())`.

> `eval` is very convenient as it allows us to include pretty much any condition in a rule. However, it's considerably slower. With other conditions, Drools can cache (remember) the results because it can figure out when these results need to change. With `eval`, Drools doesn't have this visibility. Therefore, all `eval` expressions need to be rechecked every time the rule is true.
>
> If you have to use `eval`, it's best to add it as the last condition in a rule—meaning, it will be called less often. If any of the previous conditions return 'false', then Drools shortcuts, because there is no need to check any of the remaining conditions.

from

For the examples we've given so far, we've expressed (or pushed) our information (the Java facts) into our rules. The `from` keyword allows the rule engine rules to pull information as required, for example, from a database using the Hibernate framework. Assuming that we have correctly set up Hibernate to talk to the database (a topic so vast that a whole book about it can be written), our rule can use the following syntax:

```
rule
    when
        Order() from $myHibernateObjectPassedAsGlobal.subquery
    then …
```

Righthand side—Then

Just like the When part of the rule, there are also more powerful options available on the righthand side (Then clause) of the rule. At the start of the chapter we came across simple uses of `update()` and `insert()`, but the following keywords are also valid in our rules:

- `$someHandle = insert(something)`: This form of insert works the same as `insert(something)`, that is, putting 'something' into the working memory. The difference is that we keep a hold of it (in the variable `$someHandle`) so that we can do things with it later on.

- `retract($someHandle)`: This removes a fact from the working memory. For example, we may decide to insert a fact representing a discount, only to retract it later if the customer cancels an order.

- `insertLogical(new someFact())`: At the start, `insertLogical()` works the same as insert—it puts an object into memory. The only difference is that as soon as the rule stops being true, the fact (someFact) is automatically retracted from the working memory.

- `update(object, $somehandle)`: This is similar to `update(object)`, although we can specify to the object the handle that we wish to update. If the handle is not passed (that is, the update we did previously), Drools can use a 'best guess'.

The advanced 'When...Then' options are available both in the text editor (like the previous examples) and the guided editor.

Guided editor in the JBoss IDE

Until now we've focussed on using the advanced text editor in the JBoss IDE. But it's also possible to use a guided editor, similar to the one we used in Guvnor. To use this editor, you can take the following steps:

1. Open any Drools-enabled project in the JBoss IDE, and right-click on the folder where you want to create the file.

2. From the context menu that appears, select **New | Other | Guided rule**. (You may need to filter, or open, the **drools** folder in the dialog box to see this last option.) Click on **Next**.

3. Give the new rule file (for example, `myNewRule`) a name, and click on **Finish**.

4. That's it. You should see a new tab open in the editor, as shown in the following screenshot:

The guided rule editor is very similar to the guided editor in Guvnor, which we covered in the previous chapters. It has the same 'when...then' options layout. The guided editor also has tabs to allow us to view the text that was built behind the scenes using this graphical builder.

Summary

This chapter extended the limits of what can be done with business rules. We went through almost every keyword available to us in writing rules and used them to generate a sample to help the Ooompa Loompas pack chocolate bars onto trucks. Now that we understand how the rules work, in the next chapter we will look at testing to ensure that our rules keep on working the way we intend them to.

7
Testing your Rules

We went through many samples in the first six chapters of the book, and didn't have to pay out 'real' money if we made a mistake. We could happily play with the examples, make mistakes, and learn from them. This changes when we start writing 'real' business rules. How much money would a company lose if a rule that you wrote gave double the intended discount to a customer? Or, what if your airline ticket pricing rule started giving away first class transatlantic flights for one cent?

Of course, mistakes happen. This chapter makes sure that these costly mistakes don't happen to you. If you're going through the trouble of writing business rules, you will want to make sure that they do what you intend them to, and keep on doing what you intend, even when you or other people make changes, both now and in the future.

The chapter shows how to test your rules. It begins the testing by using Guvnor. It then shows how to test rules against requirement documents using the **FIT** (**Framework** for **Integrated Testing**), and then shows how to unit test rules by using Junit. But first of all, we will see how testing is not a standalone activity, but part of an ongoing cycle.

Testing when building rules

In this book we play with the examples, and then throw them away when we've learned everything that we can from them. Real life isn't like that. It's a slightly morbid thought, but there's every chance that some of the business rules that you write will last longer than you do. Remember the millennium bug caused by programmers in the 1960's, assuming that nobody would be using their work in 40 years' time, and then being surprised when the year 2000 actually came along?

Rather than 'play and throw away', we're more likely to create production business rules in the following cycle:

1. Write your rules (or modify an existing one) based on a specification, or feedback from end users.

2. Test your rules to make sure that your new rules do what you want them to do, and ensure that you haven't inadvertently broken any existing rules.

3. Deploy your rules to somewhere other than your local machine, where end users (perhaps via a web page or an enterprise system) can interact with them.

You can repeat steps 1, 2, and 3 as often as required. That means, repeat as many times as it takes you to get the first version into production. Or, deploy now and modify it anytime later –in 1, 2, or 10 years time.

We covered step 1 (writing) in the first six chapters of this book. We will cover step 3 (deployment) in Chapter 11. Testing is what we'll cover in this chapter.

Making testing interesting

Normal testing, where you inspect everything manually, is boooooooring! You might check everything the first time, but after the hundredth deployment you'll be tempted to skip your tests—and you'll probably get away with it without any problems. You'll then be tempted to skip your tests on the 101st deployment—still no problems. So, not testing becomes a bad habit either because you're bored, or because your boss fails to see the value of the tests.

The problem, then comes one Friday afternoon, or just when you're about to go on vacation, or some other worst possible time. The whole world will see any mistakes in the rules that are in production. Therefore, fixing them is a lot more time and money consuming than if you catch the error at the very start on your own PC.

What's the solution? **Automate** the testing. All of your manual checks are very repetitive—exactly the sort of thing that computers are good at. The sort of checks for our chocolate shipment example would be 'every time we have an order of 2000 candy bars, we should have 10 shipments of 210 bars and one shipment of 110 bars'.

Testing using Guvnor

Back in Chapters 3 and 4, we used the testing facilities in Guvnor to run our first rules. We had no other way of running rules that would eventually be deployed into the enterprise systems. This is another advantage of testing—we can instantly see whether our tests are correct, without having to wait for our rules to be deployed into the target system.

At a high level, Guvnor has two main screens that deal with testing:

- An individual test screen: Here you can edit your test by specifying the values that you want to input, and the values that you expect once your rules have fired

- A package or multiple tests screen (below): This allows you to run (later on) all of the tests in your package, to catch any rules that you may have inadvertently broken

Another way of saying this is: You write your tests for selfish reasons because you need them to ensure that your rules do what you want them to do. By keeping your tests for later, they automatically become a free safety net that catches bugs as soon as you make a change.

Testing using FIT

Guvnor testing is great. But, often, a lot of what you are testing for is already specified in the requirements documents for the system. With a bit of thought in specifying various scenarios in your requirements documents, **FIT** allows you to automatically compare these requirements against your rules. These requirements documents can be written in Microsoft Word, or similar format, and they will highlight if the outputs aren't what is specified. Like Drools, FIT is an open source project, so there is no charge for either using it, or for customising it to fit your needs.

Before you get too excited about this, your requirements documents do have some compromises. The tests must specify the values to be input to the rules, and the expected result—similar to the examples, or scenarios, that many specifications already contain. These scenarios have to follow a FIT-specific format. Specification documents should follow a standard format anyway—the FIT scenario piece is often less than 10% of it, and it is still highly human-readable! Even better, the document can be written in anything that generates HTML, which includes Microsoft Word, Excel, OpenOffice, Google documents, and most of the myriad of editors that are available today.

Like the Guvnor testing, we can use FIT to test whether our individual requirements are being met when writing our rules. It is possible to run FIT automatically over multiple requirement documents to ensure that nothing has 'accidentally' broken as we update other rules.

Getting FIT

When you downloaded the samples for Chapter 6, you probably noticed three strange packages and folders that we didn't talk about at the time.

- `fit-testcase`: This folder resides just within the main project folder, and contains the FIT requirements documents that we're going to test against.

- `chap7`: This is a folder under `src/main/java/net/firstpartners`, and contains the `startpoint` (`FitRulesExample.java`) that we'll use to kick-start our FIT Tests.

- `FIT`: This folder is next to the `chap7` folder. It contains some of the 'magic plumbing' that makes FIT work. Most business users won't care how this works (you probably won't need to change what you find here), but we will take a look at it in more detail in case we want to customize exactly how FIT works.

If you built the previous example using Maven, then all of the required FIT software will have been downloaded for you. (Isn't Maven great?) So, we're ready to go.

The FIT requirements document

Open the word document `fit-testcase.doc` using Word, or OpenOffice. Remember that it's in the `fit-testcase` folder. `fit-testcase.doc` is a normal document, without any hidden code. The testing magic lies in the way the document is laid out. More specifically, it's in the tables that you see in the document. All of the other text is optional. Let's go through it.

Logo and the first paragraph

At the very top of the document is the Drools logo and a reference to where you can download FIT for rules code. It's also worth reading the text here, as it's another explanation of what the FIT project does and how it works.

None of this text matters, or rather FIT ignores it as it contains no tables. We can safely replace this (or any other text in this document that isn't in the table) with your company logo, or whatever you normally put at the top of your requirement documents.

 FIT is a **GPL** (**General Public License**) open source software. This means you can modify it (as long as you publish your changes). In this sample we've modified it to accept global variables passed into the rules. (We will use this feature in step 3.)

The changes are published in the FIT plumbing directory, which is a part of the sample. Feel free to use it in your own projects.

First step—setup

The setup table prepares the ground for our test, and explains the objects that we want to use in our test. These objects are familiar as they are the Java facts that we've used in our rules.

There's a bit of text (worth reading as it also explains what the table does), but FIT ignores it. The bit that it reads is given in the following table:

net.firstpartners.fit.fixture.Setup	
`net.firstpartners.chap6.domain.CustomerOrder`	`AcmeOrder`
`net.firstpartners.chap6.domain.OoompaLoompaDate`	`nextAvailableShipmentDate`

If you're wondering what this does, try the following explanation in the same table format:

Use the piece of plumbing called 'Setup'	
Create `CustomerOrder` and call it	`AcmeOrder`
Create `OoompaLoompaDate` and call it	`nextAvailableShipmentDate`

There is nothing here that we haven't seen before. Note that we will be passing `nextShipmentDate` as a global so that it matches the global of a same name in our rules file (the match includes the exact spelling, and the same lower-and uppercase).

Second step—values in

The second part also has the usual text explanation (ignored by FIT) and table (the important bit), which explains how to set the values.

net.firstpartners.fit.fixture.Populate		
`AcmeOrder`	Set initial balance	2000
`AcmeOrder`	Set current balance	2000

It's a little bit clearer than the first table, but we'll explain it again anyway.

Use the piece of plumbing called Populate		
`AcmeOrder`	Take the … we created earlier, and set it to have an initial balance of …	2000
`AcmeOrder`	Take the … we created earlier, and set it to have a current balance of …	2000

Third step—click on the Go button

Our next part starts the rules. Or rather, the table tells FIT to invoke the rules. The rest of the text (which is useful to explain what is going on to us humans) gets ignored.

net.firstpartners.fit.fixture.Engine	
Ruleset	`src/main/java/net/firstpartners/chap6/` `shipping-rules.drl`
Assert	`AcmeOrder`
Global	`nextAvailableShipmentDate`
Execute	

The following table is the same again, in English:

Use the piece of plumbing called 'Engine'	
Ruleset	Use the rules in `shipping-rules.drl`
Assert	Pass our `AcmeOrder` to the rule engine (as a fact)
Global	Pass our `nextAvailableShipmentDate` to the rule engine (as a global)
Execute	Click on the **Go** button

Fourth step—check the results

After running our rules, we check to see if the results are as we expected.

net.firstpartners.fit.fixture.Results		
AcmeOrder	Get current balance	0
AcmeOrder	Get initial balance	2000

The following table explains whether the results are as we expected:

Use the piece of plumbing called 'Results'		
AcmeOrder	Check the ... we created earlier, and make sure we now have a current balance of ...	0
AcmeOrder	Check the ... we created earlier, and make sure we have an initial balance of ...	2000

Clear (an optional step)

This optional step clears any of the previous steps. This means that, if we want, we can repeat steps 1 to 4 again in the same requirements document.

```
net.firstpartners.fit.fixture Clear
```

Print a summary (an optional step)

Another optional step is to print a summary of how our tests went. This is in addition to the information that will append to each of the previous steps.

```
fit.Summary
```

Footer

Finally, there is some more narrative in the footer. FIT ignores this, so you can remove or replace this if you want.

There is an important part in this footer. It's a note that the sample (that we're now using) is based on FIT, and also on a sample by Michael Neale from the Drools team—`http://fit-for-rules.sourceforge.net/`. This sample is based on GPL licenced code. My understanding (remember that I'm not a lawyer) is that you can use it internally within your organization; but if it is used outside, then you will need to publish any changes (if you made any) to the core FIT testing code.

Running FIT on our sample

So far, all we've seen is a Word document. Let's make the magic happen by running FIT against this document. In this example we're running FIT through the JBoss IDE, but it would be easy for anyone with a moderate knowledge of Java (ask your friendly technical person) to make this work by double-clicking on a Windows icon. The steps for running FIT on our sample are given as follows:

1. FIT doesn't run against the Word document, but against the HTML version of the Word document. Save your Word document as HTML. (In Word, choose **File | Save As | Web Page**.) Name the file as `fit-testcase.htm`.

 Our project already has this 'Save As HTML' step done, but don't forget to do it again if you make any changes to the FIT document, later.

2. Run the FIT test. In this case select `FitRulesExample` in the JBoss IDE (package explorer or navigator), and right-click on it. Select **Run As | Java Application** from the context menu that is dispalyed.

3. You should see a bunch of stuff in the console, beginning with `net firstpartners.chap7.FitRulesExample main` and ending with `Clearing domain objects`.

4. In between, you'll see the results of our rules firing, such as **28 right, 0 wrong, 23 ignored, 0 exceptions.** Remember that we automate our testing in order to automate our inspection of the results. So don't bother reading the console, other than to check that FIT has run successfully.

5. To see the results, open `fit-test-result.htm`. The filenames that we use (`fit-testcase.htm` and `fit-test-result.htm`) are set in the `FitRulesExample.java` file, and can be changed to whatever you want.

What just happened?

`Fit-test-result.htm` is a copy of the original FIT test case, but it has been updated with the results of our tests. If everything goes well, all of our tables should be highlighted. As an example, the fourth table where we check the results is shown as follows:

net.firstpartners.fit.fixture.Results		
AcmeOrder	Get current balance	0
AcmeOrder	Get initial balance	2000

The other main change has been our (optional) summary table. FIT has updated the output with a summary of the set of tests that it has just run. Most importantly, it's highlighted.

fit.Summary	
counts	28 right, 0 wrong, 23 ignored, 0 exceptions
input file	C:\projects-drools\chap6-sample\fit-testcases\fit-testcase.htm
input update	Thu Sep 04 22:31:39 BST 2008
output file	C:\projects-drools\chap6-sample\fit-testcases\fit-test-result.htm
run date	Thu Sep 04 22:43:44 BST 2008
run elapsed time	0:01.58

There is a small bug in the version of FIT used here (we didn't have 28 tests). But a test that fails will always be picked up, which leads us to the question, "What does a failed test look like?"

What can go wrong?

Let's imagine that our requirements document was slightly different—it said that our rules have run, and so we should still have a balance left on our order of 150 bars still to ship. In other words, table 4 of our requirements document should look something like this:

net.firstpartners.fit.fixture.Results		
AcmeOrder	Get current balance	150
AcmeOrder	Get initial balance	2000

When we save the document using **Save as | HTML** and run our FIT tests again (using the steps above), we'll notice two differences. The first indication that a test has failed is in the console of the JBoss IDE, where we'll see the message: **25 right, 3 wrong, 23 ignored, 0 exceptions**. The second change is in the FIT document, where the results table (table 4) is highlighted in dark gray. Helpfully, it shows you the actual and expected values. The following figure shows you a failing FIT test:

Net.firstpartners.fit.fixture.Results		
AcmeOrder	Get current balance	150 expected
		0 actual
AcmeOrder	Get initial balance	2000

Normally, we would revise our rules and run our FIT tests again until our requirements were met (hightlighted).

That was a failing rule. But what if something more serious happens that causes our rules to 'blow up', or throw an exception? We made a note while talking about the rules that it was important that the rule matches the name of our global variable.

What happens if it doesn't? Let's change the name of the variable in tables 1 and 3. The following table shows the setup using some made-up name:

net.firstpartners.fit.fixture.Setup	
net.firstpartners.chap6.domain.CustomerOrder	AcmeOrder
net.firstpartners.chap6.domain.OoompaLoompaDate	**someMadeupName**

The following table shows how to execute the rule using some made-up name:

net.firstpartners.fit.fixture.Engine	
Ruleset	`src/main/java/net/firstpartners/chap6/shipping-rules.drl`
Assert	`AcmeOrder`
Global	`someMadeupName`
Execute	

When we save the document using **Save as | HTML** and we run FIT again, we see an indication of problems in the console (**22 right, 3 wrong, 23 ignored, 2 exceptions**) with full details of the error in the updated FIT results document. It is shown as follows with some details removed, and others highlighted for clarity:

```
org.drools.spi.ConsequenceException: java.lang.
NullPointerException
....
Caused by: java.lang.NullPointerException
at net.firstpartners.chap6.Rule_Add_Next_Available_Shipment_Date_
0.consequence(Rule_Add_Next_Available_Shipment_Date_0.java:10)

  ... 19 more
```

When you first see this, there is too much detail (about 19 lines of technical-looking text, in this example), but the important bits are:

- The first line that tells us we have a `nullpointer` exception. As explained in the previous chapter, this is where a rule expects to have something available; but what it expects isn't there.

- The `Caused by` line indicates that the problem is in `Rule_Add_Next_Available_Shipment`, and more particularly in the consequence (the 'when' part).

Looking at the When part of `Rule_Add_Next_Available_Shipment`, we see that it contains the code `nextAvailableShipmentDate.rollForward(7)`. This assumes that our `nextAvailableShipmentDate` has something passed in to it. But it doesn't, as we've just changed the FIT rules to use a different name. Hence, it is empty, and causes the `NullPointerException` that we see.

This process of deduction would be even more impressive if we hadn't deliberately broken the rule in the first place.

Even though we change the first (and not the third) table in our FIT document, we will still get an exception, but of a different kind: `IllegalArgumentException-No domain object for key 'nextAvailableShipmentDate' exists`.

As before, the key to resolving the error is to not get scared by the large amount of detail provided, but to look for clues. In this case something is wrong relating to `nextAvailableShipmentDate`. 80% of the problems are caused by something being misspelt, or the wrong variable name being used (which is the problem in this case).

The FIT plumbing

If you're interested only in testing against requirements, then you should presume that FIT for rules 'just works' and skip ahead to the next section (on unit testing). If you're somewhat technical, you're probably wondering how FIT works under the covers. If so, read on.

In general, the classes that were mentioned in the FIT template (for example, `net.firstpartners.fit.fixture.Setup`) are the plumbing that allows the FIT framework to understand our rules code. These files can be found in the `src/main/java/net/firstpartners/fit` folder.

FIT or FIT for rules? FIT is a general-purpose requirements-testing framework that can be adapted to test almost anything. Normally, 'adapted' means a bit of work to match FIT to your code. Fortunately, as most rules follow a standard pattern, Micheal Neale (of the Drools team) has already written the adapter for you as the 'FIT for Rules' project.

The most likely scenario is that 99% of what you need is already covered by this (modified) FIT for Rules framework, but you may come across something that you would like to add, or do differently. For example, the modified framework can pass global variables to the rules, whereas the original source cannot.

The full source is available for both, so these are just pointers to get you started:

1. When we start `FitRulesExample`, Java finds our `main()` method and jumps in. This method sets up parameters (such as input and output files) and calls the `FileRunner` file (run method).

2. `FileRunner` is a part of the FIT framework—the source code is available. But as a summary, it loads the input document that we specified and scans it for tables that may contain instructions to carry out a test.

3. You'll notice that the first line of all of the tables in our FIT document start with an instruction—Setup, Populate, Engine, Results, Clear, and Summary. When the FIT framework finds one of these, it tries to find the file, and loads it.

4. All of these instruction files follow a similar format. They 'extend' another file called `AbstractRulesTesting`, which is like a template. So when we are reading a file (for example, `Setup.java`), we must remember that it also contains all of the code from `AbstractRulesTesting`. (Because many files use this common template, it saves us a lot of typing.)

5. At this point, FIT has scanned the document, found the table, and loaded the instruction file (for example, `Setup.java`). It loops through each cell in the table and calls the `doCell()` method in the `Setup.java` (or other instruction) file.

6. The `doCell()` method checks to see what sort of cell it is. It may carry out different actions depending on whether it's the first row, the first column, or any other cell.

In this way, FIT loops through the document and sets up the facts to be tested, calls the rule engine, checks the results, and then prints a summary.

Remember that we would normally write the instruction file to understand our code. It just happens that we have a set of adaptors (in FIT for Rules) that understands most of the rules-related code. If we need to modify an adaptor, we can add pretty much any Java-based code that's required.

The actual mechanics of calling the rules from FIT are the same as our previous examples. What is different in FIT for Rules is that we express our tests in Word, and (via our adaptors) FIT understands what values to pass to the rules.

Now that we understand requirements testing, let's look at testing at the next level down—unit testing.

What is unit testing?

A good enterprise computer system should be built as if it was made of Lego bricks. Your rules are only a piece of the puzzle. You'll need to go back to the Lego box to get pieces that talk to the database, make web pages, talk to other systems that you may have in your company (or organisation), and so on. Just as Lego bricks can be taken apart and put together in many different ways, the components in a well-designed system should be reusable in many different systems.

Before you use any of these components (or 'bricks') in your system, you will want to be sure that they work. For Lego bricks this is easy—you can just make sure that none of the studs are broken. For components this is a bit harder—often, you can neither see them, nor do you have any idea whether their inputs and outputs are correct. Unit testing makes sure that all of the component pieces of your application work, before you even assemble them.

You can unit test manually, but just like FIT requirements testing, you're going to 'forget' to do it sooner or later. Fortunately, there is a tool to automate your unit tests known as **Junit** (for Java; there are also versions for many other languages, such as .Net). Like Drools and FIT, Junit is open source. Therefore, we can use it on our project without much difficulty. Junit is integrated into the JBoss IDE and is also pretty much an industry standard, so it's easy to find more information on it. A good starting point is the project's home page at `www.Junit.org`.

The following points can help you to decide when to use unit testing, and when to use the other forms of testing that we talked about:

- If you're most comfortable using Guvnor, then use the test scenarios within Guvnor. As you'll see shortly, they're very close to unit tests.
- If the majority of your work involves detailing and signing off against the requirement documents, then you should consider using FIT for Rules.
- If you're most comfortable using Java, or some other programming language, then you're probably using (J)unit tests already—and we can apply these unit tests to rule testing.

In reality, your testing is likely to be a mix of two or three of these options.

Why unit test?

An important point to note is that you've already carried out unit testing in the rules that we wrote earlier. OK, it was manual unit testing, but we still checked that our block of rules produced the outcome that we expected. All we're talking about here is automating the process.

Unit testing also has the advantage of documenting the code because it gives a working example of how to call the rules. It also makes your rules and code more reusable. You've just proved (in your unit test) that you can call your code on a standalone basis, which is an important first step for somebody else to be able to use it again in the future.

You do want your rules to be reused, don't you?

Unit testing the Chocolate Shipments sample

As luck would have it, our Chocolate Shipments example also contains a unit test. This is called `DroolsUnitTest.java`, and it can be found in the `test/java/net/firstpartners/chap7` folder.

> `DroolsUnitTest.java` lives in a similar, but parallel, set of folders. It begins with `test` instead of `main`. Having these parallel sets of folders is a convention used to separate our test code from our production code.
>
> We want to run our tests before we deploy them to production, but not actually deploy those tests. By having the folders set up in this way, we fool Java into thinking that these tests live in the same package as the actual rules, yet they are still separate. This is done so that the tests don't accidentally get deployed (which is a good thing, as we don't want our tests to corrupt our production data).

Running the Junit test is similar to running the samples. In the JBoss IDE Navigator or package explorer, we select **DroolsUnitTest.java**, right-click on it, and then select **Run as | Junit test** from the shortcut menu.

All being well, you should see some messages appear on the console. We're going to ignore the console messages; after all, we're meant to be automating our testing, not manually reading the console. The really interesting bit should appear in the IDE— the Junit test result, similar to the screenshot shown below. If everything is OK, we should see the green bar displayed—success!

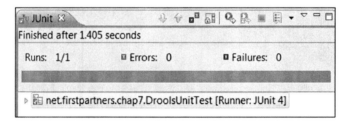

We've run only one unit test, so the output is fairly simple. From top to bottom we have: the time it took to run the test; the number of errors and failures (both zero—we'll explain the difference shortly, but having none of them is a good thing), the green bar (success!), and a summary of the unit tests that we've just run (**DroolsUnitTest**).

If you were running this test prior to deploying to production, all you need to know is that the green bar means that everything is working as intended. It's a lot easier than inspecting the code line by line.

However, as this is the first time that we're using a unit test, we're going to step through the tests line by line. A lot of our Junit test is similar to `MultipleRulesExample.java` that we ran in the previous chapter. For example, the unit test uses the same `RuleRunner` file to load and call the rules. In addition, the Junit test also has some automated checks (asserts) that give us the green bar when they pass, which we saw in the previous screenshot.

What just happened?

Probably the easiest way to understand what just happened is to walk through the contents of the `DroolsUnitTest.java` file.

Our unit code starts with the usual package information. Even though it is in a separate folder, Java is fooled into using the same package.

```
package net.firstpartners.chap7;
```

In our imports section (list of other files that we need), we have a mix of our domain objects (the facts such as `CustomerOrder`) that we used earlier for holding information. We also have the logging tools. What is new is the imports of `Assert` (part of our automatic checking tool) and importing the `junit` test (the template for our unit test).

```
import static org.junit.Assert.assertEquals;
import static org.junit.Assert.assertNotNull;
import static org.junit.Assert.assertTrue;

import java.util.HashMap;

import net.firstpartners.chap6.domain.CustomerOrder;
import net.firstpartners.chap6.domain.OoompaLoompaDate;
import net.firstpartners.drools.RuleRunner;

import org.apache.commons.logging.Log;
import org.apache.commons.logging.LogFactory;
import org.junit.Test;
```

The start of the main part of the file may be renamed to `DroolsUnitTest`, but what it does is the same. The rules are still read from exactly the same file as before.

```
public class DroolsUnitTest {

    private static Log log = LogFactory.getLog(DroolsUnitTest.class);

    private static final String NEXT_AVAILABLE_SHIPMENT_DATE =
    "nextAvailableShipmentDate";

    private static final String[] RULES_FILES = new String[] { "src/
    main/java/net/firstpartners/chap6/shipping-rules.drl" };
```

Earlier, our starting point was called `main` so that Java knew where we wanted it to start when we pressed the green **Go** button. This time, our start method is called `testShippingRules` and it's marked with a `@Test` flag so that we know it's an entry point. We can have multiple tests, each marked with `@Test`. The Junit framework will test each one in turn.

The rest of this code snippet, which involves setting up and calling the business rules via `RuleRunner`, is exactly the same as our previous 'calling the rule engine' samples.

```
@Test
public void testShippingRules() throws Exception {

    // Initial order
    CustomerOrder candyBarOrder = new CustomerOrder(2000);

    HashMap<String, Object> startDate = new HashMap<String,
    Object>();
    startDate.put(NEXT_AVAILABLE_SHIPMENT_DATE, new
    OoompaLoompaDate(2009, 02, 03));
    // Holidays
    OoompaLoompaDate holiday2 = new OoompaLoompaDate(2009, 2, 10);
    OoompaLoompaDate holiday1 = new OoompaLoompaDate(2009, 3, 17);

    // Call the rule engine
    Object[] facts = new Object[3];
    facts[0] = candyBarOrder;
    facts[1] = holiday1;
    facts[2] = holiday2;

    // A lot of the running rules uses the same code. The RuleRunner
    (code
    // in this project)
    // keeps this code in one place. It needs to know
    // - the name(s) of the files containing our rules
    // - the fact object(s) containing the information to be passed
    in and
    // out of our rules
    // - a list of global values

    new RuleRunner().runRules(RULES_FILES, facts, startDate);
```

In our previous example, once we called the rules, we printed the results out to the screen for manual inspection. This time things are different. We want to make this checking automatic. Hence, we have added following new lines in the final snippet, using `assertXXX` to check if the values that we get back from the rules are as expected:

```
    // Check that the results are as we expected
    assertEquals(
      "No more bars should be left to ship", 0, candyBarOrder
        .getCurrentBalance());

    assertEquals(
        "Our initial order balance should not be changed",
        2100, candyBarOrder.getInitialBalance());

    assertNotNull(
        "Our list of shipments should contain a value",
        candyBarOrder.getShipments());

    assertTrue(
        "We should have some Cusomter Shipments",
        candyBarOrder.getShipments().size() > 5);
  }

}
```

In general, our `assert` checks follow the format: `Assert ( "message if the value is not as we expect" , valueWeExpected, valueWeGotWhenWeRanTheTest)`

- The first line (`assertEquals`) compares the number of candy bars that should still be left to ship after our rules have fired (should be 0)
- The second line (`assertEquals`) ensures that the initial order is not changed by the rules, and remains at 2100
- The next line (`assertNotNull`) ensures that the list of shipments that we made is not empty
- The final line (`assertTrue`) checks that we have more than five shipments made to a customer

Is it best to have multiple tests or multiple asserts within a single test? It is possible to have multiple tests, such as `someTest()` methods (each marked with `@Test`), and/or multiple tests using `assertXXX` within a method. A combination of both is probably the best. Multiple asserts in one method are great when your test is difficult to set up, but the test will stop at the first assert that turns out to be false. This means you can solve the first error, but your test will then stop at the next assert that fails. Having these asserts in separate test methods shows you instantly how many problem(s) you have—at the price of having some duplicated setup code.

There is a school of thought that advocates test-first design. Write your unit tests before you write any proper rules—this acts as your specification.

Of course, all of your tests will fail at the start. However, bit by bit, you must write the rules to make them work. That way, you know when you've done what you started out to do—no more and no less. And it means that you can never 'forget' to write your tests.

It may appear strange, but it works for many people. So, it's certainly worth giving a try.

What if it goes wrong?

We were lucky that our tests worked the very first time. Unfortunately, this is almost impossible to achieve. For example, assume that we mistakenly wrote a rule that changed the initial balance.

```
assertEquals(
    "Our initial order balance should not be changed",
    2100, candyBarOrder.getInitialBalance());
```

In this case, when we come to check, our test will fail. We will get a red bar in our unit tests, detailing what has gone wrong (similar to the screenshot below). The message in our assert (**Our initial order balance should not be changed**) and other details (such as line numbers) are provided to help us trace what is going wrong. You'll also notice that the **Failures** count is now **1**.

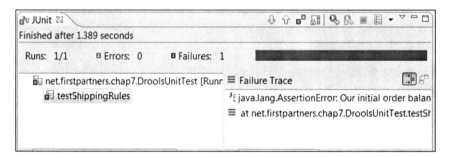

Failures and errors

So what's the difference between failures and errors? Failures are things (such as the above assert) that we explicitly check for. Errors are the unexpected things that go wrong. Remember our `NullPointerException` from the previous section in FIT? That is, the problem that we face when something is empty that shouldn't be. That exception is shown as an error in Junit with a red bar (again), along with the details of the problem to help you fix it.

It's simple—green is good and red is bad. But remember, it's always better to catch mistakes early.

Testing an entire package

Typically, you write a unit test at the same time as writing a set of rules to confirm that the functionality is 'done'.

After you're 'done', you (or one of your team) should run all of the tests in the project to make sure that your new work hasn't broken any of the rules or code that already existed. There are a couple of ways to automatically do this overnight (as part of a build control tool such as Cruise Control) as part of your build scripts (Maven, the tool installed to build the samples in this book does this for you), or you can run all of the tests from the JBoss IDE (akin to the 'run all scenarios in package' that we saw in Guvnor).

It's pretty easy to run all of your unit tests in one go. All you have to do is this:

1. From the toolbar (at the very top of the JBoss IDE) select **Run**.
2. In the dialog box that is dispalyed, select **Junit** (near the lower-left of the screen) and then click on **New launch configuration** (the icon on the upper-left of the screen, as shown in the screenshot).

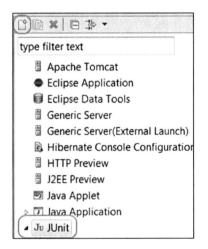

3. On the righthand side, fill in the following values:

```
Name:  MultiTest

[ ] Test  (x)= Arguments  ✈ Classpath  ▦ JRE  ⧉ Source  ▥ Environment  »₁

○ Run a single test

    Project:     chap6-sample                              Browse...

    Test class:                                            Search...

● Run all tests in the selected project, package or source folder:

    chap6-sample                                           Search...

Test runner:   JUnit 4                              ▼

[ ] Keep JUnit running after a test run when debugging


                                        Apply            Revert
```

4. Click on **Apply** (to save it, so that you don't have to go through all of the steps the next time), and then click on **Run**.

As before, the JBoss IDE will chug away for a couple of moments, and then the popup JUnit screen will be displayed. As before, if any of the multiple tests fail, you'll see a red bar, along with details of all of the items that went wrong. When all of your tests pass, you can be sure that your rules are of top quality.

Summary

Hopefully, you're now confident about testing. In this chapter we've seen how to test our rules using Guvnor, as well as using FIT for rule testing against requirements documents, and unit testing using Junit. Now that we can write and test advanced enterprise rules, let's see another rule format—rules in Excel (decision table) format.

8
Data and Rules in Excel

At the start of the book we said 'If you can understand Microsoft Excel, then you should be OK'. To prove this, we're going to devote this entire chapter to Excel.

Almost everybody understands Excel spreadsheets, or their equivalent in OpenOffice and Google Docs. All of these are simple, grid-based editors that allow us to store, edit, and share information. Spreadsheets may not be perfect, but they're popular and well-understood. First, we're going to use them to hold the data that we supply to the business rules. Then we're going to use spreadsheets to hold the actual rules in a decision table format.

Reading data from Excel

One of the basic problems that we face is getting information into and out of our business rules. Until now we've been using JavaBeans. These are great, especially if you're familiar with Java already. JavaBeans are also good if your information is already available from a technical source of data, such as a database, that Java can easily read. But JavaBeans can be time-consuming to create—more so if your information is already contained in an Excel spreadsheet.

Instead of having to create our Java Beans manually, wouldn't it be great if we could hand this spreadsheet to the Drools rule engine and say 'here you go—fire the rules against this information'. It would be even better if our rules could say something like 'If the value at cell A1 is greater than 100, then update the spreadsheet to say: value too high'. As a result of our rules firing, the spreadsheet could be updated with that message.

Fortunately, there is already an open source project called Apache POI that allows Java-based programs (such as the Drools rule engine) to read and write data from Excel spreadsheets. We'll use a simplified version, based on POI (from the Red-Piranha project), in our chapter so that we can read and write from Excel. That covers the 'store the data in Excel' requirement.

What's the difference between updating values using normal Excel formulae and updating the values using Drools, as we explain in this chapter?

For most spreadsheets, the power of Excel (and it is very powerful) is enough. But, pretty quickly, those formulae become very complex and difficult to understand, test, and maintain—the same problem of 'traditional coding' that we talked about in the previous chapters. Rules solve this problem by expressing your business rules in a clear and clean way.

If you're interested in loading high volumes of data from different formats (including Excel), fast-forward to the Smooks section in Chapter 12. The advantage of the Red-Piranha approach is that it allows us to change the formatting or colours in the spreadsheet. Smooks is better for large volumes of data, but doesn't give you the pretty colors!

Business rules for this sample

The business rules that we'll walk through in this chapter are based on the following:

- The chocolate factory needs to buy cocoa beans to make candy bars
- Because the price of cocoa beans rises and falls almost daily (an entire building in Chicago is dedicated to this market), the chocolate factory decides to make a bit of side money by trading in chocolate
- We trust certain traders more than others, so we will buy from them at a higher price—that is, we have specific prices for each broker
- We also have different selling prices for different traders, as either they have a bulk-buying agreement, or we factor in the cost of delivery

Of course, this is very simple compared to what really goes on in the market, but it's enough to show how to store both data and rules in Excel.

Getting and running the sample

Our sample that shows how to read and write Excel data (as our fact model) can be downloaded (like the last example) from Google Code at `http://code.google.com/p/red-piranha`. The file you need is `droolsbook-chap8-sample_01.zip.`. Like the previous example, unzip it to a location of your choice. The downloaded file should contain the Eclipse project, but (as before) you may need to execute the Maven command `mvn clean package` to download the required libraries to your computer.

Input

Open this project and look for the input spreadsheet. It is called `chocolate-data.xls`, and is found in the `src/main/resources` folder. When you open it, it looks something like the following screenshot—a fairly ordinary spreadsheet with one value at the top (**Current Stock**), and below that many rows, one per broker (**A Broker**, **B Broker**, and so on) with five columns. These lines are the various buy and sell offers that chocolate brokers will make to us. The five columns are contain **Broker Code**, **Buy or Sell**, **Quantity**, **Price**, and **Status** of the trade.

	A	B	C	D	E
1	**Chocolate Trading Example**				
2					
3	Current Stock	2000			
4					
5	**Broker Code**	**Buy or Sell**	**Quantity**	**Price**	**Status**
6	A Broker	TRUE	110	300	n/a
7	B Broker	FALSE	120	500	n/a
8	C Broker	TRUE	130	700	n/a
9	D Broker	FALSE	140	300	n/a
10	E Broker	TRUE	150	500	n/a
11	F Broker	FALSE	160	700	n/a
12	G Broker	TRUE	170	300	n/a
13	H Broker	FALSE	180	500	n/a
14	I Broker	TRUE	190	700	n/a
15	J Broker	FALSE	200	300	n/a
16	K Broker	TRUE	210	500	n/a
17	L Broker	FALSE	220	700	n/a
18	M Broker	TRUE	230	300	n/a
19	N Broker	FALSE	240	500	n/a
20	O Broker	TRUE	250	700	n/a
21	P Broker	FALSE	260	300	n/a
22	Q Broker	TRUE	270	500	n/a
23	R Broker	FALSE	280	700	n/a
24	S Broker	TRUE	290	300	n/a
25	T Broker	FALSE	300	500	n/a
26	U Broker	TRUE	290	300	n/a
27	V Broker	FALSE	300	500	n/a
28	W Broker	TRUE	290	300	n/a
29	X Broker	FALSE	300	500	n/a
30	Y Broker	TRUE	290	300	n/a
31	Z Broker	FALSE	300	500	n/a

The screenshot below demonstrates named ranges. Referring to cells such as 'A1' or 'B12' is great, until you have to modify the spreadsheet when you need to update all your rules.

Rather than referring to cells 'A12-E12', we can use a name such as 'G Broker Values' to refer to a range (group) of cells. If we add or remove lines from the spreadsheet, the named range will continue to point to the same set of information.

To see the named ranges in Excel, select **Insert | Name | Define** from the toolbar. You should see the **Define Name** dialog box listing all of the ranges in the current spreadsheet. In effect, there is one named range for each broker (that is, one for each line in the Excel spreadsheet), and a named range for the current stock value.

Rules

Our rules for the first sample are pretty simple and are still in the standard format that we're used to. It just prints out the values and marks cells as modified. Remember, this first sample is all about reading data from Excel.

```
package net.firstpartners.chap8;

import net.firstpartners.drools.log.ILogger

import net.firstpartners.exceldata.Cell;
import net.firstpartners.exceldata.Range;

global ILogger log;

rule "log then modify cell values"
    when
        $cell : Cell(modified==false)

    then

        $cell.setModified(true);

        //Logging message
        log.info("initial cell value:"+$cell);
end
```

Running the sample

Our main class is `ExcelDataRulesExample.java` (which is in the directory `src/main/java/net/firstpartners/chap8`). Select this Java file in Eclipse and run it in the usual way (right-click on the file, and then choose **Run as Java application**). You'll see some output in the console, but the real change is in the Excel spreadsheet, which has been copied and then modified.

This output spreadsheet is called `chocolate-output.xls`, and can be found in the main project folder. When you open it you'll see that according to our simple rule, all cells having a range name have been marked as modified. In this case, the cells are highlighted to make it clear what is going on.

	A	B	C	D	E
1	Chocolate Trading Example				
2					
3	Current Stock	2000			
4					
5	Broker Code	Buy or Sell	Quantity	Price	Status
6	A Broker	TRUE	110	300	n/a
7	B Broker	FALSE	120	500	n/a
8	C Broker	TRUE	130	700	n/a
9	D Broker	FALSE	140	300	n/a

 Copying the Excel spreadsheet and then modifying it means that even if a rule deleted all the values by accident, you still have the original spreadsheet to go back to and try again!

What's going on?

If you're not interested in the technical nuts and bolts, then skip ahead to the next section. Just remember that we can read and write information in Excel, and pass this information to our rules. Still with us? Then you're in for a treat, because we're going to explain what's just happened in the previous example. Along the way, you'll pick up information that will help you write rules that use Excel as a fact model to hold information for our business rules.

Under the covers

Our sample starts in the `ExcelDataExample.java` file. As before, the flow starts in the main method. It's fairly clear in this file where our input (`chocolate-data.xls`), output (`chocolate-output.xls`), and rules (`log-then-modify-rules.drl`) are. What is different from the previous sample is that we have a piece of code (`Rangeconvertor`) that loads the Excel spreadsheet and transforms it into a set of simple JavaBeans (Cells and Ranges). These JavaBeans are the fact model (containing the data) that we pass to our rules as normal.

Why not use the Cells and Ranges supplied by the Apache POI framework? The answer is that you can use them, but the Cells and Ranges based on Red-Piranha that we will use here are simpler. They also allow us to add methods (such as `getRangeContainsValue`) that make it easier to write rules.

We've already seen that the simple rule for this example matches against all cells, logs their contents, and marks them as modified. Our `RangeConvertor` also translates our (updated) Cells and Ranges back into a proper Excel spreadsheet. For clarity, any cell that we modify is highlighted—hence all our ranges are highlighted.

More on Cells and Ranges

When we write more sophisticated rules, we'll be matching against Cells and Ranges. These JavaBeans hold the information that we passed in via the Excel spreadsheet. Because our rules will be matching against these Cells and Ranges, it's worth looking at them in more detail.

```
▲ 🗐  Range
      ● ˢ getUniqueCellName(String, int)          3 ●   getRangeContainsValue(Object)
      ● ᶜ Range()                                 1 ●   getRangeName()
      ● ᶜ Range(String)                              ●   getUniqueCellName(int)
      ●   addPropertyChangeListener(PropertyChangeListener)  ● ▲ hashCode()
      ● ▲ clear()                                    ● ▲ isEmpty()
      ● ▲ containsKey(Object)                        ● ▲ keySet()
      ● ▲ containsValue(Object)                      ●   propertyChange(PropertyChangeEvent)
      ● ▲ entrySet()                               2 ● ▲ put(String, Cell)
      ● ▲ equals(Object)                           2 ● ▲ putAll(Map<? extends String, ? extends Cell>)
      ● ▲ get(Object)                                ● ▲ remove(Object)
   3  ●   getCell(int)                                ●   removePropertyChangeListener(PropertyChangeListener)
      ●   getCellInRange(String, int)             1 ●   setRangeName(String)
      ●   getCellName(String, int)                   ● ▲ size()
   3  ●   getCellValue(int)                        4 ●   toShortString()
      ●   getCellValueArray()                      4 ● ▲ toString()
   3  ●   getCellValueList()                       4 ● ▲ values()
```

Our **Range** JavaBean, like its equivalent in Excel, is used to hold a group of cells. The items marked on the above screenshot are the ones that we will discuss in more detail.

1. Like Excel, our **Range** has a name that we can access with the **getRangeName** and **setRangeName** methods.

2. A range is based on the Map interface. That is, our cells are stored within the range as a cell name, and then the actual cell itself. Our cell names follow the range name (for example, the first cell in the **some_name** range would be **some_name_0**), but we have convenience methods that handle this for us.

3. Our own methods for working with cells are: **getCell** (the actual cell itself), **getCellValue** (a shortcut to the value held within the list), **getCellValueList** (a list of all the values within the range), and **getRangeContainsValue** (which searches the range and returns true if the value is found).

4. We have other methods to help us print (for example, **toString** and **toShortString**), methods to help us compare ranges (**hashcode** and **equals**), and other Map methods (**size,remove, isEmpty**, and so on).

```
▲ ⊙  Cell
      ● ᶜ Cell()                                          4    ● ▲ hashCode()
      ● ᶜ Cell(String, Object)                            2    ●   isModified()
      ●   addPropertyChangeListener(PropertyChangeListener)    ● ▲ propertyChange(PropertyChangeEvent)
  4   ● ▲ equals(Object)                                       ●   removePropertyChangeListener(PropertyChangeListener)
  3   ●   getBooleanValue()                                    ●   setCellName(String)
      ●   getCellName()                                        ●   setComment(String)
      ●   getComment()                                    1    ●   setHoldingRange(Range)
  1   ●   getHoldingRange()                                    ●   setModified(boolean)
  3   ●   getIntValue()                                        ●   setValue(Object)
      ●   getValue()                                      4    ● ▲ toString()
  3   ●   getValueAsText()
```

One **Range** can contain one or more cells, depending on the Excel spreadsheet that is passed in.

1. A cell is aware of the Range that holds it (**getHoldingRange**, **setHoldingRange**).

2. When a cell is updated by any `setMethod`, the modified flag is tripped. We can read this with the **isModified** method. This is what is used later on to mark the modified cells (in Excel) are highlighted.

3. We can read or set a value with the **getValue** or **setValue** methods. We also have convenience methods such as **getBooleanValue**, **getIntValue**, and **getValueAsText** to get the values converted to yes/no, numbers, and text respectively.

4. Like the range, we implement **toString, equals**, and **hashcode** to make Cells easier to print (to the console) and easier to handle from our rules.

The actual code that converts between the Excel code and our JavaBean code (and back again) is contained in the `RangeConvertor.java` and `CellConvetor.java` files. We don't need to go into the details. But we should know that we loop through all of the named ranges in the Excel sheet, and copy the values to and from our JavaBeans as required. There are a couple of quirks in this conversion process, such as:

1. If we leave the `chocolate-output.xls` open in Excel, and run our sample again, we'll get the following error (to resolve it, simply close the file in Excel):

   ```
   Exception in thread "main" java.io.FileNotFoundException:
   chocolate-output.xls (The process cannot access the file because
   it is being used by another process)
   ```

2. Because of the way that Eclipse builds projects, if you change the input spreadsheet (`chocolate-data.xls`), you must save the Excel file (as normal) and then clean out any old versions by selecting **Project | Clean** from the Eclipse toolbar. If you don't do this before running the sample, any changes that you make will appear to be ignored.

3. If a cell is blank in Excel, then it doesn't exist. (It's a way to make the Excel file size smaller.) If a cell doesn't exist, then we can't update it with a value, even if the Rules have changed it—that's why have **n/a** in some cells rather than keeping them empty. This is a quirk in the Excel conversion code that a future version of Red-Piranha should correct.

> Red Piranha is a knowledge management tool available as an open source project on Google Code, at `http://code.google.com/p/red-piranha`.
>
> For the purposes of this chapter, Red-Piranha makes it easier to manipulate data in Excel using Drools. Drools hides the complexity of Apache POI (the code that does the actual Excel manipulation), which means that your rules could update other table-based sources of information such as Google Docs, or web pages containing HTML tables.

You may have noticed that when we invoked the rule engine (via the `DtRuleRunner` file), we passed in both Ranges and Cells (that is, we called the `ranges.getAllRangesAndCells` method). Surely, this is duplication. Because Ranges contain Cells, why not pass only the Ranges so that the rule engine can automatically read all the Cells that are contained within them? The answer is: We *can* access a cell within a range using the notation `SomeRange.getCell(1).getValue()`. But as the rule engine cannot detect changes in these second-level JavaBeans, updates to Cells made in this way will not cause other rules to fire when they should.

This restriction applies not only to Ranges and Cells, but also to any 'nested' JavaBeans that you may write on your own. Later, we'll see ways of notifying Drools about the changes to the cells. But for the moment, it's best to pass both Ranges and Cells to the rule engine. Java is smart enough to realise that they are duplicates, so we only end up with a single copy of the cell being stored in memory.

Note that both Cells and Ranges implement property change listeners to help the rule engine detect changes in values. However, because your JavaBeans may not have these, we also notify the rule engine explicitly of any changes (via update and modify calls).

In this example, contents of Cells may change, but Ranges do not. That is, the value of a cell may be updated, but the shape or the name of a range is unlikely to change.

As an aside, you may have noticed that even though we have both Range and Cell values available (in working memory) to match against, (to keep the sample simple), the current rules only match against values contained in Cells.

Sophisticated, but repetitive rules

Reading and updating an Excel file is a good trick, but our simple rule doesn't do much yet. How can we add more sophisticated rules? More importantly, if you've extended the rules from previous chapters, how do we write repetitive rules without a lot of copying and pasting? And how do we write rules in an Excel format, and not just the data, which is what we've done so far in this chapter?

Let's remind ourselves of the chocolate trading rules and write them in a more 'business rule' type format:

- When you get a **BUY** offer for **A_Broker**, compare the price of the offer against the price that you are willing to pay. If the price is reasonable, make a note to execute a buy order.

- Put in place similar buy rules for each and every broker.

- When you have a note saying **BUY**, execute the order.

- When you get a **SELL** offer for **A_Broker**, compare the price of the offer against the price that you are willing to accept. If the price is reasonable, make a note to execute a sell order.

- Put in place similar buy rules for each and every broker.

- When you have a note saying **SELL**, execute the order.

Although, there are only four types of rules (evaluate buy, execute buy, evaluate sell, and execute sell) there are potentially hundreds of duplicate rules. These rules may be simple compared to those in previous chapters, but they have a higher risk of error due to their large number. It would be better if we could set them out in a simple table format like the rules table shown in the following screenshot:

 The two images in the screenshot below are actually the same table, except split to fit into the page. Both are screenshots from the `TradingRules.xls` file that you downloaded as a part of the Chapter 8 sample.

RuleTable Evaluate the Buy Trades that we are interested in			
Check the broker name (against the range)	Check if this is a buy offer (true)	And our cell as not yet been modified	As long as the price is less than
A_Broker	true	false	300
C_Broker	true	false	400
E_Broker	true	false	500
G_Broker	true	false	200

The first part of the table shows the usual 'if' conditions. In the column which is highlighted, we check the broker name, ensure that this is a buy offer, make sure that no other rule has processed this offer, and then ensure that the price is greater than what we're prepared to pay for.

Underneath, we have the actual lines of data we use as part of these 'if' conditions. We only show four, but there are 13 as a part of the sample table, and there could be many more. These lines combine with our rules, so we can read the first line as:

> Check that our broker name is **A_Broker**. Check that it is a buy offer, and that nobody else has taken up (modified) this offer. And if the buy offer price is less than 300 then …

If we didn't have the table format, we'd have had to write out in full each of the rules from 4 to 13, or however many we have. So the decision table format is ideal for the rules that are repetitive. The structure stays the same, but the values that we are checking against change from rule to rule.

That's the 'when' part of the table. What about the other part (the 'then' part)? In real life, the screenshot below (showing the 'then' part) follows to the right of the previous table.

Update the status to –	Log what we just did with the message –	Mark Cell as updated	Mark Range as updated
Buy This	Plan to Buy from A Broker	blank	blank
Buy This	Plan to Buy from C Broker	blank	blank
Buy This	Plan to Buy from E Broker	blank	blank
Buy This	Plan to Buy from G Broker	blank	blank

Our 'then' part follows a similar format, breaking the rules into the structure (the highlighted part) and the associated values that change for each rule. The 'then' part matching against our 'when' part (**A_Broker** (the first line)) is:

- **Update the status to_Buy This**
- Log a message about what we plan to do
- Notify the rule engine that both Cells and Ranges have been updated (to see if any other rules should be fired)

Some Excel magic

The decision tables that you saw earlier are taken directly from our sample `Trading-Rules.xls`, but it looks like there is something missing. How does our technical rule engine understand the near-English language we have in the excel decision tables?

The answer is that we've used a bit of Excel magic to hide this technical complexity from the business users. In Excel 2003 and Open Office, the feature we use is called **Group and Outline** and is found under the **Data** item on the toolbar. Office 2007 has this feature under the **Group** item on the ribbon.

1 2		A	B	C	D
	1			**Chocolate Trading Rules**	
+	7				
	8			RuleTable Evaluate the Buy Trades that we are interested in	
+	12		Note: This rule table checks broker specific prices (Buy)	Check the broker name (against the range)	Check if this is a buy offer (true)
	13			A_Broker	true
	14			C_Broker	true
	15			E_Broker	true
	16			G_Broker	true
	17			I_Broker	true
	18			K_Broker	true

Clicking the '+' sign at the far left of the screen shows the hidden technical mapping. With the lines unhidden, we can begin to see what is really going on.

Grouping and hiding columns is not the only visual trick that we can use to make data entry easier. We can use formatting and colors in cells, borders, and comments—all of which are used on this sample. We can also use more advanced features such as merged cells and dropdowns for selecting values from a predefined list.

In general, Drools just ignores these and reads the basic Excel table in black and white.

1 2	A	B	C	D	E
1					
2			**Chocolate Trading Rules**		
3			RuleSet	net.firstpartners.chap8	
4			Notes	This decision table is to regulate the buying and selling of chocolate beans	
5			Import	net.firstpartners.exceldata.Cell,net.firstpartners.exceldata.Range	
6					
7					
8			RuleTable Evaluate the Buy Trades that we are interested in		
9			CONDITION	CONDITION	CONDITION
10			$r:Range		
11			eval($r.getRangeName().equals("$1"))	eval($r.getCell(1).getBooleanValue()==$1)	eval($r.getCell(4).isModified() == $1)
12		Note: This rule table checks broker specific prices (Buy)	Check the broker name (against the range)	Check if this is a buy offer (true)	And our cell as not yet been modified

Decision tables behind the scenes

A lot of the lines that we've just displayed contain the rule syntax that we've used in the previous chapter. We'll take a run through the information at the top of our decision table file and the first two decision tables. Remember that we're writing these rules to match against the `chocolate-data.xls` fact model (containing the data), which we loaded at the start of this example.

 Keep in mind that decision tables are just a mechanism to help generate our rules. Behind the scenes, the rules themselves get translated into the rules syntax that we're familiar with.

Header information

In Chapters 5 and 6, we saw a list of items that go at the top of our rules files. These items can go into the header table, which always starts with a **RuleSet** declaration, as we can see in the screenshot below.

RuleSet lets Drools know where the header table begins, and everything else is ignored (for example the **Chocolate Trading Rules** title is not read). **RuleSet** also lets Drools know which package these rules live in, although we do import additional JavaBeans for this example (the ones that represent our Ranges and Cells). Our **Notes** line is ignored as it means nothing to Drools. We could also have used items such as 'global' and 'function' in this part.

Chocolate Trading Rules

RuleSet	net.firstpartners.chap8
Notes	This decision table is to regulate the buying and selling of chocolate beans
Import	net.firstpartners.exceldata.Cell,net.firstpartners.exceldata.Range

RuleTable—Evaluate the buy trades

Drools ignores everything else in the Excel file, until it comes to a section marked as **RuleTable**, where it expects to find rules laid out in the specific decision table format. The text following **RuleTable** is used to autogenerate the rule names, so be careful with the name that you use.

RuleTable Evaluate the Buy Trades that we are interested in			
CONDITION	CONDITION	CONDITION	CONDITION
$r:Range			
eval($r.getRangeName().equals("$1"))	eval($r.getCell(1).getBooleanValue()==$1)	eval($r.getCell(4).isModified() == $1)	eval($r.getCell(3).getIntValue() < $1)
Check the broker name (against the range)	Check if this is a buy offer (true)	And our cell as not yet been modified	As long as the price is less than
A_Broker	true	false	300
C_Broker	true	false	400
E_Broker	true	false	500

The first part of the decision table is the **CONDITION** cells, which makes up the 'when' part of the rule. In this case, we have one variable definition and four conditions to be matched before the rule fires. Note the use of parameter variables in the unhidden part of the rules. **$param1** or **$1** means take the first value from the cells below and use it as part of the comparison in the rule. The following table explains the different conditions shown in the above screenshot:

- **CONDITION $r:Range**: Only match against Ranges in working memory.

- **CONDITION eval($r.getRangeName().equals("$1"))**: Matches the name of this range against the parameter from the cell below (for example **A_Broker**, **B_Broker**, and so on).

- **CONDITION eval($r.getCell(1).getBooleanValue()==$1)**: Matches the first cell of this range against the parameter (this value is **true** for all lines). Remember that the first cell of data is the **Buy / Sell** flag.

- **CONDITION eval($r.getCell(4).isModified() == $1)**: Checks that the fourth (that is, last) cell in our Range—'modified' flag—is equal to the parameter (that is, this parameter is false for all lines). Remember that the last cell of **data** that we pass in (from the data spreadsheet, which was the first spreadsheet mentioned in this chapter) is **Status**, which starts out as **N/A**.

- **CONDITION eval($r.getCell(3).getIntValue() < $1)**: Checks that the third cell in our data range (the price that we offered for the chocolate beans) is less than our parameter (which varies from broker to broker).

 Decision tables can use more than one parameter. For example, $2 means take the second value within the data cells in the same column of the spreadsheet. For example, if a data cell had values of 10, 20 then $1 would have a value of 10, and $2 would have a value of 20. (Note that the two values are separated by a comma.)

As a reminder, `eval()` can take any calculation, as long as it returns a true or false answer. It's great for text and calculations. The downside is that it's not as efficient, but that's OK for a small ruleset like the one in this example.

The second part of this decision table (**ACTION**) gives the 'then' part of the rules, which includes the following:

- **ACTION $r.getCell(4).setValue("$1");**: Sets the value on the fourth cell in the data range (the status) to our param, which is always **Buy This**
- **ACTION log.info("$1");**: Logs the message from the following table
- **ACTION update($r.getCell(4));**: Pings the rule engine to let it know that cell 4 in our data has been updated
- **ACTION update `($r);`**: Pings the rule engine to let it know that the entire Range has been updated

ACTION	ACTION	ACTION	ACTION
$r.getCell(4).setValue("$1");	log.info("$1");	update($r.getCell(4));	update($r);
Update the status to _	Log what we just did with the message _	Mark Cell as updated	Mark Range as updated
Buy This	Plan to Buy from A Broker	blank	blank
Buy This	Plan to Buy from C Broker	blank	blank
Buy This	Plan to Buy from E Broker	blank	blank

The above screenshot will generate three rules. Each rule will use the same structure, but will have the values embedded in it. To demonstrate this, the following is the rule that will be generated for the first line, for **A_Broker**:

```
rule "Identify the Buy Trades that we are interested in_12"
    when
            $r:Range(eval($r.getRangeName().equals("A_Broker")))
            eval($r.getCell(1).getBooleanValue()==true)
            eval($r.getCell(4).isModified() == false)
            eval($r.getCell(3).getIntValue() < 300)
    then
            $r.getCell(4).setValue("Buy This");
            log.info("Plan to Buy from Y Broker");
            update($r.getCell(4));
            update($r);
    end
```

There will be similar rules generated for each and every line in each of our decision tables. This sample generates 13 in total, one for each line of this table.

RuleTable—Execute the buy trades

We can have multiple RuleTables on one Excel spreadsheet. Each starts with the keyword **RuleTable**, and then follows the same decision table format. For example, take a look at the next decision table, which takes trades marked **Buy This** and actually executes the trade. (That is, the first table says we are interested in buying, but this second rule table is where money changes hands.)

The format (once we unhide or ungroup the technical parts) is the same as before, even if we've only one line of rules rather than the 13 we had previously. It also has two conditions and three actions.

RuleTable Execute the Buy Trades	
CONDITION	CONDITION
$r:Range	$output:Range
eval($r.getRangeContainsValue("$1"))	eval($output.getRangeName().equals("$1"))
Check the broker name (against the range)	Check that we have a place to output called
Buy This	Current_Stock

The conditions are:

- **CONDITION: $r:Range , eval($r.getRangeContainsValue("$1"))**: Only matches lines of data that have been flagged with param 1 (**Buy This**).
- **CONDITION: $output:Range , eval($output.getRangeName() .equals("$1"))**: Fires this rule only if we have a place to put our output (that is, a cell or range in our data sheet called **Current Stock**).

ACTION	ACTION	ACTION
$output.getCell(1).setValue($1);	$r.getCell(4).setValue("$1");	log.info("$1");
Adjust the current stock value (plus)	Update the status to _	Log what we just did with the message _
$output.getCell(1).getIntValue()+$r.getC{	Trade Executed (Buy)	Executed Trade

The actions are:

- **ACTION: $output.getCell(1).setValue($1);**: Increases the value of our current stock (the cell we previously identified as **$output**) by the amount of stock we have just bought. You can demonstrate the formula passed as params by using the calculation listed in the (white) param cell as **$output. getCell(1).getIntValue()+$r.getCell(2).getIntValue()**.
- **ACTION: $r.getCell(4).setValue("$1");**: Updates the status of this trade on the Excel spreadsheet to the param that we pass (that is, **Trade Executed**).
- **ACTION: log.info("$1");**: Logs what we just did to the console.

Other rule tables

We have two other rule decision tables in our sample `TradingRules.xls` file. These deal with identifying the sales offers that we wish to take up and the execution of those sales. The format of these two tables is very similar to the two rule tables above (**Evaluate Buy**, and **Execute Buy**). Of course, there is a minor difference — we are selling chocolate beans rather than buying.

Mixing rules and decision tables

While reading the previous rules Excel file, you may have wondered where the log object that we used in the previous rules actually comes from. In other chapters we had to declare a global variable (that our rules had a connection to the outside world, including the screen or console to actually print or log messages onto) and pass it in our logging object. In our `DecisionTable.xls` file we don't have this, but why?

The answer is that as we run this example, we load a second traditional rules file (`log-rules.drl`). This file is optional, as we could have used a global variable in the header section of our Excel rules file, but it's a good way of showing a mixture of rules and decision tables. After all, Drools translates them behind the scenes to be in the same format.

A good rule of thumb is to put the business rules stay in Excel and keep the more expressive, but more technical, 'plumbing' in the `.drl` (standard rule) format.

Looking at the `log-rule.drl` file, you'll see that it contains the imported file `global ILogger log` and two rules, which are:

1. A rule that matches **against unchanged** cells and logs (but does not modify) the contents.
2. A rule that matches **against changed** cells and logs (but does not modify) the contents.

Remember that both our Cell and Range JavaBeans have a modified `toString()` method to make logging easier. The logging object (`Ilogger`) also comes from the Red-Piranha project. It prints everything to the console, but also saves it (if we ask it to) as a part of our Excel output file.

Running the Chocolate Trading example

To run the DecisionTable-based Chocolate Trading example, open `ExcelDataRulesExample.java` in Eclipse (it's in the same directory as the sample that we ran in the previous chapter, `src/main/java/net/firstpartners/chap8`). Before we run it (by selecting menu option **Run | Run As | Java Application** from the Eclipse toolbar), we note that there are a couple of obvious similarities and differences in this example file:

- As before, our input file is called `chocolate-data.xls` and our output goes to `chocolate-output.xls`

- Unlike before, we load two rules files: the Excel decision table that we've just looked through (`TradingRules.xls`), and a standard rules file (`log-rules.drl`) that shows that we can mix and match decision tables with the 'traditional' rule format that we're used to

Like most of the examples in the book, your PC will pause for a couple of seconds, print out lots of messages to the console, then show the line, **ExcelDataRulesExample - Finished** when done.

Opening the output file (`chocolate-output.xls`), we see that only some of the cells have been updated (highlighted) in line with the more sophisticated business rules in this example.

Chocolate Trading Example				
Current Stock		590		
Broker Code	**Buy or Sell**	**Quantity**	**Price**	**Status**
A Broker	TRUE	110	300	n/a
B Broker	FALSE	120	500	Trade Executed(Sell)
C Broker	TRUE	130	700	n/a
D Broker	FALSE	140	300	n/a
E Broker	TRUE	150	500	n/a
F Broker	FALSE	160	700	Trade Executed(Sell)
G Broker	TRUE	170	300	n/a
H Broker	FALSE	180	500	Trade Executed(Sell)
I Broker	TRUE	190	700	n/a
J Broker	FALSE	200	300	Trade Executed(Sell)
K Broker	TRUE	210	500	Trade Executed (Buy)
L Broker	FALSE	220	700	n/a
M Broker	TRUE	230	300	Trade Executed (Buy)
N Broker	FALSE	240	500	n/a
O Broker	TRUE	250	700	n/a
P Broker	FALSE	260	300	n/a
Q Broker	TRUE	270	500	n/a
R Broker	FALSE	280	700	Trade Executed(Sell)
S Broker	TRUE	290	300	Trade Executed (Buy)
T Broker	FALSE	300	500	Trade Executed(Sell)
U Broker	TRUE	290	300	n/a
V Broker	FALSE	300	500	Trade Executed(Sell)
W Broker	TRUE	290	300	n/a
X Broker	FALSE	300	500	Trade Executed(Sell)
Y Broker	TRUE	290	300	n/a
Z Broker	FALSE	300	500	Trade Executed(Sell)

The following cells are updated:

1. The **Current Stock** is updated, as both our "execute buy" and "execute sell" rules modify the total.

2. Status fields for individual offers that we have taken up are highlighted, with a **Trade Executed (Buy/Sell)** message.

3. Status fields for individual offers that we have not taken up remain white, with the value unchanged.

4. All other cells remain white, as they have not been modified by our rules.

Logging information is printed to the Eclipse console. More usefully, there is a second tab in the output spreadsheet (`Chocolate-Output.xls`), with logging only from the rules. An extract of this is shown as follows (highlights in bold):

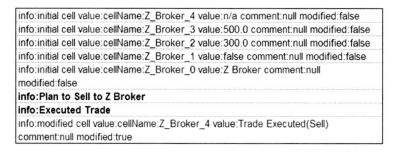

```
info:initial cell value:cellName:Z_Broker_4 value:n/a comment:null modified:false
info:initial cell value:cellName:Z_Broker_3 value:500.0 comment:null modified:false
info:initial cell value:cellName:Z_Broker_2 value:300.0 comment:null modified:false
info:initial cell value:cellName:Z_Broker_1 value:false comment:null modified:false
info:initial cell value:cellName:Z_Broker_0 value:Z Broker comment:null
modified:false
info:Plan to Sell to Z Broker
info:Executed Trade
info:modified cell value:cellName:Z_Broker_4 value:Trade Executed(Sell)
comment:null modified:true
```

Before we go through what is happening when these rules fire, we'll go back to basics. We will look through the main log file (in the Eclipse console) to explain what just happened, from start to finish.

What just happened?

The first thing that we see in our console log when we run `ExcelDataRules.java` is that our sample finds the source Excel file (containing the buy and sell data) and converts it to Cell and Range JavaBeans (which we looked at in detail earlier)—just like the very first example in this chapter.

```
ExcelDataRulesExample - found file:chocolate-data.xls
```

It then logs all Cells and Ranges, and so on, for each broker and range listed in our Data Excel spreadsheet.

```
============ Excel Cell Contents In =========
ExcelDataRulesExample  - Range:A_Broker
A_Broker_2: cellName:A_Broker_2 value:110.0 comment:null modified:
false
A_Broker_3: cellName:A_Broker_3 value:300.0 comment:null modified:
```

```
false
A_Broker_0: cellName:A_Broker_0 value:A Broker comment:null modified:
false
A_Broker_1: cellName:A_Broker_1 value:true comment:null modified:false
A_Broker_4: cellName:A_Broker_4 value:n/a comment:null modified:false
...
```

The sample then loads the 'traditional' style rule file, before loading the decision table.

```
DtRuleRunner   - Loading file: log-rules.drl

...

found file:TradingRules.xls
```

After it loads the decision table, it compiles it into the standard rule format. Our sample converts our Excel-based decision table to rules and logs the output—like the extract we see below. We saw one of the 26 evaluate buy-sell rules earlier in this chapter. This is the 'execute sell rule', once it has been translated. (This will probably be at the end of the set of the rules that is output to the log.)

```
#From row number: 68
rule "Execute the Sell Trades_68"
    when
          $r:Range(eval($r.getRangeContainsValue("Sell This")))
          $output:Range(eval($output.getRangeName().equals
        ("Current_Stock")))
    then
          $output.getCell(1).setValue($output.getCell(1)
        .getIntValue()-$r.getCell(2).getIntValue());
          $r.getCell(4).setValue("Trade Executed(Sell)");
          log.info("Executed Trade");
    end
```

If we have an error (that is, because of incorrect decision table format), it normally gets flagged here. Often, it can help to look at the rule format that is printed out, to help you identify the error.

The next step in our example is to insert global variables, of which we have only one in this example—a handle to the object that we use for logging.

```
Inserting handle to logger (via global)
```

And then we call our rules.

```
DtRuleRunner - === Calling Rule Engine ===
```

At this point, in our rules, our Excel output matches the console output. As before, we have no control over the order in which our rules fire. For example, the first set of rules to fire concern the last broker in the list (**Z_Broker**).

> You may have noticed from the console output that rules are not executed in the order in which they appear on the decision table. Rather, just like the other rules that we have seen, they are executed in the order that the rule engine deems best.
>
> Remember that your rules will fire if something is true. So if you find yourself writing rules that are sequence-dependant, think again.

The cells are updated with the help of the following steps:

1. The initial rule (from the drl file) logs the initial cell values.

    ```
    ExcelLogger - initial cell value:cellName:Z_Broker_4 value:n/a
    comment:null modified:false
    ExcelLogger - initial cell value:cellName:Z_Broker_3 value:500.0
    comment:null modified:false
    ExcelLogger - initial cell value:cellName:Z_Broker_2 value:300.0
    comment:null modified:false
    ExcelLogger - initial cell value:cellName:Z_Broker_1 value:false
    comment:null modified:false
    ExcelLogger - initial cell value:cellName:Z_Broker_0 value:Z
    Broker comment:null modified:false
    ```

2. The evaluate Sell rule fires (from the decision table).

    ```
    ExcelLogger - Plan to Sell to Z Broker
    ```

3. The execute Sell rule fires (from the decision table).

    ```
    ExcelLogger - Executed Trade
    ```

4. The modified cell logger fires (from the drl file).

    ```
    ExcelLogger - modified cell value:cellName:Z_Broker_4 value:Trade
    Executed(Sell) comment:null modified:true
    ```

5. This pattern repeats itself for each of the brokers until we have evaluated all of the buy/sell rules.

6. It is at this point (as the rules have finished firing) that Excel and the console log diverge again.

    ```
    DtRuleRunner - ==== Rules Complete ====
    ```

7. We now log a snapshot of the cell values after all of the rules have fired.

    ```
    ExcelDataRulesExample - ==== Excel Cell Contents Out ====
    ... cell contents ...
    ```

Now, our JavaBean to Excel Data file convertor (in the `RangeConverter.java` file) outputs its messages. You'll notice that:

- Only the cells marked as modified will be updated.

- Only one update is made to the current stock (even though it has changed multiple times — once for each stock trade that we fired). This is because the Excel updater only converts the finished set of values.

```
CellConvertor  - UpdatingCell:B_Broker_4 value:Trade
Executed(Sell) as String
CellConvertor  - UpdatingCell:Current_Stock_1 value:590 as Number
CellConvertor  - UpdatingCell:F_Broker_4 value:Trade
Executed(Sell) as String
CellConvertor  - UpdatingCell:H_Broker_4 value:Trade
Executed(Sell) as String
CellConvertor  - UpdatingCell:J_Broker_4 value:Trade
Executed(Sell) as String
CellConvertor  - UpdatingCell:K_Broker_4 value:Trade Executed
(Buy) as String
CellConvertor  - UpdatingCell:M_Broker_4 value:Trade Executed
(Buy) as String
CellConvertor  - UpdatingCell:R_Broker_4 value:Trade
Executed(Sell) as String
CellConvertor  - UpdatingCell:S_Broker_4 value:Trade Executed
(Buy) as String
CellConvertor  - UpdatingCell:T_Broker_4 value:Trade
Executed(Sell) as String
CellConvertor  - UpdatingCell:V_Broker_4 value:Trade
Executed(Sell) as String
CellConvertor  - UpdatingCell:X_Broker_4 value:Trade
Executed(Sell) as String
CellConvertor  - UpdatingCell:Z_Broker_4 value:Trade
Executed(Sell) as String
```

- Although it's not noted in the log file, behind the scenes we add the log output to our output Excel file, and save everything to disk, by starting with the line.

```
// update the excel spreadsheet with our log file
excelLogger.flush(wb, EXCEL_LOG_WORKSHEET_NAME);
```

8. Finally, we see a final message saying that everything is complete (and it is time to open the `chocolate-output.xls` file to see what the output looks like).

```
ExcelDataRulesExample  - Finished
```

Have a go

The whole point of loading our rules and data from Excel is to make them easier to modify and maintain. So go on, have a go yourself! Modify the above example as follows:

- Change the sample so that it uses different quantities and prices, and see the effect.

- Add a check to our sell rules to ensure that we cannot sell more chocolate than we have in our current stock. Hint: Our `execute_sell` rule already obtains a handle to the current stock. We can use this as part of an additional condition to the `evaluate_sell` rule.

- Take a data spreadsheet from your business and use it instead of the data sheet (`chocolate-data.xls`) used in this sample. Hint: When writing the rules, try to make small changes to one rule at a time.

When 'having a go', remember to execute a 'clean project' command in Eclipse (if you are making modifications to Excel), and make sure that you don't keep your `chocolate-output.xls` file open (or you'll get the Java `FileNotFoundException` error that we highlighted earlier).

Summary

This chapter, behind all of the details, was pretty simple. We used Excel spreadsheets (Cells and Ranges) as our fact model, instead of the write-your-own-JavaBean approach that we took earlier. Then we used Excel spreadsheets to hold decision tables in order to make repetitive rules easier to write.

In reality, we can use this new capability in three ways:

- Use Excel as our data model, with a standard rule (`.drl`) file
- Use Excel to hold our rules, and JavaBeans to hold our data
- Use Excel to hold both rules and data

There are several ways of handling rules and data. Use the one that makes it easy for you to handle your project. In the next chapter, we'll again try to make things simpler by using DSLs and Ruleflow.

9
Domain Specific Language (DSL) and RuleFlow

People new to rule engines are often confused by two things: the syntax of the rules, and the fact that the rule engine (and not you) decides the order in which your rules are fired. This chapter will show some ways of making both of these things easy to understand.

In the previous chapter, we saw how to use Excel decision tables to make it easier to write rules. This chapter takes off from the 'easy to write rules' theme. Although writing rules in Excel is good, wouldn't it be much better to write them in a language that is closer to English, or whatever human language you prefer? **Domain Specific Language (DSL)** gives you this option.

The other point of confusion is the order in which rules are fired. Wouldn't it be great to draw a workflow diagram to see and control which (groups of) rules should fire, and when? Ruleflow gives us this control.

We'll come to Ruleflow shortly, but first we'll look at how to use DSLs.

What is a Domain Specific Language (DSL)?

Every profession has its own language, or what is called a jargon. Although, on the surface a jargon may appear to be related to English, it's often incomprehensible to outsiders. If you've watched ER, Grey's Anatomy, House, or any of the other medical dramas on TV, you know what I mean. You will understand this better with the help of the following example:

Doctor to nurse:

> Give me sterilised scalpel number 4, spreaders—the patient's cardioangiogram is showing traces of acute defibrillation.

In plain English, this means:

> *Give me a knife now, this guy's having a heart attack.*

One of the reasons why each profession, or domain, has its own specific language (or DSL) is that it conveys information much more precisely and concisely. A more cynical view would be that domain terminology allows professionals to baffle clients and charge more. But obviously, nobody in the IT industry would ever take advantage of that fact!

The fact is that business and other professionals speak one language. Our rules, even though they are 'plainer English', are written (so far) in another language. If we want to capture the business knowledge from the professionals, we need to speak the language of the business users. This is where DSLs provided by Drools come in.

Imagine that we could write our rules in a form similar to the extract that follows. This extract is pretty easy to understand without any technical knowledge. This would be a good thing, because more people would be able to review and maintain the rules.

```
rule "Check Patient for Heart Attack"
    when
            There is a Patient
                    - appears not to be breathing
                    - has no pulse
                    - is white or blue in the face
        then
            Call for Assistance
                Start CPR
    end
```

You've been reading this book long enough now to know that the next line after 'imagine ... ' is usually 'but of course you can!'. And **expanders** are a key part of how we do it.

Expanders

Something needs to convert the near-English rules (like the previous sample) into the more formal or standard rule (DRL) format that we're used to seeing. That's the Drools expander. The concept is simple:

1. We start with the near-English business rules. They are saved in a text file with a `.dslr` extension, to make it clearer to us what the file contains.

2. The `rulefile` contains a statement similar to `expander chocolate-trading. dsl`. So Drools knows how to translate the near-English file into our standard rule file format.

3. Using the DSL file, Drools finds the English text and replaces it with a more technical rule language.

4. Once this find-and-replace process is complete, we will have a file (in memory, not on disk) containing our standard rule language. It is similar to the DRL rules that we saw in earlier chapters.

5. Drools can then execute the rules in this DRL as before.

The actual process is even more powerful than find and replace, given that we can use regular expressions (also known as regex) and wildcards. For example, `h\?t` would match (then replace) all three-letter words beginning with "h" and ending with "t"-for example, "hat", "het", "hit", "hot", "hut", as well as the more nonsensical words with endings such as "hbt", "hct", and so on.

How does Drools know which expander or DSL file to use? Our (near-English) rules file tells Drools which file is required, using a statement such as `expander my-dsl-file-name` near the top of the rules (`.dslr`) file.

The process of taking a more readable file, converting it to a rules file, and then applying those rules as appropriate, may seem familiar. It's the same sort of process used in the Excel-based decision tables from the previous chapter. Like decision tables, DSLs can automatically convert a human-friendly format into something more Drools-like, and then fire the generated business rules as appropriate.

If we had a medical DSL in place, this find-and-replace process would result in the following business rule (in Drools syntax):

```
rule "Check Patient for Heart Attack"
    when
            $patient : Patient(
                    breathing == false ,
                    pulse == false
                    (face == blue or face == white)
                    )

    then
        $hospital.callForAssistance();
        $patient.startCPR();
end
```

The DSL format

What is the format of the DSL that will convert the 'medical' rule to a Drools rule, and vice versa? The format looks something like the following plain-text file, so that you can view it with almost any editor. The file will have a `.dsl` extension.

```
# Match against the when part of our medical rules

[when]There is a Patient  = $patient : Patient()
[when]-has no pulse = pulse==false
[when]-appears not to be breathing = breathing== false
[when]-is {color1} or {color2} in the face = (face == {color1} or face == {color2})

# Our possible medical actions in the 'when' part

[then]Call for Assistance= $hospital.callForAssitence();
[then]Start CPR=$patient.startCPR();
```

The format allows a pretty simple find-and-replace process, using the following parts:

1. Comments (lines beginning with #) are ignored, although they are useful for explaining what is going on. Similarly, whitespace and blank lines are also ignored, but laying out the file cleanly using whitespace makes it a lot more readable.

2. The basic format of the file is [when] or [then] (something to find = something to replace). The [when] or [then] part means that we will only match against the left (when) or right (then) part of the rule, as appropriate.

3. For example, [when] There is a Patient = $patient: Patient() means, find the text There is a patient in the when part of our rule, and replace it with the more Drools-like language $patent : Patient() (that is, match against all patients in working memory).

4. If the next line starts with a '-' (for example, -has no pulse = pulse==false), then Drools is smart enough to add a filter to our rule in case of a match in the original file. This means that we end up with $patient : Patient(pulse==false), which will match against all patients with no pulse. This allows us to mix and match the conditions on our rules without having to specify every possible combination in our DRL translation file.

5. The [when] find {value} = replace {value} allows you to specify a value in your original rule, which will get passed to the final translation. For example, -is {color1} or {color2} in the face means we can reuse this DRL translation for other colors (specified in the 'English' .dslr rules file) later.

6. The find-and-replace mechanism works in a similar way for translating the [then] part of the rules from 'near-English' to the more technical Drools language.

Other DSL editing options

The DSL is just a text file, so we can edit it in Notepad. There is another option for editing a DSL file in the IDE—the guided editor. If you open a DSL file in the JBoss IDE, you'll see something similar to the following screenshot:

Language Expression	Rule Language Mapping	Object	Scope
There is a Patient	$patient : Patient()		[condition]
-appears not to be breathing	breathing== false		[condition]
-has no pulse	pulse==false		[condition]
-is {color1} or {color2} in the face	(face == {color1} or face == {color2})		[condition]
Call for Assistance	$hospital.callForAssitence();		[consequence]
Start CPR	$patient.startCPR();		[consequence]

Description:

Expression: Edit
Mapping: Remove
Object: Add
Sort by: ▾ Sort
Copy

- There are three main sections to the editor: a place for the DRL **Description** at the top, a table showing existing entries in the DSL, and a space at the bottom to add new entries. The latter space also has buttons to **Edit, Remove, Add,** or **Copy** entries, as well as an option to **Sort** the existing ones.

- **Language Expression** is what we will **Find** in the original rules file. **Rule Language Mapping** is something we will **Replace** it with to generate our Drools technical file. This find-and-replace mechanism is similar to the one we looked at in the text editor.

- We also have **Scope ([condition]** or **[consequence])**, which is just another name for **[when]** or **[then]**, which we looked at previously.

- What is new is the **Object** field. This object takes the full name of a JavaBean, including the package (for example `net.firstpartners.Patient`). This allows autocompletion (that is, pop-up suggestions) when we are writing the rules that use this DSL in Guvnor or the IDE.

The IDE editor saves the DRL file in the text format that we looked at earlier. So, we can switch back and forward between the two editors as required.

Writing DSLs

Imagine that you had to write your own language, from the very beginning. Where would you start? You could try using an existing dictionary as your inspiration, but you're likely to map too many words that you don't really need. Or, you could make it up as you go along, but users would get frustrated with the many delays while you add yet another word to your language. Remember that the ideal is to have a more-or-less stable language that users can easily understand so that it is easier for them to write their rules. So, what are you going to do?

The answer is iteration. You (as a 'knowledge engineer' who understand rules and DSLs) write the first 10, 20, or 100 rules, adding the elements that you need to the DSL, as you go. Over time, you'll find that your DSL becomes more and more stable, needing fewer additions to cope with each additional rule. At this point, you can hand over the DSL to your business users (with much mentoring and training) and the users can start writing their own rules based on the (near-stable) DSL.

Of course, picking a representative sample of rules will make writing the initial DSL much more effective. Staying around to pick up the occasional mapping that your rule writers need to add, will make them a lot happier. It also helps to have tests written against your rules (as described in Chapter 7) so that you know instantly if any of the changes that you are making breaks anything.

Let's look at this process, using a sample that we saw in the last chapter.

[🖊️ As there is a lot of crossover and code reuse, the samples for this chapter can be downloaded from the Chapter 8 sample at `http://code.google.com/p/red-piranha`.]

Meet the sample

Do you remember the rule in the DRL file that we had in the previous chapter—the one that logged the contents of Excel cells? At the start of `log-rules.dsl`, it looked something like the following:

```
package net.firstpartners.chap8;

import net.firstpartners.drools.log.ILogger

import net.firstpartners.excel.Cell;
import net.firstpartners.excel.Range;

global ILogger log;
rule "print cell initial values"

    when
            $cell : Cell(modified==false)

    then
        //Logging message
            log.info("initial cell value:"+$cell);
end
```

Our first step is to change the file name to `log-rules.dslr`, and create a blank DSL file called `cell-logging.dsl`. We link the two by adding an expander statement to the DSLR file (`expander cell-logging.dsl`).

Once we add the expander statement, we've got a problem: Drools expects to match everything between `when` and `end` against what it finds in the DSL. The problem is that the DSL is (for the moment) just a blank file. The lines are marked with '>' so that they are taken as they are. Our `.dslr` file will now look as follows:

```
package net.firstpartners.chap8;

import net.firstpartners.drools.log.ILogger

import net.firstpartners.excel.Cell;
import net.firstpartners.excel.Range;

expander cell-logging.dsl

global ILogger log;

rule "print cell initial values"

    when
```

```
>              $cell : Cell(modified==false)
     then

         //Logging message
>              log.info("initial cell value:"+$cell);
     end
```

For this iteration, we know that we need to put in the entries for the two lines marked with '>'. Starting with the 'then' part, we add the following lines to our DSL:

```
#Cell Selection Rules
[when]There is a Cell = $cell: Cell()
[when]-unmodified = modified==false
[when]-modified = modified==true
```

To cover the second-to-last line (log.info) we add some more lines to our DSL file:

```
# Logging rules
[then]Log the cell contents = log.info("Cell value:"+$cell);
```

Now that we have a DSL ready (at least for this iteration), we can update our rule file with more English-language rules. Because we've also changed the package declaration inline with this chapter's name, the sample now looks like this:

```
package net.firstpartners.chap9;

import net.firstpartners.drools.log.ILogger

import net.firstpartners.excel.Cell;

import net.firstpartners.excel.Range;

global ILogger log;

# We must reference the dsl that we are using
expander cell-logging.dsl

rule "print cell initial values"

    when
            There is a Cell
                    - unmodified
      then
          Log the cell contents
End
```

In real life, once we were happy that this was working, we would carry out some more iterations. We would do this by covering other methods available on the Cell Object, and perhaps the Range Object as well.

Running the DSL example

This example (with simple cell logging) is ready to run, as part of the example that you downloaded in the previous chapter. The start point is the `DslChocolateTradingExample` Java file found in the `net/firstpartners/chap9` folder. If we run it (right-click on the file, and then select **Run as | Java application** from the shortcut menu), we'll see all of the following values from the Excel input file being logged:

```
ExcelLogger  - Cell value:cellName:Z_Broker_4 value:n/a comment:null
modified:false
ExcelLogger  - Cell value:cellName:Z_Broker_3 value:500.0 comment:null
modified:false
ExcelLogger  - Cell value:cellName:Z_Broker_2 value:300.0 comment:null
modified:false
ExcelLogger  - Cell value:cellName:Z_Broker_1 value:false comment:null
modified:false
```

Note that in the `DslChocolateTradingExample`, we specify (again) the DSL file that we are using.

```
new RuleRunner().runStatelessRules(RULES_FILES,DSL_FILE,    ranges.
getAllRangesAndCells(), globals,    excelLogger);
```

You'll notice that in the log file, both the rule file and the DSL file are loaded.

```
RuleRunner  - found rule file:log-rules.dslr
RuleRunner  - found dsl file:cell-logging.dsl
```

Guvnor and DSL-based rules

Domain-specific languages aim to make business users' life easier by allowing them to write rules in a format they're familiar with. On the other hand, Guvnor is a web editor intended for business users editing rules. What could be more perfect than combining the two?

From what we already know, it's pretty simple to start writing DSL-based rules in the Guvnor Web editor.

1. Open up the Guvnor web editor, as you did in Chapter 3.
2. Create a new package (`net.firstpartners.chap9`) to hold our information, like we did in Chapter 4.

3. Export our fact model that contains the Cell and Range JavaBeans from Eclipse (the JBoss IDE) and import them into Guvnor under the `net.firstpartners.chap9` package (as you did in Chapter 4).

```
logging-rules.dslr ⊠

package net.firstpartners.chap9;
import net.firstpartners.drools.log.ILogger
import net.firstpartners.excel.Cell;
import net.firstpartners.excel.Range;

global ILogger log;

# We must reference the dsl that we are using
expander cell-logging.dsl

rule "print cell initial values"
    when
        There is a Cell
            - unmodified
    then
        Log the cell contents
end

View source    Validate
```

4. Create a new DSL and give it the same name as the one in Eclipse (`Cell.logging.dsl`). Under the **chap9** package, set the category to **anything**. Copy and paste the contents of our Eclipse-based DSL file into this package, and save the package. You can create a new DSL under the same menu as **Create a new rule**.

5. From the same menu (and in the same package), create a new DSL business rule (using the text editor) and name it `logging-rules.dslr`. Copy and paste the values from the Eclipse (the JBoss IDE) file of the same name.

The file in Guvnor will now look similar to the above screenshot. Clicking on the **Validate** button will show the following success message:

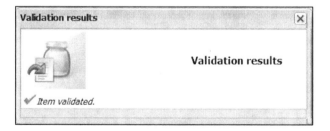

While editing your dslr rule, pressing the *Ctrl+Space* keys will enable the autosuggest feature, which is shown in the following screenshot:

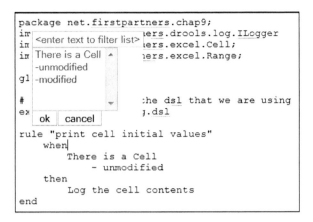

```
package net.firstpartners.chap9;
im                              ers.drools.log.ILogger
in  <enter text to filter list> ers.excel.Cell;
in  There is a Cell  ▲         ers.excel.Range;
    -unmodified
gl  -modified

#                               :he dsl that we are using
ex  ┌──────┬────────┐           j.dsl
    │  ok  │ cancel │
    └──────┴────────┘
rule "print cell initial values"
    when|
          There is a Cell
               - unmodified
    then
          Log the cell contents
end
```

So far, in this chapter, we've looked at DSL (Domain Specific Language) to make our rules easier to understand. Ruleflow also makes our rules more understandable. We'll take a look at that, now.

Ruleflow

One of the key features of a rule engine is that we have no control exactly when our rules will fire. Our rules simply become available to fire (because the 'when' conditions have been filled), and the rule engine decides the best order in which to execute them. We may drop hints about the rules that have higher priority (using Salience), but the sort of 'fine-grained' controls that we have in other languages are (for good reason) not there. This is a good thing as it makes the individual rules simpler, reusable, and easier to understand. However, there are business situations where we may need to group our rules and control when they fire.

For example, for a mortgage application (which we'll call Homeloan) you may have several hundred business rules. These might be naturally grouped by the state of the loan application: rules that fire in the initial enquiry (for example, to provide a quick quote), rules that fire when the application is received (for example, to make sure that all of the paperwork is in order), rules that fire when the loan is drawn down (for example, to ensure that the money is sent out correctly), rules that fire every month (for example, to calculate interest and accept a loan repayment), and rules that fire if the loan goes into arrears or if there is a change in the interest rate.

It would be possible to write our rules to check the status of the application, for example:

```
When
    Mortgage application is in 'Monthly Loan Repayment State'
    And (some other conditions unique to this business rule)
    ......
Then
    Carry out monthly interest calculations
```

This goes on for each and every one of our several hundred rules. The problem with this is that if our business flow changes (for example, if our bank decides that there is an exciting new opportunity in the subprime lending market), then we have to change each and every one of the business rules to reflect this. Next, we test all of the rules to make sure that none of them inadvertently fire at the wrong time.

The alternative is to map our business flow graphically, like the following diagram. At a glance, we can now see what the sequence of rule firing is:

- We start at **Initial Enquiry** and allow those rules to fire.

- If the **Initial Enquiry** is followed up, then we loan the money.

- After passing through a join point, we make a decision based on the question: Are there any loan repayments outstanding? If yes, we give our rules that calculate the loan interest the chance to fire.

- There is a (non) rule action to collect repayment before rejoining the previous point.

- This time, if we don't have any repayments outstanding, we allow the **Complete Loan** rules to fire, before ending the Ruleflow.

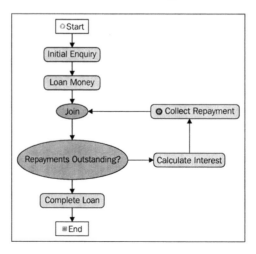

Understanding the Ruleflow in a diagram is far easier than deciphering the information buried in individual rules.

Ruleflow is not workflow

Notice that in the previous section we didn't say 'and at stage X the rules fire'. What we said was 'at stage X we give the rules a chance to fire'. It's still up to the rule engine to decide which rules are the most appropriate to fire. Your rules are still rules, except that effectively another condition has been added to the 'when' part—checking that the Ruleflow is pointing to the group that our rule is in.

It's worth repeating this statement again. Ruleflow is not workflow. It might look similar (for example, the JBoss jBPM workflow product has similar diagrams), but it is subtly different. Let's look at the differences between the two:

- Workflow says exactly what will happen at each stage in the process. As soon as the workflow reaches a step, we will fire the actions associated with it.

- Ruleflow says what *might happen* at each stage in the process. The rule engine selects the rules that actually fire.

It is possible to set individual rules to fire at each step in the flow (just like traditional workflow). But if you find yourself wanting to do this, then you're really not using a rule engine in the best way. It is better to mark a group of rules (and not a single rule) to fire, and then let Drools do its rule-engine stuff.

If you do need traditional workflow, you've got plenty of choices. From JBoss alone you have **jBPM (java Business Process Management)** and Drools (with enhanced workflow features in Drools 5, which we will introduce in Chapter 12).

Both JBoss workflow products integrate well with the rule engine. For example, when we have a decision node (to choose what the next step is) we can use the rule engine to make this decision.

Whatever you do, don't be tempted to write your own workflow—there's no need to do so with hundreds of open source and commercial workflow engines to choose from.

That Homeloan example again

To create a sample like the Homeloan, right-click on a project in the JBoss IDE and select the **New | other | Ruleflow** menu option. You'll be shown a blank drawing page (where you can draw your Ruleflow) with the following icons available on the lefthand side of the screen. To compose your Ruleflow, select the icons that you want to use, and then use **Connection Creation** to tie them together.

The available steps in our Ruleflow are:

- **Start**: Every flow should have only one start. Naturally enough, this is where our Ruleflow begins.

- **RuleFlowGroup**: Our **RuleFlowGroup** has a name. When our Ruleflow reaches this point in the flow, rules belonging to this Ruleflow group (and only those rules belonging to this group) will be given the chance to fire.

Property	Value
Name	RuleSet
RuleFlowGroup	Evaluate Loan

- **RuleSet:** If you look at the **Property** tab at the bottom of the screen, you see additional information about each icon. In this case we can see that the display name of the icon is **RuleSet**, and that **RuleFlowGroup** (which we will use shortly to tie our Ruleflow to our rules) is **Evaluate Loan**.

- Remember that all icons, and not just the **RuleSet**, have properties that you can view and change.

- **Action**: In our Homeloan flow we have a step that was more suited to the traditional programming task (**Collect Repayment**). This could be printing a letter, or sending an XML message to another bank, requesting payment. Although this can be done via our rules (as it's calling the standard Java code), it's better to be able to state it as a clear step in our flow.

- **Split**: Only the simplest flows run in a straight line from start to finish. Splits and joins allow the flow to branch and reconnect. As we saw in the Homeloan sample diagram, splits and joins allow us to create loops in the Ruleflow. Splits can allow the flow to go down one path or another, or even down both paths. The decision about the path is rule-based.

- **Join:** This action allows multiple branches to come back together. We can specify to wait for all branches to come back the **Join,** or just wait for one of them one.

- **Milestone**: This is a wait state—waiting until specified conditions become true. The expressions used to specify the wait state are the same as those on the lefthand side of a rule. The flow will be held until this condition is fulfilled.

- **SubFlow**: This executes the flow in another Ruleflow file. The name of that other Ruleflow file is specified via the **Properties** tab.

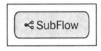

- **End**: Every flow should have only one end point. Naturally enough, this is where our Ruleflow terminates.

It's not just the icons that have properties. If you select the entire Ruleflow (by clicking on a blank area of the diagram), we can set properties for it as well.

Property	Value
Connection Layout	Shortest Path
Id	mortgage-ruleflow
Name	homeloan
Package	net.firstpartners.chap9
Version	

In this case, we see that the ID of Ruleflow is **mortgage-ruleflow** and it is a part of the **net.firstpartners.chap9** package. There are also fields to set a version number and to give the Ruleflow a more human-readable name (in this case, **homeloan**).

After drawing your diagram and making connections between the Ruleflow steps (select two workflow steps, right click, then choose create connection from the context menu that appears). It's always useful to validate the diagram (so that you catch any errors now, rather than when you try to execute the flow for the first time). To validate the diagram, right-click anywhere in the whitespace of the Ruleflow diagram and select **Validate** from the context menu. Drools will notify you of any errors that it finds in the Ruleflow.

> Just because your Ruleflow validates correctly doesn't necessarily mean that it will run without any errors. There are many things that can still go wrong at runtime. Validation is still a good way of reducing the chances of having errors.

Linking rules to Ruleflow

So far, we drawn a few Ruleflow diagrams and stepped through the different actions that we can add to the Ruleflow. But how does Drools know which rules are available to fire at each step in the Ruleflow?

The answer is simple. We tag our rules with the name of the Ruleflow group that they belong to. (Remember that we set the Ruleflow group name as a part of the Ruleflow diagram.) By doing this, we end up with a rule looking something like this:

```
rule 'YourRule'
   ruleflow-group 'evaluate loan'
   when
     ...
   then
     ...
   end
```

This way, when our flow gets to the `evaluate loan` Ruleflow group, we know that we have at least one rule that is available for firing. Whether the rule fires or not will depend on the conditions attached to the `when` part of the rule.

There are other Ruleflow-related attributes that we can add to our rules. These are as follows:

- `agenda-group` is just another term for Ruleflow group.
- `auto-focus true` allows the rule to capture the focus if no Ruleflow-group is selected.

- `activation-group "some-name"` is an activation group from which only one rule in can fire. You can think of it as a more sophisticated form of `no-loop true`, which acts on groups instead of single rules.

There is a final part to tying rules and Ruleflow together, but first we need a quick lesson in stateful applications.

A quick introduction to stateful applications

Most of the rules examples that we've seen are stateless. This means they run, fire the rules, print the values, and then terminate. When we run the example again, they 'forget' that they have been run before and produce exactly the same output.

Most real-life applications are stateful. How angry would you be if you'd logged into your web based online banking, only to find the application had forgotten about the money that you'd lodged in your account the last time you logged on?

In a normal application, such as an online banking web site, we need to remember what users did last (Are they logged in? What account are they looking at? Are they in the middle of making a payment? and so on). If we do not remember this data, users would get annoyed about having to repeat themselves at every step. It would also lead to some pretty complicated screens, to allow users to enter all of the information at once. Instead, we allow users to enter information in several steps, and remember where they are each time.

In an application designed to be used by computers, we don't have to worry about this. We can force the computer to give us all of the information required in one go, for example username, password, bank account to take money from, bank account to give money to, the date on which to execute the transaction, and so on. This is actually easy for a computer, because we make one call to our banking service and we are told whether our transaction has succeeded or failed. It's also easier for us to build our service.

Each service (transferring money, booking flights, or executing share trade) does only one thing.

Because each service 'forgets' everything after each call, we don't need to worry about trying to remember what we were doing before.

Because we have no memory, stateless applications (and services) are very scalable. We can make several copies of the same service and put them in a pool. Any client can talk to any service—no waiting for a particular server to become available.

In summary, stateless applications are simpler and scale better. Stateful applications, although harder to design and build, are more user-friendly. There are scores of books dedicated to explaining which design to choose and how to build them. But for the time being, there is one important reason why we've introduced stateful applications.

Stateful rules and Ruleflow

In all of our previous examples, we've fired our rules in a stateless manner. That is, we pass all of the information that we need to our rules, allow the rules to fire, and then get the final result back. There is no 'state', and nothing to remember, as everything is fired in one go.

You may recall the following line from previous examples:

```
runStatelessRules(RULES_FILES,DSL_FILE, facts, globals, logger);
```

Notice that no value is returned by this piece of code, nor do we need it. We fire our rules in one go, and our facts (for example, cells in the Excel spreadsheet) are automatically updated.

Stateless rule sessions are fine for our simple examples, where everything is completed in a few seconds. But what about our mortgage application Ruleflow, where the process can last for days, weeks, or even months? We will have to call our rules in a stateful way to remember the way we left things the last time we invoked the rule engine.

 Stateful and stateless rules are almost the same. The only difference is the manner in which we call the rule engine.

The code extract (from `RuleFlowExample.java` in the `net firstpartners chap9` package or folder) shows us how. It also shows that while we gain the power of having stateful rules, it takes a bit more work on our part to call the rule engine.

```
StatefulSession session = new RuleRunner()
        .getStatefulSession(RULES_FILES,
         null,
         RULEFLOW_FILE,
        ranges.getAllRangesAndCells(),
        globals,
            excelLogger);

session.startProcess(RULEFLOW_ID);

session.fireAllRules();
```

This code does a few things, such as:

- It uses our `RuleRunner` to load the rule file.

- Like before, it passes in our facts (the Cell JavaBeans), globals, and a handle to the logger. It also passes a handle to the Ruleflow file (so that Drools knows what process we wish to use).

- Unlike before, rules are not fired at this point. Instead, we get a `session` back — that is, a handle to the rule engine, with everything loaded and ready to go.

- Our second line of code starts the Ruleflow process by calling the `session.startprocess` method. This simply puts the token at the start of the Ruleflow because no rules are fired as yet. The `RULEFLOW_ID` that we pass in is the one that we set in the properties screen of our Ruleflow (for example, **mortgage Ruleflow**).

- The final line of our code (`session.fireAllRules`) starts our rules. The difference between the rules firing in this and the previous samples is that the Ruleflow is guiding which groups of rules become available to fire, and when. As before, when all of the possible rules have fired, our fact objects (the Cell JavaBeans) are updated, and control returns to our program.

The rest of the code example (for example, the code that converts the values from Excel to JavaBeans and back again, the logging, and so on) remains the same as the code we've used in other examples.

There are a lot of other things that we can do with the Drools session, and not just Ruleflow. For example, as we step through the web pages for a Homeloan application, we can have Drools working in the background to ensure that all rules remain true, by updating the facts. We'll cover this truth-maintenance capability in more detail in the next chapter.

Summary

This chapter aimed to make our rules both easier to use, and more powerful.

We started with a DSL, or domain specific language. By using DSLs, business rule editors can write near-English rules in a language suited to their profession. Drools then does the hard work of finding and replacing these rules, using an expander, so that we end up with a more technical rule that we can execute in the normal way.

Ruleflow also makes our rules easier to understand. It allows us to extract the flow that might otherwise be hidden in our rules. We saw how to create the Ruleflow diagram, and how to run it as part of a stateful rules session.

In our next chapter, we'll see how to take these new rules capabilities and deploy them as a part of a real-world application.

10
Deploying Rules in Real Life

All of the previous chapters have shown you how to do many useful things with business rules—including how to write them in the Guvnor, the IDE, excel spreadsheet, and the near-English DSL formats. All of this is useless unless you can make the results of your hard labour available to end users who will interact with your business rules in some way. To make this possible, you need to get your business rules off the computer where you wrote them and onto a production server. It's like a teenager leaving his or her home for the first time and making his or her way in the wider world.

What we need to do is **deploy** our business rules.

One size fits all architecture

If you were building a house, you'd employ an architect to design it for you before anybody started working on the site. That way, the bricklayers, plumbers, joiners, and electricians would know what the finished product will look like and can plan their work accordingly. Most computer systems cost far more than your average house (that is, when you include the cost the wages of the people involved in the IT project). So it makes sense to take a little time to prepare the architecture for these systems as well.

Fortunately, most computer systems these days are web based; that is, they use web pages to gather input from users and to display the result. It doesn't matter if these web pages can be seen only within your company or organisation, or by the world at large—both use the same underlying technology. There are entire bookshelves (or the online equivalent) devoted to the best web architecture, but pretty much all of the designs contain a similar core, as shown in the following diagram:

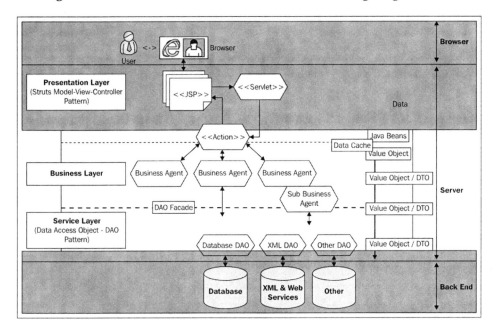

- Most web systems take information from the user (at the top of the diagram), do something with it (the white area in the middle of the diagram), and store it in a database (at the bottom of the diagram).

- The grey areas at the top (**Browser**) and bottom (**Back End Database** and other systems) are outside our immediate control. We have to 'talk' to them. But, typically, we're stuck with whatever web browser or database someone else has chosen.

- The part that we can control is in the middle, labelled **Server**. A server is simply a computer dedicated to running our software and making it available over the Web.

- Our system on the server is built in three layers: the **Presentation Layer**, the **Business Layer**, and the **Service Layer**.

- These three layers are like a sandwich. Standard technologies make up the **Presentation Layer** (which shows web pages to the user) and the **Service Layer** (which talks to databases and other 'backend' systems). The more interesting sandwich filling (unique to our system) is the **Business Layer** right in the middle of the diagram.

- As you'd expect from the name 'business rules', the **Business Layer** is where the business rules normally reside .

There you have the one-size-fits-all architecture. Now, what are you paying all those overpriced consultants for?

What needs to be deployed?

The architecture diagram contains a lot more than examples based on simple rules, which is what we've been looking at until now. There are a lot of pieces that make up a full Enterprise web system. Many of these should already have been installed as a 'one-off' by the friendly system administrators in your IT department. Others are up to you to provide.

Let's look at the parts of the solution that you'll need:

- Server: An application needs a machine to run on. This could be a box tucked away under somebody's desk (not ideal), a real server plugged into a rack somewhere (better), or a 'virtual' server hosted by an IT company or a secure third-party hosting company (better again).

- Operating system (OS): Our server is useless without the basic instructions that make it work. This would most likely be Windows (a version similar to what is on your desktop PC), Linux, or some other variant of UNIX. For the purpose of Java-based rules, our application can deploy on any of these.

- Java application server: We talked about deploying this on a desktop PC back in Chapter 2, when installing JBoss. This gives our application a 'home' to run on and provides common services such as security, database access, and a web server.

- Application: This consists of the non-rules Java code, web pages, and other configuration. This is pretty much everything except the business rules, as depicted on our 'one size fits all' architecture diagram. The application is often deployed as a `.war` (web archive) file, a type of ZIP file.

- In some cases the configuration files may be deployed separately, to allow easier changes later. (That is, you only have to update a single file, rather than the entire application.)

- Support libraries (such as web frameworks or drivers to allow us to talk to databases) are often deployed as part of the **WAR (Web Archive)** file, but can be deployed separately. The choice will often depend on the instructions provided with the library.

- Rules: The business rules that form the core of the system. To a large extent, the other components are deployed purely to support the rules.

In general, the server, OS, Java, and the application will be supplied by your IT department (with input from you). The web application may be provided by you, or by the development team that you are working with. The development team will also specify the support libraries required (and where on the Internet they can be obtained). Rules will be developed by you.

Rules as code or data?

Should business rules be embedded as a part of the application code that doesn't change very often? Or are rules more like your application data (for example, pricing lists), which you expect to change on an almost daily basis? Depending on your answers, you will deploy your rules very differently. The answer, somewhat confusingly, is that rules are 'both'.

- Rules are as powerful as the normal code and should be treated in the same way. (For example, before deployment, any changes should be thoroughly tested.)

- Rules are as easy to change as data because: first, they live outside the 'normal' application; and second, rule engines are expressly designed to allow easy changes to the business rules.

Organisations will typically have two sorts of deployment processes, which are as follows:

1. A heavier, more rigorous, process for the deployment of code as, traditionally, getting it wrong has been at best embarrassing, and at worst very, very costly.

2. A lighter process for deploying data changes—after all, the application is changing data itself all the time—such as saving user profiles in a database.

Remember that it is also possible to store rules in a database, even though most of the examples in this book store the rules in a standard text file. For example, hidden within the Guvnor is an Apache Jackrabbit repository. This repository can use an industry standard database (such as Oracle, Sybase, MySql, or Microsoft SQL Server) as its storage area.

Perhaps the best way of summing this up is that rules give you a lot of power, and many deployment choices; so be careful how you use them. Whatever view you take, any changes to your rules in the 'big bad world' of production, or a live system, should be part of a standard, well-documented process.

Deployment process

We know how to write our business rules. We also know about the other pieces of the application puzzle (or at least we know who to ask them for). And we've decided whether we want to treat our rules as code or as data. Now, how do we get them from our computer (where we have written them) to the production server (where the entire company, or world, can interact with them)?

What we need is a deployment process.

If you don't have a deployment process, the worst case scenario is that you have to edit the rules on the production server. In doing so, you not only risk breaking an application that users are using, but you also risk not having a backup copy.

A slightly less bad scenario is that you edit the rules on your own PC, and then put them live. If you have no process to manage this transfer, you risk making a mistake. And your mistake may not be recognized until several days later. How do you return to the last known good version of your rules?

What we need is a deployment process. So what does a proper deployment process look like? Although there are many variations, at their core they contain the features shown in the following diagram:

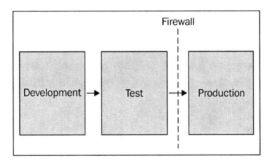

The first surprising thing that you encounter is that three separate computers are used in the deployment process. One (maybe your local PC) is where you write your rules. Another is the production server, which is a server accessible to the end users. But the rules aren't deployed directly from development to production. They get there via a test box—a server that is as similar to the production server as possible. It allows verification of the code that we are about to deploy, without disrupting users.

We need a separate test server to verify our application (and rules). The main reason for this is that other people will need to test your rules before they go live. No matter how careful you are, you might miss something. Having a third-party test for your rules provides an additional level of confidence.

The second group of people involved in the deployment process are the system administrators. It is unlikely that you will move the code between the various servers—it will more likely be the sys admins who do the job for you. Their role is to ensure the stability of these servers, and not just to put your application live. Expect plenty of questions from the sys admins about differences between versions, the underlying software requirements, step-by-step instructions on how to install the software, and which repository to find the code to deploy in.

What's a repository?

One of the questions the system administrators will ask you is "Are you storing your source code in a repository?" Now, what's a repository? And why do they care—after all you're deploying the finished, compiled product, not the source code?

The problem with storing your files on a local file system is that if you delete a file accidentally, it's very difficult to recover. Yes, you have the recycle bin, but what happens if that is full? What happens if you delete a portion of a file, save it, then only realize your mistake five minutes later?

A repository solves this versioning problem. It allows you to save a complete history of all of the changes that you have made and roll back to whichever version you choose (should this prove necessary). By allowing the merging of files, an entire team can co-operate on developing an application. There are many repositories available from many suppliers, including Microsoft, and Subversion.

You'll remember that Guvnor has a built-in repository, and take advantage of this later in the chapter. This repository stores only rules and items directly related to rules. For version control of the other items in our application, we would still need a full repository.

Deploying rules

Just to complicate things further, there are many options for how we can deploy the rules. They are as follows:

1. We can deploy the rules as plain-text source files—similar to the approach used in the examples in this book. Although this is perhaps the simplest approach, we will need the Drools compiler as a support library. This means that there can be problems, which we will find only after we deploy.

2. One alternative is to compile the rules and the dependent objects into a binary package. It is this package that is deployed on the server. This approach needs an extra step during our compile or build process, but it will find problems sooner.

3. A third approach is to pull the rules from the Guvnor repository. Although this is convenient, this approach doesn't always have the 'somebody else checks your rules before deployment' step. It is easy (perhaps far too easy) to push changes to your rules to the production.

There are further variations on the above three themes. They are listed as follows:

- We can mix and match any, or all, of these three solutions
- We can add or remove individual packages (or the entire rule base consisting of multiple packages) before, or during, our running of the rules
- When deploying source files, we can pre-check for syntax errors, but still allow rules to be compiled on the production server
- We can deploy our rules as code (as an integral part of the application) or as data (that is, build our application to check often for rule-changes)

Remember that Drools is pretty powerful. It can cope with rules swapping in and out, even when the rules are running as a part of long-term stateful rule session. We can also serialize (akin to freeze-drying) all of the Drools objects. This means we can de-serialize them later—a bit like adding water again to bring the rules and other Drools objects back to life. Serialisation means that 'live' rules can be sent over the network, and stored in a database for later use, and so on.

Push or pull?

In a normal deployment style, we 'push' the items to be deployed from the development PC or repository to the test server, and finally to the production server. The following diagram shows push deployment:

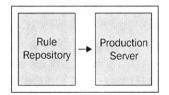

The copy, or deployment, (as shown by the arrow) is often a manual copy of the rules files. This is great because the copy will often be managed by system administrators, and they will ask you tough questions (such as 'Are you really sure?') before they deploy. This push style fits very well with treating rules as traditional code.

On the other hand, aren't rules meant to be dynamic? What if we want to make a small change to a business rule, which is after all designed to change frequently? Do we have to wait for a system adminstrator to be available? Will all of the questions they ask just get in the way?

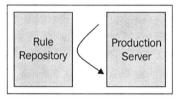

The pull style is meant to be more dynamic than this. In it, the production application using the rules will check every 'x' minutes, or hours, or days to see if there is a new set of rules in our rule repository. If so, it 'pulls' the new rules into the application. This process is similar to Windows Update, and can happen automatically, behind the scenes. A Drools component called 'RuleAgent' is provided to help build these kinds of systems.

The pull style works best if you are treating your rules as data that changes often. It also works best if the kind of changes you are making to your rules preclude costly mistakes—the sysadmin's 'Are you sure?' question comes from hard-earned experience. Remember that there is no 'best' deployment mechanism, but only the one that works best for your project.

Loading our rules

Whether we push or pull our rules to the live system, or deploy the rules a plain text of a pre-compiled or processed binary, we've got the same problem: How does our application actually load the rules we give it? In our previous examples, we've glossed over this process while we concentrated on what the rule engine was doing. Now it's time to take a detailed look at how we call the rule engine from Java.

Looking inside RuleRunner.java

Almost all of our samples have used some variation on the `RuleRunner.java` file to do the hard work of calling our rules. The good news is that the process is the same, which means that you can reuse it in your own projects. The code in `RuleRunner` will cover the following scenarios in which we have to:

- Load rules in a stateless manner
- Load rules in a stateful manner
- Load decision tables

- Load rules with DSL
- Load rules with Ruleflow

Helper methods

Firstly, we'll look at the code that all of these scenarios will use. The following code identifies our package, imports the other files that we will need, defines some constants (the XLS file extension, which is unlikely to change any time during the life of the program), and also defines the `RuleRunner()` method—it makes `RuleRunner` a JavaBean. Although this is not vital in the book samples, it does make the code more reusable.

 If you're happy being just a business rule author, you're unlikely to need the mechanics of rule loading to the detail we're going to discuss here. On the other hand, if you're a rule and Java developer—read on. We're going to talk about lots of useful stuff.

```
package net.firstpartners.drools;

import java.io.FileNotFoundException;
import java.io.IOException;
import java.io.InputStream;
import java.io.InputStreamReader;
import java.io.StringReader;
import java.util.Collection;
import java.util.HashMap;

import org.apache.commons.logging.Log;
import org.apache.commons.logging.LogFactory;

import org.drools.RuleBase;
import org.drools.RuleBaseFactory;
import org.drools.StatefulSession;
import org.drools.StatelessSession;
import org.drools.rule.Package;
import org.drools.compiler.DroolsParserException;
import org.drools.compiler.PackageBuilder;
import org.drools.decisiontable.InputType;
import org.drools.decisiontable.SpreadsheetCompiler;

import net.firstpartners.drools.log.ILogger;

public class RuleRunner {
    private static final String XLS_FILE_EXTENSION = ".xls";
    private Log log = LogFactory.getLog(getClass());

    public RuleRunner() {
    }
```

The imports fall into the following four broad categories:

- Standard Java objects, such as exceptions (errors) when a file is not found or cannot be opened (`IOException`), and utilities for reading files (`InputStream`, `InputStreamReader`, `StringReader`). It also includes Java standard collections and a Hashmap (a collection of name-value pairs).

- Objects from Apache, which provide many useful open source utilities. In this case, we import the logging utilities. These help us print messages about what is going on in our samples.

- Next, we import the Drools objects. We've seen them before—a `RuleBase` (or compiled set of rules) and a `RuleBaseFactory` to help us load the rules from a package. We have stateful and stateless sessions (working copies of the rules), as well as compiler for both standard and decision table based rules.

- Finally, we import other Java files from the project—in this case, a utility that we use to help write log entries for our rules.

The next section contains helper methods that are used by the stateful and stateless rule loaders. You'll see that these are marked private, that is, only other methods within the same file—the public `runStatelessRules` and `getStatefulSession` methods that you will recognize from the samples in previous chapters. The main helper method used is `loadRules`, which finds the multiple rule files we pass into it, as well as any DSL or ruleflow files that we specify.

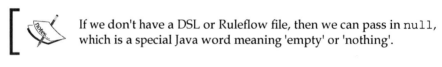 If we don't have a DSL or Ruleflow file, then we can pass in `null`, which is a special Java word meaning 'empty' or 'nothing'.

```
private RuleBase loadRules(String[] rules,
                            String dslFileName,
                            String ruleFlowFileName)
                throws Exception{
    RuleBase localRuleBase = RuleBaseFactory.newRuleBase();
    PackageBuilder builder = new PackageBuilder();

    for ( int i = 0; i < rules.length; i++ ) {
        String ruleFile = rules[i];
        log.info( "Loading file: " + ruleFile );

        //Check the type of rule file, then load it
        if(ruleFile.endsWith(XLS_FILE_EXTENSION)){

            loadExcelRules(ruleFile,builder);
        } else {
```

```
                   loadRuleFile (ruleFile,dslFileName,ruleFlowFileName,
                   builder);
         }

     Package pkg = builder.getPackage();
     localRuleBase.addPackage( pkg );

     }

     return localRuleBase;
  }
```

Within the method, there are three main rules-related features that are highlighted in the code above. They are:

1. The line beginning with `for (...)` loops though all of the names of the rule files that we pass in.

2. The line beginning with `if ( ... XLS_FILE_EXTENSION)` checks to see if our rule file is an Excel decision table. Depending on the answer, it calls a helper method to load a normal, or an Excel, rules file.

3. All of the rules files loaded by the helper method are added to a package (`builder.getPackage`), and then combined into a single rulebase (`localRuleBase.addPackage`).

The `loadRuleFile` method (which loads DRL rules) is called by the `loadRules` method. However, it only takes the name of a single `drl` rulefile as a parameter (as well as the `dsl` and `ruleflow` files).

```
    private void loadRuleFile(String ruleFile,
                              String dslFileName,
                              String ruleFlowFileName,
                              PackageBuilder addRulesToThisPackage )
              throws DroolsParserException,
              IOException{

    //This method is more flexible in finding resources on disk
    InputStream ruleSource = RuleRunner.class.getClassLoader()
                                .getResourceAsStream(ruleFile);

    //We must be able to find all rule files
    if(null==ruleSource){

            throw new FileNotFoundException
                    ("Cannot find rule file:"+ruleFile);

    } else {

            log.info("found rule file:"+ruleFile);

    }
```

```
//Check if the user has passed in a DSL
if(dslFileName!=null){

    //Load the rules, expanding them using the DSL Specified
    InputStream dslSource = RuleRunner.class.getClassLoader()
                            .getResourceAsStream(dslFileName);

    //We must be able to find all rule files
    if(null==dslSource){
            throw new FileNotFoundException
                    ("Cannot find dsl file:"+dslFileName);
    } else {
            log.info("found dsl file:"+ dslFileName);
    }


  //Load the rules, using DSL
      addRulesToThisPackage.addPackageFromDrl(
                  new InputStreamReader(ruleSource),
                  new InputStreamReader(dslSource));

} else {

    //Load the rules, no DSL
    addRulesToThisPackage.addPackageFromDrl(
            new InputStreamReader(ruleSource));
}

//if we've specified a ruleflow, add this to the package
if(ruleFlowFileName!=null){

    //Load the rules , expanding them using the DSL Specified
    InputStream ruleFlowSource =RuleRunner.class.getClassLoader()
                        .getResourceAsStream(ruleFlowFileName);

    //We must be able to find all rule files
     if(null==ruleFlowSource){
            throw new FileNotFoundException
                    ("Cannot find dsl file:"+ruleFlowFileName);
    } else {
            log.info("found dsl file:"+ ruleFlowFileName);
    }

      addRulesToThisPackage.addRuleFlow(
              new InputStreamReader(ruleFlowSource));
}
}
```

Notable steps highlighted in this method are:

1. The Java method for locating and loading the `RuleRunner.class`. `getClassLoader().getResourceAsStream(ruleFile)` file. Rather than being hardwired to a specific location, this file allows Java to search in the locality for files of the specific name. This is especially useful if this code is running as a part of a web application.

2. We try to load the rule file using this technique, and then throw an exception (error message) if the file cannot be found.

3. We check to see if a DSL has been passed in (`dslFileName!=null`). If yes, we call the Drools method `addPackageFromDrl(ruleSource, dslSource)`. If there no DSL file specifed, we call the more simple `addPackageFromDrl(ruleSource)` method.

4. We check to see if a ruleflow file has been specified (`ruleFlowFileName !=null`). If yes, we load and add it to the package by using the Drools method `addRuleFlow( ruleFlowSource)`.

The Excel equivalent of this method is `loadExcelRules`. This method takes the name of the Excel decision table that we wish to load, and the name of the package that we want to add it to.

 This example doesn't accept a Ruleflow file to keep things simple. It is possible to use Ruleflow with Excel decision tables in a similar way as normal DRL rule files are used.

```
private void loadExcelRules(String excelRuleFile,
                        PackageBuilder addRulesToThisPackage )
           throws DroolsParserException, IOException{

    //This method is more flexible in finding resources on disk
    InputStream xlRuleSource = RuleRunner.class.getClassLoader().
                            getResourceAsStream(excelRuleFile);

    if(null==xlRuleSource){
        throw new FileNotFoundException
            ("Cannot find file:"+excelRuleFile);
    } else {
        log.info("found file:"+excelRuleFile);
    }

    //first we compile the decision table into a whole lot of rules.
        SpreadsheetCompiler compiler = new SpreadsheetCompiler();
        String drl = compiler.compile(xlRuleSource, InputType.XLS);
        //Show the DRL that is generated
```

```
        log.debug(drl);

        ////same as previous - we add the drl to our package
        addRulesToThisPackage.addPackageFromDrl(
                                    new StringReader(drl));
    }
}
```

This method also finds the named Excel file by using the `getResourceAsStream` `(excelRuleFile)` technique. However, there are two new lines (highlighted). They are explained as follows:

1. We create a `SpreadsheetCompiler` helper object (kindly provided by the Drools project).

2. We call the `compile` method on this helper object to transform the Excel-based decision table into the DRL format, which we are familiar with. Just to prove that our rules are now in the DRL format, we even print them to the screen by using the `log.debug` statement.

Once done, we add the rules to the package provided, which is similar to what we did for the DRL source rules.

Public methods

All of these methods are going on 'under the covers', because the examples from previous chapters don't use them directly. In fact, unless you want to modify the behavior (for example, to add Ruleflow to rules based on decision tables), you might never need this amount of detail. What you will do in your project, like in our examples, is call one of the following methods:

- `runStatelessRules`
- `getStatefulSession`

As with the samples in the previous chapters, stateless rules are simpler as they fire once, and then give you a result immediately. Stateful rules, though more complex, are good for long-lived rules where we will update records and get results multiple times.

Stateless

The `runStatelessRules` method takes the following parameters:

- An array of text names — these are the rule files that the sample will search for, and then load.
- The `dslFileName` as text (string), or null if it is empty.

- The facts that we wish to pass to the rule engine—a collection of JavaBeans.

- A collection of global objects, such as name/value pairs, and so on.

- The `ruleFlowFileName` as text (string), or null if it is empty.

- A handle to the logger helper object. This allows the rules to print out what is happening.

> Remember that the difference between facts and globals is that facts are designed to be updated as a result of business rules firing (and will cause other rules to fire in turn). Globals, on the other hand, are more for 'reference' data that may or may not change.

To see an example of how this method is called, look at the `ExcelDataRulesExample` again. (It's part of the samples in Chapter 8.) The complete details of the `runStatelessRules` method:

```
/**
 * Run the rules
 * @param rules - array of rule files that we need to load
 * @param dslFileName - optional dsl file name (can be null)
 * @param facts - Javabeans to pass to the rule engine
 * @param globals - global variables to pass to the rule engine
 * @param logger - handle to a logging object
 * @throws Exception
 */
public void runStatelessRules(String[] rules, String dslFileName,
                        Collection<Object> facts,
                        HashMap<String,Object> globals,
                        String ruleFlowFileName,
                        ILogger logger)
            throws Exception {

    RuleBase masterRulebase=
            loadRules(rules,dslFileName, ruleFlowFileName);

    //Create a new stateless session
    StatelessSession workingMemory =
                        masterRulebase.newStatelessSession();

    for (String o: globals.keySet()){

      log.info( "Inserting global name:"+o+" value:"+globals.get(o));
            workingMemory.setGlobal(o, globals.get(o));
    }
    //Add the logger
```

```
        log.info("Inserting handle to logger (via global)");
        workingMemory.setGlobal("log", logger);

        log.info("==== Calling Rule Engine ====");

        //Fire using the facts
        workingMemory.execute(facts);

        log.info("==== Rules Complete =====");
    }
```

The key features of this method (highlighted above) are:

1. Load the rule, or DSL, or ruleflow file, by using the `loadRules()` helper method.
2. From the loaded `RuleBase`, create `StatelessSession`. This is a one-time scratchpad based on the rules, which is unique to this session.
3. Into this `StatelessSession`, add the globals in a loop (starting at the `for ...` line). The logger helper object is also added as a global.
4. Fire the rules, passing in the facts using the Drools method `workingMemory.execute(facts)`.

When the rules fire, the facts (JavaBeans) are updated. So when this method finishes, the rest of our Java code has access (via these JavaBeans) to the 'answers' that the rule engine comes up with.

Stateful

The stateful method takes almost the same set of parameters as does the stateless one. But there are two points of difference: we don't pass in the facts to it, and the stateful method returns a value (whereas the stateless method returns nothing). The returned value is `StatefulSession`. By returning this, we have a handle to the memory. This handle gives us the state of the rules, and allows us to come back to update that state with new facts later, if needed.

```
/**
 * Run the rules
 * @param rules - array of rule files that we need to load
 * @param dslFileName - optional DSL file name (can be null)
 * @param ruleFlowFileName - optional (can be null)
 * @param facts - JavaBeans to pass to the rule engine
 * @param globals - global variables to pass to the rule engine
 * @param logger - handle to a logging object
 * @throws Exception
 */
```

```
public StatefulSession getStatefulSession(String[] rules,String
                                          dslFileName, String
                                          ruleFlowFileName,
                                          HashMap globals,
                                          ILoggerlogger)
                throws Exception {
                        RuleBase masterRulebase=loadRules
                                (rules,dslFileName,ruleFlowFileName);

//Create a new stateful session
StatefulSession workingMemory = masterRulebase.newStatefulSession();

for (String o : globals.keySet()){

    log.info("Inserting global name: "+o+" value:"+globals.get(o) );

    workingMemory.setGlobal(o, globals.get(o));
}
//Add the logger
log.info("Inserting handle to logger (via global)");
workingMemory.setGlobal("log", logger);

return workingMemory;
}
```

Two differences are highlighted in this method. Firstly, we use
`newStatefulSession()` to get a working memory (scratchpad). This stateful session
can be called more than once.

Secondly, the method is actually shorter than its stateless equivalent. The reason is
that we set up the rules, but don't fire them. So if we're using this method (as in the
`RuleflowExample.java` file from Chapter 9), you'll see that you have to do the hard
work in the Java code that calls this method.

This 'hard work' is familiar, and explains why we don't have to pass in the facts. We
have to insert ourselves in the calling method. An example of the calling code is
as follows:

```
Collection<Object> allRangeValues = ranges.getAllRangesAndCells();

for (Object fact: allRangeValues){
                statefulSession.insert(fact);
```

Finally, we also need to remember to call the rules:

```
statefulSession.fireAllRules();
```

Alternative method—RuleAgent

Drools provides an alternative method for loading the rules, based on the `RuleAgent` (found in the `org.drools.agent` package). The `RuleAgent` helper can make your code simpler, as long as you follow the `RuleAgent` way of deployment. However, you don't get as much flexibility as you do with the code samples above. Typically, this means that pre-compiled (binary) packages of rules fit quite well with the way the Guvnor web editor works.

The way the `RuleAgent` works is through code plus a properties file. Your code calls the `RuleAgent` helper, similar to the following (remember that you will have `import org.drools.agent.RuleAgent` at the top of the file):

```
RuleAgent ra = RuleAgent.newRuleAgent("/RuleAgent.properties");
RuleBase rb = ra.getRuleBase();

// now get a stateful or stateless sessions from RuleBase as before
```

The `RuleAgent.properties` text file referred to in the above code snippet looks similar to the following:

```
poll=60
NewInstance=false
name=SomeNameUsedInLogging
dir=/my/dir
file = alternativeToDir
url=http://myfirstUrl http://anotherURLIfNeeded
localCacheDir=file://c://temp
```

Most of the options in the properties file are straightforward, as follows:

- `Poll = 60`: This causes the RuleAgent to check for updates every 60 seconds.
- `NewInstance`: If this is true, and there is an update to the rules, then only new sessions that are created will pick up the new rules. The previous sessions will remain unchanged.
- `name`: This is the name that is used in logging.
- `dir`, `file`, or `url`: The location where the binary package of rules can be located. `url` can be used to point directly to Guvnor.
- `localCacheDir`: The `RuleAgent` will keep a local copy in case the remote URL is temporarily unavailable.

Web deployment

Normally, you'd expect that we will take what we've just learned and use it to deploy an example on the Web. However, you could be using one of the hundreds of Java web frameworks. Each of those web frameworks would be worthy of a book in itself. Instead, we'll provide a set of notes about what to expect. These notes are not meant to be exhaustive, but to give you an idea of the steps involved in deploying Drools as a part of the web framework of your choice.

Each of these frameworks has three major points of integration with JBoss Rules. These are as follows:

- How do we package the project (with Rules and the Drools Libraries) so that it gets deployed to the web server?
- In which folder do we save the rules files in the web project?
- Where in the web framework do we call the rules code (seen previously in this chapter)?

For our walkthrough, we'll use the Appfuse framework (which uses Spring under the covers). The quick run-through also assumes that you have the MySql database installed from `http://dev.mysql.com/downloads/` — the community edition will do fine. The next few pages assume some knowledge of Java web development due to the complexity of the subject.

 Why Appfuse? Underneath, it uses the popular Spring MVC framework. But it gives you a choice of web frameworks. It also generates most of the applications automatically, for immediate results — a bit like Ruby on Rails. More information on the Appfuse project is available at `www.appfuse.org`.

Maven for packaging

Previous chapters have used Maven as a build tool, mainly for setting up Eclipse projects. It can do a lot more, including pulling down Appfuse from the Web, creating the package structure for the project, and deploying the code to the web server. This can be seen with the help of the following steps:

1. Open a command window. Use Maven to download Appfuse, and create a standard project.

   ```
   mvn archetype:create -DarchetypeGroupId=org.appfuse.archetypes-
   DarchetypeArtifactId=appfuse-basic-spring -DremoteRepositories
   =http://static.appfuse.org/releases -DarchetypeVersion=2.0.2 -
   DgroupId=net.firstpartners.chap10 -DartifactId=chap10-sample
   ```

2. Change the director to the folder created in the previous step using the `cd chap10-sample` command.

3. Use Maven again, this time to generate a project skeleton, with the command `mvn war:inplace`.

4. Create an Eclipse project by using `mvn eclipse:eclipse`, and then open the project in Eclipse.

In the project structure, you'll see the place where we can save our rules files and other resources, under the `resources` folder, as shown in the screenshot below. By default, Maven expects this standard structure. The following figure shows the RuleFile location:

5. Maven can also run a test web server - `mvn jetty:runwar`. When the message **[INFO] Started Jetty Server [INFO] Starting scanner at interval of 3 seconds.** appears in the console, open a web browser at `http://localhost:8080/login.jsp`. You will see the following web screen, or sample app, generated by Appfuse. If you want to log in and play around, enter **admin** as both the **Username** and the **Password**.

6. Stop Maven (by pressing *Ctrl+C* in the command window), when you're finished playing with it.

7. Now that we have a web application up and running, it's time to start adding Drools. In Eclipse, we'll modify the `pom.xml` file so that the web project knows where to find the Drools libraries. Rather than supplying the full details here, just copy and paste the `<dependencies>` section from the `pom.xml` file in the sample from Chapter 8.

8. Next, we need to add the code that calls JBoss Rules (that is, the code we saw previously in this chapter and in the samples). Typically, this is in the Java file (controller of the model-view-controller pattern) where the values submitted by the user on the Web have already been converted into JavaBeans. By happy coincidence, these JavaBeans are very suitable for passing into the rule engine.

9. More details on how to add a controller for Appfuse-Spring-MVC can be found at `http://www.appfuse.org/display/APF/Using+Spring+MVC`. The file that we will modify according to these instructions is `PersonFormController`. In summary, this file (`PersonFormController`) extends another file (`BaseFormController`), and adds one method (that we will use to call the rules):

```
public ModelAndView onSubmit(HttpServletRequest request,
        HttpServletResponse response, Object command,
        BindException errors)
throws Exception {
    log.debug("About to call Rules...");
        //Place the code to call rules here, exactly
    as previous examples
    return new ModelAndView(success);
}
```

10. Within the updated `PersonFormController`, add the code that calls the rule engine—a copy-and-paste job from the examples in Chapter 9 should work. The trickiest part for this code is the rules (DRL) file. However, as long as the rules file is included in the Web Archive (WAR) file that contains the application, the code in our previous sample, `getClassLoader().getResourceAsStream(ruleFile)`, should find it.

11. Generate the web application ZIP file by using `Mvn War`, and deploy it to your favorite web application using the instructions that come with it.

 Remember—this isn't meant to be a complete web application development tutorial. Rather, it's meant for people familiar with Java web development to be able to add rules to their applications. If you're not familiar with web development, it may give you some idea of the required steps.

So, let's answer the three big previous questions, here:

- How to package the project? The answer is: Use Maven standard functionality (or an equivalent from another Java build framework) with the Drools libraries specified as a part of the build script (for example `pom.xml`).

- In which folder do we save the rules files? The answer is: In the `resources` folder of the Java project.

- Where do we call the rules code? The answer is: We call it from the Java code, typically the controller class. If you followed the instructions that come with Appfuse, whenever you click the **Submit** button on the web browser, the framework will eventually cause the above rule code to be executed.

Look again at the 'one size architecture fits all' diagram at the start of this chapter. As promised, the code we have just seen fits right in the middle of the picture, in the **Business Layer** of the system.

Summary

This chapter has shown you how to deploy your business rules in the real world. We looked at the pieces that made up an entire web application, and where our rules fit into it. We saw the various options for deploying rules as a part of our application, and also the team that's involved in the process. Once deployed, we looked at the code that will load and run the rules—both home-grown, and those created using the standard RuleAgent. Finally, we saw how to combine this into a web project using the framework of your choice.

11
Looking under the Cover

In the previous chapters, we've treated the rule engine as a 'black box'. We've described what goes in and what comes out, but not what happens 'under the covers'. In this chapter, we open the box and explain how a rule engine works. We demonstrate how it is a faster and easier-to-maintain solution than traditional coding methods. We'll also introduce debugging and other ways of seeing what is going on inside the rule engine in real time, as it happens.

In this chapter, we will cover the following topics:

- Rule engine concepts
- Logging
- Rete
- Debugging rules

Rule engine concepts

To understand what we're seeing when we look inside the rule engine, we first need to understand a couple of rule engine concepts, including a repetition (in more depth) of something we first covered back in Chapter 1.

Facts or objects

Facts are pretty straightforward. They're the container that we use to transport information into (and out of) the rule engine. You'll remember that because facts are standard JavaBeans (we compared them to Lego blocks), a lot of the code already in your organisation can be used for this purpose. Or, you can write your own—such as the `CustomerOrder` and `ChocolateShipment`.

An 'object' is just another term for a fact (it's where the term **Object Orientated Programming** or **OOP** comes from). Earlier, we saw how we can insert, update, and retract (remove) facts or objects from the rule engine, and how the rules would react as a result.

Or rather, we inserted, updated, and retracted the facts from the **Working Memory**, and saw the **Agenda** and **Activations** change as a result. All three of these are parts of the Drools Rule Engine, and are a critical part of what happens 'under the covers'.

Working memory

To keep things simple, all of the examples that we've given until now have been about a 'single user'. That way, we could treat the rule engine and working memory as almost the same. In real life, the sorts of Enterprise Applications that use rules will have many people calling rules at the same time. If all of these people shared the same memory, then things could get pretty confusing. (Imagine if the rules returned somebody else's bank balance!) The solution is to give everybody their own workspace, or working memory.

 If you're used to working with web servers, you will notice a similar problem and a similar solution—each user who is interacting with the server has his or her own unique session, which is isolated from any other user's session.

We touched upon working memory when we used stateful sessions as a part of the ruleflow, but working memory is also behind the stateless session. Both stateless and stateful sessions are types of working memory. In both cases, working memory acts as a scratchpad, unique to each user, which contains all of the knowledge (facts) that Drools has been told about the case. When we insert, update, or retract a fact, it's the working memory that changes. Likewise, when a rule inserts, updates, or retract a fact, it's the working memory that changes.

Let's repeat it because it's important: Rules change facts in the working memory. Because of the way that Java works, even though our facts are a part of working memory, the code that passed in the values still has a 'handle' to them. Thus, it automatically knows about the changed values.

Pattern matching, Agenda, and Activations

You'll remember the spreadsheet below from Chapter 1. It is about the business rules for the chocolate factory. It's far simpler than the Excel-based decision tables that we used later in the book. In the following table, the first three columns represent the 'when' part of the rule, and the final, fourth column shows the actions to be taken:

Highlighted are the rules that become available to fire whenever we sell more than 30,000 Chocolate Crunchie bars. This pattern matching (identifying the relevant rules for any given situation) is a core part of Drools, and something that rule engines do very well.

In real life we would insert facts to the rule engine (or rather, to working memory), telling the rule engine that all those candy bars have been sold. As soon as we did so, the rule engine would identify the relevant rules via pattern matching. These rules would become 'active' or ready to fire. So, *Activations are rules that are ready to fire, and Agenda is the list of all of these activations.*

Conflict resolution

Note that we didn't say Activations 'are rules that fire' but 'rules that are ready to fire'. Just because there are facts in the working memory that match a rule (that is, a rule *could* fire) doesn't mean that the rule will fire. The first question, which might not be obvious from the chocolate factory sample, is which rule amongst the six highlighted ones will fire first?

Because (at a simple level) only one rule fires at a time, Drools needs to decide which of these rules should fire first. To make this decision, let's introduce an idea called **conflict resolution**.

 Strictly speaking, more than one rule can fire at a time, especially if you have multiple working memories. Within the working memory, the Rete algorithm optimises the matching and firing process.

As soon as the 'when' part of the rule it satisfied, it is added to the Agenda as an Activation. This creates a list of rules that are available to fire. If there is only one rule Activation on the agenda, there is no need for conflict resolution—it is fired straight away. If there are two or more rules, conflict resolution is used to put an order to the list.

By default, conflict resolution decides the order of priority in the following manner:

1. **Salience**: Back in Chapter 5, we came across salience as a rule attribute that we could add via Guvnor (or the other rule editors). Under this conflict resolution method, a rule with a higher salience value will be closer to the top of the agenda, and thus more likely to fire. Remember that salience only changes the order of rules whose 'if' part matches the current facts. If this doesn't happen, you can increase the salience if you wish.

2. **Recency:** If salience doesn't resolve the rule agenda order, then Drools looks at Recency, or how many times a rule has fired previously. The more the rule has fired, the higher it will be on the agenda.

3. **Complexity:** A rule with more conditions in the 'when' part will be more specific, that is, it will be fussier when it fires. On the other hand, when it does fire, it is likely to be more relevant to the current situation. Therefore, the more complex rules tend to move toward the top of the agenda.

4. **LoadOrder:** If none of the first three strategies work, then the fallback situation is to use the LoadOrder of the rules—that is, rules that got loaded first get fired first. Because we can load rules from many different files, we can implicitly state which blocks of rules are more important than others. If you need to refresh your memory, look at `RuleRunner.Java`, from the previous chapter.

Although this is the default conflict resolution strategy, it is possible to change the methodology employed. There can be good reasons for doing this, but in general, a well-written set of rules shouldn't need this level of fine-tuning.

A more dynamic Agenda

The order in which rules/Activations appear on the Agenda is critical. This is because only the first rule on the Agenda is guaranteed to fire, even though all of the other rules on the Agenda match the current set of facts in the working memory. The other rules may fire in turn, but only if an earlier rule hasn't changed the facts in the working memory. This means that rules can be dropped from the Agenda before they get a chance to fire, because there are no longer valid.

> Let me explain how housework and chores get done in my home. My wife gives me a list of tasks to complete — wash the dishes, brush the floor, and put out the bins. By the time I finish washing the dishes, my wife has lost patience and has already brushed the floor — so that's no longer on my 'to-do' list. On the other hand, she has now asked me to tidy up the yard and wash the car, so that gets added to the list.
>
> Think of the 'to-do' list as the Drools Agenda and you'll get an idea of the dynamic addition or removal of 'rules to fire' from the list.

Truth maintenance

We change the working memory by inserting and removing facts. Changes in working memory cause rules to match, get added to the agenda, and fire. Because rules can also insert, remove, or update the facts in the working memory, a rule firing can cascade and cause other rules to be added to the agenda and subsequently fire. These rules, in turn, can cause further rules to become active and fire.

What is going on here is the process of **truth maintenance**. Given a set of facts, the rule engine applies the appropriate business rules and modifies the facts as necessary. If the newly-changed facts mean that other business rules come into play, then they are applied. Eventually, all necessary rules are fired, and the facts stored in the working memory represent the truth, or at least the truth as understood by our business rules.

Any change in facts (for example, if a user submits more information about his or her insurance application) causes new rules to come into play, in an attempt to maintain the truth.

Truth maintenance is a bit like playing pool (or snooker) because of the following reasons:

1. You take a shot, hitting the white cue ball (that is, introduce a new fact to the system).

2. The rules of physics are applied and the ball rolls across the green baize, and bounces off the cushions.

3. It may hit another ball (that is, cause another rule to fire). The rules of physics are applied again, and now two balls are moving.

4. These may hit other balls (more facts getting introduced, more rules getting fired, and more balls getting moved — although slightly more slowly), until eventually the whole system (all the balls on the table) is still again.

5. The truth (according to the laws of physics) has been maintained! Or at least, until another player takes a shot.

This 'rules changing facts causing other rules to fire' process can lead to rules getting caught in a loop. Rule 1 changes a fact, which causes rule 2 to fire, rule 2 changes a fact, which causes rule 1 to fire, and so on. There are a couple of features in Drools that help to avoid this. Marking a rule with an attribute of 'no-loop' means the rule cannot cause itself to fire. In Ruleflow, Agenda groups control the amount of rules available to fire. Writing the conditions (the 'when' part of the rule) as precisely as possible also helps to avoid this scenario.

If you're a programmer, truth maintenance is a fundamental difference to any language you may have used before. With those languages, you (the programmer) have to ensure that your code gives the correct results. With Drools, the rule engine ensures that the result is always consistent with the business rules that you have given it.

Back to the future (with chocolate shipping)

We've just looked at a couple of make-believe rules from the chocolate factory. Wouldn't it be great to see some real rules and use it to see the internals of the rule engine that we've just talked about? Fortunately, our Chapter 11 example allows us to do just that (this example is available for download from the same site as the previous samples, `http://code.google.com/p/red-piranha/`).

This sample is the same as the chocolate factory that we saw back in Chapter 6, but with some extra code that makes it easier to see the internal happenings in the rule engine. The following are the basic rules found in the `shipping-rules.drl` file:

- A rule to confirm (print out) the OoompaLoompa holidays is passed, as a fact, to the rule engine

- A rule matches against unfilled customer orders, and starts sending out shipments of 210 units at a time

- A rule adds an estimated date to these new shipments of chocolate

- A rule adjusts this shipment date if it falls on a day that the OoompaLoompas take as a holiday

- A rule ensures that we don't overshoot on the last shipment, adjusting it so that only the remaining balance is sent

Running the Chapter 11 example is similar to before. Open `EventRulesExample.java`, right-click anywhere in the file, and select **Run As | Java Application** from the context menu that appears.

> The sample comes with an Eclipse project, so you should be able to open it with **File | New Project**, and then select the folder to which you unzipped the sample. If this doesn't work (for example, you are using a newer version of Eclipse since the book came out), you can regenerate the project with Maven (assuming that you have it installed). Open a command window (Dos Prompt) at the folder containing the project (the one containing `pom.xml`). After executing the command `mvn eclipse:clean eclipse:eclipse`, refresh or reopen the project in Eclipse, and everything should be set up correctly.

After running the sample, you should get output similar to the following in the Console window as before, ending the schedule that we have calculated.

Shipment amount:210 date:03/02/2009 chocolate bars left in order:1790

Shipment amount:210 date:11/02/2009 chocolate bars left in order:1580

Shipment amount:210 date:17/02/2009 chocolate bars left in order:1370

....

Shipment amount:210 date:24/03/2009 chocolate bars left in order:320

Shipment amount:210 date:31/03/2009 chocolate bars left in order:110

Shipment amount:110 date:07/04/2009 chocolate bars left in order:0

Logging working memory

We've used logging in our earlier examples to print what is going on to the Console. The output above, showing the shipment amounts, is a good example of this. Mostly, this is our own logging statement. Although we can add logging statements that get output when the rules fire, until now we've treated the decisions by the rule engine about which rule to fire as taking place in a 'black box'. Wouldn't it be great to look inside and see which rules are getting fired, and why?

The main difference between the example in this chapter and the one in Chapter 6 is that the code in `RuleRunner.Java` has been modified to display what is going on internally in the rule engine. The main lines that have been added to this file are:

```
// create a new Working Memory Logger, that logs to file.
WorkingMemoryFileLogger wmLogger = new
                         WorkingMemoryFileLogger(workingMemory);
// Set the log file that we will be using
wmLogger.setFileName("event-log");
....

//Fire using the facts
workingMemory.execute(facts);

//stop logging
wmLogger.writeToDisk();
```

It's not a big change. The snippet above has only four lines of code, of which (`workingMemory.execute`), we're familiar with one already. What happens is:

- We create a new `WorkingMemoryFileLogger`, passing in a handle to the working memory that we want to log

- We set the name of the log file in which the information will be written (in this case `event-log`)

- We fire the rules as normal, using `workingMemory.execute`

- When the rules have fired, we write the log to disk using `wmLogger.writeToDisk`

In real life the log file can become very large, so be careful to disable the logging of production systems. At the simplest level, this means commenting out the above code (by placing '//' in front of it).

Looking at the working memory log

Assuming that you ran the sample in the previous section, you'll already have the `event-log.log` file generated. This file should sit at the root of the project (just under the `chap11-sample` folder in Eclipse, next to the `pom.xml` file).

 Eclipse doesn't display changes to files by default, so you may need to refresh the project to see the changes. To refresh your project in Eclipse, select the project name, then press the F5 key or choose **File | Refresh** from the main menu.

If we open this file, we'll see something similar to the following text:

```
<object-stream>
  <list>
    <org.drools.audit.event.ActivationLogEvent>
      <activationId>Chocolate Shipment [1]</activationId>
      <rule>Chocolate Shipment</rule>
      <declarations>$CustomerOrder=Initial Chocolate Order:2000
itemsStillToShip:2000 shipments:none-listed(1)</declarations>
      <type>4</type>
    </org.drools.audit.event.ActivationLogEvent>
    <org.drools.audit.event.ObjectLogEvent>
      <factId>1</factId>
      <objectToString>Initial Chocolate Order:2000
itemsStillToShip:2000 shipments:none-listed</objectToString>
      <type>1</type>
    </org.drools.audit.event.ObjectLogEvent>
    <org.drools.audit.event.ActivationLogEvent>
      <activationId>confirm holidays [2]</activationId>
      <rule>confirm holidays</rule>
      <declarations>$holiday=17/03/2009(2)</declarations>
      <type>4</type>
    </org.drools.audit.event.ActivationLogEvent>
    <org.drools.audit.event.ObjectLogEvent>
```

Drools Audit Log Viewer

Not very readable, is it? To understand what the working memory log is showing, we need to use the Drools Audit Log View.

To open this view in Eclipse, select **Window | Show View | Other | (Drools Folder) Audit View** from the toolbar. You should see an empty version of the above window. The window is empty as we haven't told the viewer where our working memory log file is.

See those icons at the top right of the **Audit View** window? Click on the file icon (it's the highlighted one on the left, looking like a piece of paper) and choose the audit log that we opened earlier.

Now the window looks a bit more like the **Audit View** in the diagram above. But what does it actually mean? Working through the list, you'll see that the first item in the log is where the initial chocolate order is inserted into memory. The icon is a green square.

Because the rules start firing as soon as the facts are inserted, (before the second fact is inserted) an Activation is immediately created for the `Chocolate Shipment` rule. The icon is a right-facing arrow.

The third line in the log is the second object being inserted (one of the OompaLoompa dates passed in as a holiday), causing another activation to be created for the rule `confirm holidays`.

A couple of lines later, we see the first rule—the one that confirms holidays—actually being executed. The icon is a blue diamond.

> ◆ Activation executed: Rule confirm holidays

In total, there are three activation executions in this part of the log. Note that the executions are not in the order in which they were created, but in the order that Drools deems fit when it resolves the conflicts. As the third rule is the `chocolate shipment` rule, we immediately see an object update in the log. The icon for an object update is a yellow square.

> Object updated (1): Initial Chocolate Order:2000 itemsStillToShip:1790 shipments:

The line immediately following this in the log is a new rule/Activation created (as a result of this object being created). The line immediately after that is interesting—it is another object insertion (we've seen those before). Because the object (a shipment) has been created or inserted by a rule (the `chocolate shipment` rule), with an existing object being changed, the following line has a new Activation created (`shipment` rule).

> ◢ ▫ Object inserted (4): Shipment amount:210

Even in this simple example, there are a couple of hundred lines, so we'll skip them and move on. Before we do this, it's a good time to mention the **show cause** functionality in the **Audit View**. To activate it, right-click on the log and select **Show Cause** from the context menu.

> ◢ ◆ Activation executed: Rule Chocolate Shipment $CustomerOrder=Initial Chocolate Order:2000 ite
>   ◢ Object updated (1): Initial Chocolate Order:2000 itemsStillToShip:1790 shipments:
>   ⇨ Activation created: Rule Chocolate Shipment $CustomerOrder=Initial Chocolate Order:200
>   ◢ Object inserted (4): Shipment amount:210 date:null chocolate bars left in order:1790
>   ⇨ Activation created: Rule Add Next Available Shipment Date $ChocolateShipment=Shipme
> ◢ ◆ Activation executed: Rule Add Next Available Shipment Date $ChocolateShipment=Shipment a
>   Object updated (4): Shipment amount:210 date:03/02/2009 chocolate bars left in order:1790

For this example, we clicked on the **Object updated (4)** and the action that caused it is highlighted. As it happens, what caused the update was the action in the previous screenshot (that is, the object that had just been inserted by the rule).

The previous section talked about conflict resolution when there are more than two rules on the Agenda available to fire. Near the very end of the audit log is an example of this happening.

```
◆ Activation executed: Rule Chocolate Shipment $CustomerOrder=Ini
    Object updated (1): Initial Chocolate Order:2000 itemsStillToShip
▲ ▪ Object inserted (13): Shipment amount:210 date:null chocolate b
    ⇨ Activation created: Rule Add Next Available Shipment Date $
    ⇨ Activation created: Rule Don't ship more than the customer or
◆ Activation executed: Rule Don't ship more than the customer order
▲   Object updated (13): Shipment amount:110 date:null chocolate b
    ⇦ Activation cancelled: Rule Add Next Available Shipment Date
    ⇨ Activation created: Rule Add Next Available Shipment Date $
```

The conflict happens where the two right arrows (that is, rules that are on the Agenda) fire one after the other. The rules are **Add Next Available Shipment Date** and **Don't ship more than the customer order**.

Obviously, this conflict is resolved as one of these rules is activated and fired in the next line: the **Don't ship more than the customer order** rule. This section also shows an Activation cancellation—the second line from the bottom of the screenshot. The icon for a cancellation is a left-facing arrow.

There is another icon, not shown in the above samples, when an object or fact is removed from the working memory. The icon for fact removal is a red square.

Other icons not shown in this diagram, but which might appear in your audit log, are:

- Drools logo icon: Rule or rule package added or removed
- Process icon: Ruleflow started or ended, or Ruleflow group activated or deactivated

Rete algorithm

The Rete algorithm is at the heart of the events that we just saw in the audit log. The one-line explanation of Rete is:

Rete makes rules run incredibly fast by sorting the rules in such a way that when facts change, the rule engine knows instantly which rules need to fire.

The Rete algorithm is a bit like the algorithm used by Google for searching the entire Web. You don't need to know how it works to use it, but it's nice to have a vague idea. If you want to know more than the overview here, there are hundreds of pages on the Web, including *Dr Charles Forgy 1974 to 1979 original papers*, where he first outlined Rete—just do a Google search for *Charles Forgy Rete Algorithm*.

If I was to write a rule engine, and didn't know about Rete, I would do it incredibly badly. I would probably write a series of loops checking each part of my business rules every single time a fact might have changed, including every time a rule fires.

For example, the shipping rules have 5 rules, with 3 facts, each holding about 4 values. In my loop (which I would have to run every time something changed) that would be 60 values (5x3x4 = 60) that I need to check after every single change. That's 60 values checked hundreds or thousands of times, over the life of a simple application.

That's not going to scale very well—a medium-sized sample would have 100 rules, with 20 facts in total, holding about 4 values each. This becomes 8000 items to be checked, and checked repeatedly. Even if we check 2000 items a second, it comes to a 4-second delay each and every time something changes, which can be very frequent in an enterprise application.

> Don't laugh at this description. If you've written any code, you've probably made the same mistake yourself (I have).
>
> Think of the hundreds of 'if…then' statements that you have scattered throughout your code, and imagine them gathered together in one place, often getting called more than once. Sounds a bit more like the example above? That (along with other optimisations) is why rule engines are often more efficient than the equivalent 'traditional' code.

It's just as well that I don't write rule engines. Let's try again.

Mostly, the checking of facts is slow because there are duplications in the checks. For example, if both rules use a common shipment date, the same fact will get checked twice for changes. What if we spent a bit of time grouping the rules so that one check will do everything for both rules?

Rete in action

One example of this grouping is shown in the following screenshot, from the Drools IDE. It shows the shipping rules from our example, but displayed as a **Rete Tree**. To view this yourself, open the `Shipping-rules.drl` file as normal. Using the tabs at the bottom of **Rete View**, click on **Rete Tree**.

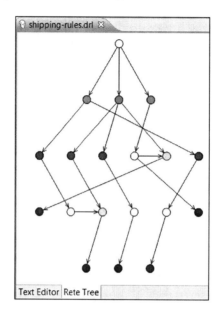

While this looks complicated, the concepts are simple. Drools (the white node at the top) has analyzed the 'when' part of the five shipping rules, and picked out the facts (the three red nodes on the second line), and the fields on those facts (the four blue nodes, most of the third line). These are then connected via the green and yellow nodes on the third and fourth line, (used to cache the previous values to further reduce the amount of checks that we need) to the black nodes (the rules that can fire) at the very bottom of the diagram.

> Remember that when we were running our previous examples, there was a noticeable pause before the rules fired. This was the time taken to construct the Rete network from the rules. It's a trade off—a slight pause at the start, compensated for by by a greatly-increased performance later.

To analyze which rule needs to fire, all that Drools has to do is to start at the top node and, depending on what has changed, walk down the tree until it gets to the black node (representing the 'when' part of the rule) to fire. That's the hard bit done. Firing the rule once it's been decided is more or less standard Java.

> To find out more information on each node, click on it in the **Rete Tree View**. If you have the property view open in Eclipse (from the toolbar, select **Window | Show view | Properties**), you'll see the name of the fact/field/rule displayed.

To give an example of this 'walking the Rete tree', imagine that a shipment date changes on one of the shipments. The path that Drools will follow is shown below. From these five nodes, one is standard Drools (the one at the top), and the next two are 'real' checks on the fact and field respectively. The fourth node is an internal connector. The final node is the actual rule that will fire.

In this example, when the shipment date changes, instead of the of the 60+ checks previously required, now only two checks need to be done (in the second and third nodes).

Two checks are obviously faster than 60 (or 8000 in the larger sample), especially if they are repeated 100 times. The actual Rete algorithm is much more sophisticated (and faster) than we describe. Drools has further optimizations that make the process faster still—it's easy to optimise business rules when they are written in standard 'when...then' format.

Debugging rules

Now that we understand how a rule engine works, let's take a peek at its internals, in real time.

This book has shown you how to print logging statements to the console to see what is going on in your rules. It has also shown you how to use the working memory logger to show you what is happening within the rule engine. But these methods are 'after the fact'—the rules have completed and we are trying to reconstruct what has happened, long after the program has finished. What if we want to see rules firing and values changing as they happen?

What we need is debugging. Debugging is like pausing a movie on a DVD player. Normally, we would run our program (movie) from end-to-end using the play (run) button. If we don't like the movie (program) we can halt it by clicking on the stop button (or pressing *Ctrl+C*). If we need to take a break we can pause it, and maybe change a few of the movie options such as to view it in widescreen, or to switch the director's commentary on or off, and so on.

If you've already debugged Java programs, you'll recognise the above description. The tools we're about to describe are very familiar. But how we do start to debug the rules?

Normally, we can only debug rules when running them through the Eclipse IDE. To start debugging, we need to do the following two things:

1. We need to tell the Drools IDE that we want to run the rules in a debug mode, and not just run straight through (which is how we've run our examples up to this point).

2. We need to tell Drools where to 'pause'. Although it is possible to debug right from the start of the program, telling Drools to run until it hits a 'breakpoint' saves us from trawling through hundreds, or thousands, of lines of code to get to the bit that we're interested in.

When the debugger hits the breakpoint in our code, it will pause the program and allow us to see a snapshot of the frozen program. When we're ready, we can continue the program, or step through it one line at a time.

Debugging rules in the Eclipse IDE

If you have the rules project for Chapter 11 already open in Eclipse, then we're almost ready to start debugging. We'll first set the breakpoints—where we want the debugger to pause:

1. Make sure that the project has **Drools Nature** enabled. To do this, right-click on the project name, and then select **Convert to Drools Project** from the context menu. This command will only switch on Drools. So if you're not sure, it does no harm to do this again.

2. Open the rules file (`ShippingRules.drl`) as normal and go to where we want the debugger to pause.

3. Select the line where we want to place the breakpoint. (In our sample, scroll down to the second-to-last line of the `Chocolate shipment` rule.)

4. In the lefthand margin of the editor, right-click and select the command **Toggle breakpoint** from the context menu.

The screen should now look like the following screenshot (with the new breakpoint circled in red).

 Using this technique, we can also set breakpoints in Java code — for example, at more or less any line after the `main[]` method in `EventRulesExample.java`. This is the method of debugging that programmers reading this book will be familiar with.

```
⊜rule "Chocolate Shipment"
    when
        $CustomerOrder : CustomerOrder
    then
        //Add a new shipment into the
        ChocolateShipment ChocolateShi
        modify($CustomerOrder){
            addShipment(ChocolateShipm
        }
        //notify the working memory of
        insert( ChocolateShipment );
        //Logging message
        log.info("Fired Customer Shipm
    end
```

If you try clicking elsewhere in the rules file, you'll notice that *you can only add breakpoints in the consequence (then) portion of the rules*. This is because of the way that the Rete algorithm works — effectively, the 'when' parts of the rules are shared at run-time. Even if we could set a breakpoint in the 'when' part, the Drools IDE would have no way of knowing which of the shared rules we wished to examine.

Now that we've told the Drools IDE where to pause for debugging, we need to start the application in debug mode. This is almost, but not quite, the same as running the application normally.

1. Open the start point of the application (`EventRulesExample.java`).
2. Start debugging by right-clicking and selecting **Debug as | Drools Application** from the context menu.

The program will now start running (much more slowly!) in debug mode. It is important to debug the program as a **Drools Application** (and not a standard debug application), otherwise the breakpoints that you set in the rules will not be noticed and the program will continue (slowly!) right until the very end.

 A typical program will run five to ten times slower while debugging because of the additional checks (such as 'Do I need to stop now?') that need constantly to be made.

Rules debug perspective

When you started debugging, you may have been asked the question **Debug perspective is normally associated with this action—do you wish to switch to it now?** Click on **Yes**, and Eclipse will look like the example shown in the following screenshot. You can always switch later, manually, by selecting the Eclipse Toolbar and going to **Window | Open Perspective | Other | Debug**.

Both actions leave a button on the toolbar (top right of the picture) to make switching perspectives easier the next time.

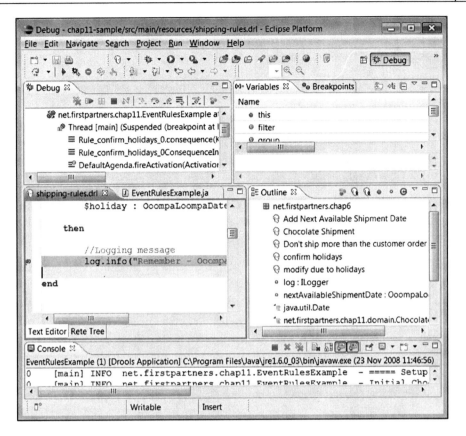

Previously, we opened views (such as the logging console) to give us more information about the project. Perspectives are just bundles of views that are displayed whenever we carry out a specific activity. Previously, (although we didn't know it) we were using the editing perspective. Now that we're debugging, it's useful to see our project from a different angle. The normal perspective is great for editing or writing files. The debug perspective (that we're looking at now) is great for debugging projects.

At first, the debug perspective looks very different from the one that we are used to. However, if we look at the screen from the bottom up, we'll see that two-thirds of the bottom screen looks familiar. It contains the following:

- The **Console** (the bottom panel): Like before, this shows text that has been output from the program
- The **Editor** (the middle left panel): This is for editing the `Shipping-Rules.drl` file, with the current line (where the program is paused) highlighted
- The **Outline** (the middle right panel): This shows an outline of the rules within the current file

The top two panels are new to this view. On the top left is the debug view (as shown in the screenshot below). For the moment, ignore the video type controls at the top of the panel, and look at the main panel instead. This main panel shows the stack trace.

When we start a program, our `main` method calls another method, which in turn calls another method until the breakpoint that we set is reached (and the program pauses). It's a bit like those Russian dolls—one method call fits inside another, and that call that fits inside another, and so on.

```
Debug ✕
▲ EventRulesExample (1) [Drools Application]
  ▲ net.firstpartners.chap11.EventRulesExample at localhost:60840
    ▲ Thread [main] (Suspended (breakpoint at line 18 in Rule_Chocolate_Shipment_0))
      ≡ Rule_Chocolate_Shipment_0.consequence(KnowledgeHelper, CustomerOrder, FactHandle, ILogger)
      ≡ Rule_Chocolate_Shipment_0ConsequenceInvoker.evaluate(KnowledgeHelper, WorkingMemory) line
      ≡ DefaultAgenda.fireActivation(Activation) line: 554
      ≡ DefaultAgenda.fireNextItem(AgendaFilter) line: 518
      ≡ ReteooWorkingMemory(AbstractWorkingMemory).fireAllRules(AgendaFilter, int) line: 475
      ≡ ReteooWorkingMemory(AbstractWorkingMemory).fireAllRules(AgendaFilter) line: 449
      ≡ ReteooStatelessSession.execute(Collection) line: 162
      ≡ RuleRunner.runStatelessRules(String[], String, Collection<Object>, HashMap<String,Object>, String,
      ≡ EventRulesExample.main(String[]) line: 68
    C:\Program Files\Java\jre1.6.0_03\bin\javaw.exe (23 Nov 2008 14:47:08)
```

We read the stack trace from the bottom up. In this case it is an `EventRulesExample`, called the `RuleRunner`, which called various Drools files (`Retoo`, `Default Agenda`, and so on), which in turn called our rules (`Rule_Chocolate_Shipment_0.consequence`).

At the top of the debug panel is a DVD-like control panel, which allows you to stop, start, and step through the program one line at a time (a bit like the 'forward by one frame' feature on most DVD players. The main icons or buttons are as follows:

- Resume (the green arrow) — continue until next breakpoint is reached, or the code ends
- Pause (greyed out): Pause the code that is running before it hits the next breakpoint
- Terminate (the red button): Stop the debug session.
- Arrows: Allow you to step through the code one line at a time

```
(x)= Variables ☒    •• Breakpoints

Name                          Value
1 ⊙ $CustomerOrder            CustomerOrder (id=23)
      currentBalance          1580
      initialBalance          2000
   ◢   shipments              ArrayList<E> (id=50)
      ◢   elementData         Object[10] (id=64)
         ▷ ▲ [0]              ChocolateShipment (id=29)
         ◢ ▲ [1]              ChocolateShipment (id=61)
               itemsStillToShip   1580
               shipmentAmount     210
               shipmentDate       null
         ◇ modCount           2
            size              2
2 ⊙ log                       ConsoleLogger (id=25)
   ◢   log                    Log4JLogger (id=36)
      ▷   logger              Logger (id=40)
      ▷   name                "net.firstpartners.drools.log.ConsoleLogger"
3 ⊙ ChocolateShipment         ChocolateShipment (id=61)
      itemsStillToShip        1580
      shipmentAmount          210
      shipmentDate            null


Shipment amount:210 date:null chocolate bars left in order:1580
```

The other new panel is the **Variables** view, which is on the top right of the debug perspective (as shown in the screenshot above). This shows the variables (value placeholders) in our rules. More precisely, it shows only the variables that the current rule (highlighted in the editing window) has access to.

The variable view gives us a window into the program in real time. If we step through the rules line by line, we can see the values being updated step by step.

The format of the screen is a 'treeview', that is, there are three top-level variables (as used by this rule) — $CustomerOrder, a handle to the logger, and an individual chocolate shipment that is the process of being created by the current rule. The panel at the very bottom shows more detail on the currently-highlighted value (the chocolate shipment).

The three JavaBeans highlighted in the above variable view are as follows:

1. **Customer Order**: The same fact that was inserted by the Java code and updated by the rules. Remember that it contains the current and the initial balance, and a list (array) of all of the shipments as the rules create them. In the current snapshot there are two shipments that are already populated in the list (elements **[0]** and **[1]**). Each of these elements is a **ChocolateShipment** JavaBean (containing the shipment amount). Because this snapshot is taken before the set shipment date has had a chance to fire, the shipment date is null or empty.

2. **log**: This is a global variable, as passed in when we called the rule. It is displayed in this view. Even through it is a global variable, it is passed in to the rule.

3. **ChocolateShipment**: This is the same JavaBean that we are in the process of creating in this rule. (That is, it is the same chocolate shipment that has been added to the list at position number **[1]**.) Given that it's 'work in progress', the **shipmentDate** is **null** (empty).

> Behind the variable view is a tab **Breakpoint**. This shows all of the sets in the rules and Java code. It is far easier to find them here than having to search through multiple files.

Other Drools views while debugging

There are other views available to help you while debugging. All of these can be added to the current view using the following option from the toolbar: **Window | Show View | Other | Drools**:

- Working memory: A live snapshot of the working memory, similar to the variables view above

- Agenda View: A list of the rules that are available to fire (and the order) in real time, as you step through the rules

- Rules: A list of the rules that have been loaded

When to log, when to test, and when to debug

Debugging, testing, and logging are all useful tools to help you understand what is going on with your rules. But when it is best to use each of these tools can be explained as follows:

- Logging is used the most. This is especially true when using a toolkit such as Log4j or Apache Commons, where it can be turned on and off via a configuration file with little or no perceptible impact on performance.

- Writing a test is proactive, and will catch errors before the users do. It also has the advantage that once it is written it goes on working, and keeps checking for a recurrence of the problem, and alerts you if required.

- Debug is the most powerful feature. However, once you've solved the problem, most of the effort is lost; and if a similar problem happens in the future, you're likely to have to start again from the beginning.

Summary

This chapter opened up the internals of the Drools rule engine so that we can understand concepts such as truth maintenance, conflict resolution, pattern matching, and the rules Agenda. We explored the Rete algorithm, and why it makes rules run faster than most comparable business logic. Finally, we saw the working memory audit log and the rules debug capabilities of the Drools IDE. The next chapter uses this power and knowledge to take advantage of some of the more advanced features.

12
Advanced Drools Features

So far we've covered several big topics such as what a rule engine is, why we would want to use one, and where you can download the Drools Rule Engine. We wrote rules using the Guvnor web editor and the more sophisticated JBoss IDE, before testing those rules using a variety of tools. We used Excel to hold both rules and data, and wrote our own DSL and rule flows. Not only that, we also looked under the covers to see some rule engine internals and understand how we would go about deploying rules in real life.

This chapter is a bit different from the earlier chapters. It is a level up from the introductory chapters as it presents additional information about the topics already covered in those chapters. A lot of information comes from the latest version of Drools. Although these features are stable and can be used in production systems, they may undergo substantial enhancements by the time you read this.

We will cover the new features of Guvnor. They include a new more powerful API for calling the rule engine from Java, the ability to load data, create Java Beans dynamically, **Complex Event Processing (CEP)**, and Drools Solver. We also explain some more under-the-cover features such as backward/forward chaining, controlling conflict resolution, and Rule Engine Standards (JSR-94).

Let's start with Drools Fusion—Complex Events Processing.

Pigeons, Drools, and Complex Event Processing

Pigeons (the birds that flock around city squares and parks) aren't known for being clever. So it may strike as strange that they appear in a book about business intelligence. However, during the Cold War, the Soviets (allegedly) trained pigeons to inspect ball-bearings on the production line. The pigeons would sit in comfortable little boxes while the shiny silver ball-bearings steamed past on a conveyor belt. If the pigeon spotted any that were defective, they would peck a button and the broken bearing would be gone. Since the fall of the Berlin Wall, all of the pigeons have been gainfully re-employed at Google (`http://www.google.com/technology/pigeonrank.html`).

Thankfully, the pigeons didn't go to work at a bank in the city. (Have you ever seen anything with feathers drive a Ferrari?) Although the pigeons would be very good at responding to simple market events (if market is up then sell, and if market down then buy), more complex analysis escapes them. For example, consider a situation where the market is down for 30 minutes. The shares in Acme corp are down by more than 10% than the average. But if you see three buy orders for that share in the last 60 seconds, then you may think that the market is about to turn, and hence buy shares in Acme corp.

Never mind the pigeons. Even most humans would find that difficult—think about trying to read the stock ticker prices (the ones you see rolling across the screen at MSNBC) for all stocks, while trying to hold the buy and sell information for the last 30 minutes in your head. And do that not only for one, but for a hundred different types of shares in the market. You have to do this while keeping an eye on your own trading position so that you're not exposed to one sector of the market (for example, keeping enough cash, and not too many property or technology shares). No wonder most traders make their millions and burn out before they're 30—that sort of **Complex Event Processing** (CEP) will wear you out.

Most IT applications are like pigeons; they can only handle simple events. Press the button. Do something. The way to make millions is to design applications that can handle these complex events, and apply sophisticated business rules to the (evolving) situation. You have to do it quickly enough (milliseconds) to seize the opportunity before somebody else does, and keep on doing it as long as the market is open.

CEP is what Drools Fusion provides.

Implementing Complex Event Processing using Fusion

There are a lot of 'under the cover' changes to the latest version of Drools. These allow it to handle the volume of events that happen (often all at once) during CEP. However, from the end user point of view using CEP is strangely familiar to:

1. Writing facts (Java Objects).
2. Writing rules — same as before.
3. Notifying Drools of events (in the same way as we asserted facts previously — facts and events are interchangeable in many ways).

The third step is similar to asserting the facts, which we've done before. The difference is that events will be in greater number (especially in a stock market trading system) than the facts. And there will (potentially) be no limit to the amount of events that can happen, while we will tend to have a good idea of the number of facts that we will encounter. Fortunately, the upgrades to Drools during the latest version are specifically intended to handle large volumes of multiple events.

Although we can manually assert the events into working memory, one optimization for complex event handling is to set the working memory to listen to a stream, and automatically pipe the event from one to the other. Even with this shortcut, our solution using CEP will involve the following three files:

1. The Java file describing the event object being used: It is a simple JavaBean, which is the same as the facts in the previous examples (that is, the facts could be used as events if desired).
2. The Rule file: It imports rules and other assets (as before), declares the events used in the rules, and connects them to any event streams that the rules listen to.
3. The Java code in the application: It loads the rules, either inserts the events or links it to the stream specified, fires the rules and then does something with the results.

We'll work through this based on a sample from the Drools code, `StreamsTest.java`. This is a unit test, but shows how CEP works in practice. We'll start with the JavaBean file.

```java
public class StockTick {

    private int tradeNumber;
    private String stockName;
    private int price;
    private long currentTimeMillis;

    public StockTick(int tradeNumber, String stockName, int price, long
    currentTimeMillis) {
            this.tradeNumber=tradeNumber;
            this.stockName = stockName;
            this.price = price;
            this.currentTimeMillis = currentTimeMillis;
    }
    public int getTradeNumber() {
            return tradeNumber; }
    public String getStockName() {
            return stockName;}
    public int getPrice() {
            return price;}
    public long getCurrentTimeMillis() {
            return currentTimeMillis;  }
}
```

Note that this class is immutable — once it's created it cannot be changed. In real life, events once occurred can't be altered, so the reasoning behind this feature is understandable.

This 'immutability' is implanted in two parts in the code above: The first part is that values that can only be set when the JavaBean is created (the line starting with `public StockTick(int tradeNumber, String stockName, int price, long currentTimeMillis)`). The second is that there is no 'set' method on the JavaBean, but there are methods beginning with 'get' to read the values. There is no chance to change an event that has already happened.

The second file is the rules file, an example of which is given as follows:

```
package org.drools;

import org.drools.StockTick;

global java.util.List results;

declare StockTick
    @role( event )
end

rule "Test entry point"
when
    $st : StockTick( company == "ACME", price > 10 ) from entry-point
StockStream
then
    results.add( $st );
end
```

This rules file has the usual package, import, and global statement. The three lines beginning with `declare StockTick` are new. They take the `StockTick` JavaBean we declared in the previous file, and let the rule engine know that we want to treat it as an event.

The rule matches all the events from the external stream where that event concerns the ACME stock, and where the price is greater than 10. When fired, the `then` part adds it to a `results` list—declared as a global variable at the top of the rules file.

The second new part in the rule file is in the `when` part of the rule beginning with `from entry-point StockStream`. We have met the `from` keyword before. It allows us to reach outside the rules' working memory (for example, to values in a database using the Hibernate framework) and allow those values to trigger rules. In this case, the source of those values is an event stream called `StockStream`. The code that calls the rule engine will supply this stream.

An extract of the application code with the complete file is available at `http://anonsvn.labs.jboss.com/labs/jbossrules /trunk/drools-compiler/ src/test/java/org/drools/integrationtests/StreamsTest.java`. Most of what has been removed is package and import statements (most of the Drools classes referred to can be found in the `org.drools` package, or subpackages under it, from the Drools core library). The code is in the form of a unit test, that is, it has `assert` statements to check the results of the rules; these statements have also been removed in the interest of clarity.

The first method loads the rules base using the new Drools API (we will talk more about this API shortly). It searches the classpath for a given file name, loads it as a rule file, and then returns Drools `Knowledgebase` based on that rule file.

```
private KnowledgeBase loadKnowledgeBase(final String fileName)
throws IOException, DroolsParserException
{
  KnowledgeBuilder kbuilder =
                    KnowledgeBuilderFactory.newKnowledgeBuilder();

kbuilder.add(
ResourceFactory.
newClassPathResource(fileName,getClass()),ResourceType.DRL);

KnowledgeBase kbase = KnowledgeBaseFactory.newKnowledgeBase();
     kbase.addKnowledgePackages( kbuilder.getKnowledgePackages() );

return kbase;
}
```

The second important method in the file is the one that uses these rules to 'do something'. It's called `testEventAssertion()`. You may remember from Chapter 7 that unit tests such as this will have every method starting with 'test', and will be called by the framework. In real life, this method would most likely be called something similar to 'call rules', but the contents of the method will be similar.

```
 public void testEventAssertion() throws Exception {
// read in the source using the method explained previously
// and the rules file (drl) we featured earlier
KnowledgeBase kbase = loadKnowledgeBase( "test_EntryPoint.drl" );

KnowledgeSessionConfiguration conf = new SessionConfiguration();
        ((SessionConfiguration) conf)
        .setClockType( ClockType.PSEUDO_CLOCK );

StatefulKnowledgeSession session = kbase.newStatefulSession( conf );

final List results = new ArrayList();

session.setGlobal( "results", results );

   StockTick tick1 = new StockTick(
 1, "DROO", 50, System.currentTimeMillis() );
   StockTick tick2 = new StockTick(
                  2, "ACME", 10, System.currentTimeMillis() );
StockTick tick3 = new StockTick(
                  3, "ACME", 10, System.currentTimeMillis() );
StockTick tick4 = new StockTick(
                  4, "DROO", 50, System.currentTimeMillis() );
```

```
......
WorkingMemoryEntryPoint entry =
          session.getWorkingMemoryEntryPoint( "StockStream" );

entry.insert( tick1 );

  ......

   session.fireAllRules();
}
```

In this artificial sample we create the four events ourselves, and then stop them. In real life, there would be another application constantly passing us events over a longer period. These events can be passed by another Java thread, a web service, or passed over a network connection.

Several important things are going on in this method:

1. The rules (that we saw earlier) are loaded into a Drools `knowledgebase` object using the helper method which we have just reviewed.

2. We create configuration settings. Since this is a test, here we want to use a clock that we have more control over, rather than one that is tied to an internal system clock. This is important in situations (such as testing, where you have multiple rule servers, or you need to 'replay' events later) where you cannot guarantee that the time will be exactly as you expect. A pseudo clock gives us control over this situation.

3. Using this configuration, a `StatefulKnowledgeSession` is created — similar in concept to the stateful session that we met earlier. A global variable (results) is passed to this session.

4. Next, four events (of type `StockTick`) are created. Each time we create a `StockTick`, we must pass the stock tick number, the stock name, the price, and the current system time.

5. We get a handle to the `StockStream` from the recently created `StatefulKnowledgeSession`, using the `getWorkingMemoryEntryPoint()` method.

6. Using the handle to the `StockStream`, we pass in the `StockTick` events. Passing in the `StockTick` events is exactly the same as passing in facts to the working memory. The advantage of using the stream method is its speed, as only rules that listen to events will inspect the newly inserted objects.

7. When we've inserted all of the objects, we allow the rules to fire by calling `session.fireAllRules` again. Once the rules have finished firing, the objects (such as the global variable results that we passed in earlier) are updated and become available for use in the rest of the Java code.

If this unit test runs correctly, only one event will match the rule and cause one line to be added to the results list.

 If you look at the test on the web site, you'll see that the actual line for inserting events contains a reference to an item called a facthandle. It is a simple handle to the object after we pass it to the rule engine. It's useful for testing (and other advanced situations), but does not change the meaning of the line from the one described on the previous page.

This simple example only hints at the power of complex event processing. For example, instead of fireAllRules used in the example, we could have called fireUntilHalt. This is more suitable for situations (such as events) where we neither know the number of objects or events that may come our way, nor the timescale in which they will be made available to us. FireUntilHalt is more suitable for these situations. Typically, there would be two threads to your program (that is, the computer is doing two things at one time). One thread is similar to the code in the example above, and calls fireUntilHalt. The other is listening for events and adding them to the working memory. At a time of our choice (for example, we choose to stop trading on the stock market) we call halt() and the rules will no longer fire, even if the events continue to happen.

More powerful events

The events syntax in the previous sample is fairly simple. Primitive events are those events in which there is no restriction of duration, no need for two events to occur in or out of sequence, or to occur within a particular time window. To add these kind of complex restrictions to the when part of the rule, you can use coincides, before, after, meets, overlaps, during, starts, and finishes as special Drools keywords. They can help in filtering your rules. The following is an example:

```
when
    $st : StockTick( company == "ACME", starts > '01/01/2009' )
    from entry-point StockStream
```

There is also the option for sliding time windows. For example, to match all events in the last 60 seconds, the syntax has to do the following:

```
StockTick( ) over window:time( 60 )
```

This will match all of the StockTick events that happened in the last 60 seconds.

A detailed list of the syntax is available in test_CEP_TimeRelationalOperators. drl file at http://anonsvn.labs.jboss.com/labs/jbossrules/trunk/drools-compiler/src/test/resources/org/drools/integrationtests/test_CEP_ TimeRelationalOperators.drl.

Inline beans

For the above sample, as with every other sample in the book, we've had to create a JavaBean to hold the information going into and out of the rule engine. Although writing this JavaBean is relatively straightforward, it still involves writing code in Java. As we saw, this is nothing to be scared of, but it is something you hardly want to do while writing your rules.

The latest version of Drools can help you with this problem. It allows you to declare beans within your rule files, and use those beans exactly as we did in other samples. Declaring an inline bean is fairly straightforward.

```
global …

declare SomeJavaBeanName
    javaBeanId : long
    name : String
    quantity : Integer
    price : double
end

rule …
```

In this extract we declare the `SomeJavaBeanName` bean with fields of `javaBeanId` (number, long), `name` (string or text), `quantity` (number, integer), `price` (number, double). The field types (String, double, and so on) are the same types used in the real JavaBeans.

Inline beans are ideal for event handling, especially where the event is coming from an external source. In this case, we change the above bean definition to include `@ role( event )` as follows:

```
declare SomeJavaBeanName
    @role( event )
    javaBeanId : long
    …
```

Loading data when your beans don't exist—Smooks

Declaring the bean inline is great for editing, but how does the rest of the system know the structure of the bean? If no JavaBean exists in a `.java` file, then Enterprise Java has no way of knowing what information it can pass in or out, the names of these fields, and the type (for example, text or numbers) of these fields.

As we've already seen in Chapter 8, the solution for this is providing the data in a standard format (such as Excel). This means that we know the format the data will be provided in, so that we can concentrate on the data rather than the format. In real life, we need to deal with other formats such as XML (a stricter form of HTML that makes up web pages, useful for data transportation), **CSV (Comma Separated Values)** — the most basic Excel format, and other proprietary formats. That's where the Smooks framework comes in.

 If Smooks can handle data from Excel, then why use the method suggested back in Chapter 8? The answer is that Smooks is better at handling data. But given that it uses CSV instead of Excel files directly, it's not so good at keeping the format of the Excel file.

Smooks is an open source Java framework that exists independently of Drools. Smooks is a Java Framework/Engine for processing XML and non-XML data (CSV, EDI, Java, JSON, and so on). You'll need to add the Smooks library to your project in order to use the functionality it provides.

To put it simply, Smooks loads the Excel (CSV), XML, or any other file and generates the events declared as inline beans in the rule file. It maps everything from the source file to the inline bean using the configuration that you provide in `smooks-config.xml`. Once the data is loaded as an inline bean, it is asserted into the working memory. Then the rules that we have written have a chance to fire. The Java code to do this is standard Drools, with one line telling Drools to use Smooks to load the incoming data.

```
//Load the rules into a rulebase and get a session as before
PackageBuilder packageBuild = new PackageBuilder();
packageBuild.addPackageFromDrl( new InputStreamReader( getClass().
getResourceAsStream( "myRuleFile.drl" )) );

RuleBase ruleBase = RuleBaseFactory.newRuleBase();
ruleBase.addPackage( packageBuild.getPackage() );

StatefulSession session = ruleBase.newStatefulSession();
// Load Smooks using the Config file
Smooks smooks = new Smooks( "smooks-config.xml" );

//Tell Drools-Smooks the point in our file that we want to start
loading data.
DroolsSmooksConfiguration conf = new DroolsSmooksConfiguration( "
someJavaBeanName ", null );

// Prepare a (Stateless) Session using the Smooks and Drools conf
DroolsSmooksStatelessSession smooksSession = new
DroolsSmooksStatelessSession( session, smooks, conf );

//Get a handle to the data file
javax.xml.transform.Source xmlSource = new StreamSource( getClass().
```

```
getResourceAsStream( "name-of-data-file.xml") )

//Load the data (and allow the rules a chane to fire)
smooksSession.executeFilter(xmlSource);
```

Once the rules have fired (following `excecuteFilter`), the Java code has a chance to inspect global rule variables. Thus, they get a handle to the result.

Mostly what we want to do is map the incoming XML (or other format) directly to the inline bean that we created in the rule file. In the following XML extract most of the names correspond directly to the names in our inline bean:

```
<someJavaBeanName>
    <javaBeanId>123</javaBeanId>
    <name>Onions</name>
    <quantity>72</quantity>
    <price>1.2</price>
</someJavaBeanName>
```

The `smooks-config.xml` configuration file to do this mapping can be quite sophisticated. For more information on how to use all of the available power, visit the Smooks web site at `http://www.smooks.org/`.

From pigeons to biscuits—Drools Solver for your local supermarket

Stock market trading might appear to be a little exotic. How about another trading problem that is causing the manager of your local supermarket to scratch his or her head?

Supermarkets, no matter how big they are, have a limited amount of shelf space. Obviously, supermarkets want to make as much money as possible. So, they want to stock the most profitable products on their shelves. However, even if chocolate bars are the most profitable line, a supermarket full of nothing but chocolate bars isn't going to make many sales. Even the most ardent chocolate fans are going to need things such as milk, bread, and cheese. So what mix of products will make the supermarket the most money?

Supermarkets have detailed information on the amount of sales in each of their stores—those barcode scanners do more than just give you your bill. They track each and every item sold in the shop. The barcode information also includes the most basic list of must-have items of the customers. The supermarket knows how much shelf space it has in any particular store and also the profit margin on each product. But this information doesn't tell the store manager how much money the store could potentially make if they had a different mix of goods on the shelves.

Part of the problem in answering the question about the best mix of products is that there are many potential factors involved—there are 100,000 products in a typical supermarket, and there are about 1,000 different ways of displaying them (top shelf, end shelf, back of store, next to the milk) in different combinations. (Does beer really sell well if it is placed next to the baby nappies as the urban legend has it?)

In classic mathematical or computing terms, this is similar to the 'travelling salesman' problem, where it is technically possible to calculate the answer. Even with computers more powerful than they are today, it would take you about 100 years to get an answer; and another 100 years to calculate it all over again if another type of beer is released in the market.

Once you tell this to the supermarket manager, you realize that (s)he would be happy even if you found a slightly better way of placing the products than the current situation. It may not be the best solution, but it's good enough to get him his bonus. And good enough solutions are something that Drools Solver can help with.

How Drools Solver works

At a very simplistic level, the way Drools Solver works is as follows:

1. One correct solution is supplied at the start—the current mix of products on the supermarket shelves.

2. Alternative solutions are generated either randomly or via an algorithm that is most likely to provide usable results.

3. Impossible solutions (for example, milk not being stored in refrigerators) are discarded. These hard constraints are expressed as rules.

4. The remaining solutions are scored using business rules. The scoring (or soft constraints) is also expressed as rules.

5. The best available solution is used when we loop back to step 1.

This process repeats until either a certain time period has elapsed, or until Drools Solver cannot find a better solution.

The Solver could have been written without using business rules, but the addition of Drools makes it so much better.

- Clear rules: What combinations are allowed, and how we score alternatives is clearly stated.

- Scalable rules: The Drools Rete Algorithm means that adding additional rules will only add milliseconds to the time required, and will not double the time needed (as per traditional solutions). This is especially important when the calculations are run repeatedly (as happens within the Solver).

- Optimized calculations: Drools detects the change from a previous to new scenario, and can carry out only those calculations required. That is, it does not need to recalculate everything from scratch.

Implementing a Solver

A full Solver solution is provided as part of the Drools examples on the download site (on which the solution below is based). Implementing the five steps given above is relatively straightforward.

Steps 1 and 5 are provided by implementing the Solution interface. This, like most of the files mentioned in this section, can be found in the `org.drools.solver.core` package (or its subfolders).

 We did warn that this chapter was more advanced than the previous ones! Although we'll explain concepts to a non-technical level, you'll probably need to have some Java experience (or know somebody who does) to actually implement the examples.

Think of an interface as a template guiding you to fill in the gaps and complete the solution—in general, this 'complete template' is contained in a second Java file. In this case, `getFacts()` returns the JavaBeans representing the goods on the shelves of the supermarket as we begin our analysis. The `cloneSolution()` method allows step 5 to copy any better solution (that is, save a good copy while it tries to improve it even further).

```
public interface Solution {
    Collection<? extends Object> getFacts();
    Solution cloneSolution();
}
```

Running the solver is easy. We create a configuration, load the configuration file, and then start the Solver (which may take some time).

```
XmlSolverConfigurer configurer = new XmlSolverConfigurer();
configurer.configure("SolverConfig.xml");
Solver solver = configurer.buildSolver();

The configuration file ties the remaining parts of the solution
together. The Comments explain what each part means.
<!--Name of the file containing the solver business rules used for
rating the alternatives-->
<scoreDrl>SolverRulesFile.drl</scoreDrl>

<!--How we compare the various solutions - Simple is one of the three
```

```
built in options, or can build or own -->
<scoreCalculator>
<scoreCalculatorType>SIMPLE</scoreCalculatorType>
</scoreCalculator>
<!-Finish solving after 2 minutes, or after 100 attemps, or after we
have achieved the perfect score-->
<finish>
    <finishCompositionStyle>OR</finishCompositionStyle>
    <maximumMinutesSpend>2</ maximumMinutesSpend>
    <maximumStepCount>100</maximumStepCount>
    <feasableScore>0.0</feasableScore>
</finish>
<!-Name of the Java File that generates alternative solutions-->
<selector>
    <moveFactoryClass>NameOfMoveFactory</moveFactoryClass>
</selector>

<!-An accepter filters out the most crazy alternatives. This is
expressed as a score - trial and error will give a value that works
best -->
<accepter>
    <completeSolutionTabuSize>1000</completeSolutionTabuSize>
</accepter>
<!-which of the best alternatives do we use - in this case take the
alternative with the highest score from the rules - ->
<forager>
    <foragerType>MAX_SCORE_OF_ALL</foragerType>
</forager>
</localSearchSolver>
```

The MoveFactory is another Java class that implements another interface or template (although there are other files that help in the background as 'abstract' and 'super' classes). The most important method is createMoveList, which is a list of the items that we wish to swap on the supermarket shelves in search for a better solution. It takes the implementation of the Solution interface as a parameter that we created earlier.

```
public interface MoveFactory
    extends LocalSearchSolverAware,
            LocalSearchSolverLifecycleListener {
    List<Move> createMoveList(Solution solution);
}
```

The LocalSearchSolverAware and LocalSearchSolverLifecycleListener files referenced are other interfaces. The methods (not listed here) that implement the Solution interface help the Solver avoid 'dead ends' that appear to be good solutions. We did not look at them in detail.

The following is an example of a rule file mentioned in the config file, which shows 'hard' constraints, such that beer and nappies should not be on the same shelf:

```
rule "Stock items cannot be placed on the same shelf"
    when
        $item1 : StockItem($shelf : shelf, name =="beer");
        $item2 : StockItem (shelf == $shelf, name =="nappies");
    then
        insertLogical(new UnweightedConstraintOccurrence(
                "Incompatible objects on shelves", $item1, $item2));
end
```

The match against the facts in the when part is the same as usual—remember all of the facts provided by the solution are inserted into the working memory, and updated as we cycle through the alternative solutions.

The then part shows how to communicate the fact that nappies and beer should not sit side by side on the same shelf. We insert a new UnweightedConstraintOccurrence into the working memory. There are similar constraints (such as IntConstraintOccurrence) which allow us to communicate a score on how good the rules think the current solution is.

> InsertLogical is similar to insert, except that the object will automatically be removed if the 'when' part is no longer true.

With all these pieces in place, Solver loads the initial solution, generates and evaluates alternative solutions, and then repeats the process until it decides to stop.

More information on Solver

Of course, the actual implementation of Drools Solver is much more sophisticated. More information is available in the Drools documentation. (See Chapter 2 for more details on where to obtain this.) When reading this documentation you may come across a line that might puzzle you.

> It's recommended to use drools in forward-chaining mode [...] This is a huge performance gain.

Forward and backward chaining are key (if advanced) rule engine concepts. So perhaps now is a good time to introduce them.

Forward and backward chaining

You use forward and backward chaining in real life—except that you don't know it yet.

- Forward chaining is where you have the instructions, but you don't know the end goal of where the instructions are taking you. For example, it's like following the driving instructions on your SatNav or GPS where somebody else has entered the end coordinates.

- Backward chaining is where you have an end goal in mind, and need to work out how you get there. For example, if you need to go to the supermarket and work out the best way to drive there, then the way you work out the route is an example of backward chaining.

Drools is a hybrid rule engine because it allows both forward and backward chaining. Most of the examples in this book have used forward chaining. Backward chaining tends to either happen accidentally, or when we need to answer the question, 'Which is the set of facts that could lead us to a particular situation?' The Miss Manners example from Drools can be configured to show backward chaining behavior.

Forward and backward chaining is important because of its effect on performance. Backward chaining is very powerful, but much slower.

To explain this, consider the example of the tangle of wires behind your television set. There are probably power cables from your TV, DVD, satellite, games console, and Wi-Fi leading to the power sockets in the wall.

- If we want to confirm that the TV is plugged in (forward chaining), all we need to do is pull the power lead at the back of the TV, and confirm that the lead that is plugged in moves.

- If we want to confirm which gadgets are plugged in to where, we need to test each and every cord. This is why backward chaining is much slower.

Forward and backward chaining is implemented using the Rete algorithm, and can fill the entire contents of a book in itself. But if we did that, we'd miss the chance to touch on another important 'under the covers' topic of how Drools implements conflict resolution, and what you can do to configure it.

Changing the conflict resolution methodology

In the previous chapter we met with a problem with rule engines. If there is more than one rule available to fire on the Agenda, how do we decide which one goes first? This is especially important as the first rule to fire might cause the subsequent rules to be removed from the agenda, and hence prevent them from firing.
The solution was conflict resolution—an in-built method that comes with Drools. It uses this methodology to resolve which rule fires first. But what if we want to change this methodology?

The code sample below shows how we do this (this happens behind the scenes without us needing to change it). Normally, the current order of conflict revolvers is based on salience (number), last fired, rule simplicity, and then rule order. Adding the following code will allow you to tweak the conflict resolution strategy of your rule engine:

```
ConflictResolver[] conflictResolvers =
   new ConflictResolver[] {
SimplicityConflictResolver.getInstance(),
SalienceConflictResolver.getInstance(),
      RecencyConflictResolver.getInstance(),
   LoadOrderConflictResolver.getInstance()
   };

CompositeConflictResolver resolver =
   new CompositeConflictResolver(
      conflictResolvers);

businessRules = RuleBaseLoader.loadFromUrl(
   BusinessLayer.class.getResource(
      BUSINESS_RULE_FILE),resolver);
```

In this case we've made simple rules (that is, fewer conditions in the when part) that are more likely to fire first. We've done that by building up an array of the conflict revolvers that Drools offers us in the *order of importance* that we want. Then we add this array (list) together in a `CompositeConflictResolver`. Finally, when we load the rules, we pass in the `CompositeResolver`. When the rules fire, conflicts (if any) are resolved using the strategies in the order that we specify.

Like forward and backward chaining, it's important to be aware of the conflict resolution strategy. Likewise, in everything but the most advanced situations, you shouldn't need to change it. So if you find yourself tweaking the conflict resolution, double-check that the problem isn't in your rules. Make sure you have a good set of unit tests around your rules. When fixing one rule, make sure that you don't inadvertently break others.

Standard rule engine API—JSR 94

The standard rule engine API, **JSR-94 (Java Specification Request)**, like conflict resolution, will come up in conversation soon after you bring up the topic of rule engines with your colleagues. JSR-94 is the Java standard API for dealing with rule engines in almost the same way as the Java Database Connectivity (JDBC) is the Java standard way of connecting Java to databases. So why is this piece of information tucked away in the very last chapter?

- JSR-94 only specifies how we call the rule engine, and not the syntax of the rules themselves. There is no rules standard similar to ANSI SQL (for databases) to specify the format.

- Even when calling rule engines, JSR-94 gives you only a subset of the power of Drools (or most other rule engines).

Although there is no standard rule format, it is possible for Drools to mimic other commercial rule engine syntax (such as Blaze) using Domain Specific Language (DSL). At the time of writing you'll need to write this DSL yourself, but given the open source nature of Drools, expect much progress in this area. For example, Drools Clips emulation is already in an advanced stage.

If you choose to use the JSR-94 syntax, you'll need to add an additional library—drools-jsr94.jar—to your project. The code to load and fire the rules in the standard manner is very close in concept to the examples we saw earlier, even if the terminology used will look something similar to the extract below. This code sample is how the sample from Chapter 6 (remember those ChocolateFactory rules?) would look using JSR-94.

```
//Specify the exact provider of the JSR-94 driver
Class.forName("org.drools.jsr94.rules.RuleServiceProviderImpl");
// Get the rule service provider from the provider manager.
RuleServiceProvider provider = RuleServiceProviderManager.getRuleServi
ceProvider("http://drools.org/");

// Get a handle to the Administration API-
RuleAdministration ruleAdministrator = provider.
getRuleAdministrator();
LocalRuleExecutionSetProvider ruleExecSet = ruleAdmin.
getLocalRuleExecutionSetProvider( null );

// Create a Reader for the drl
URL drl = new URL("shipping-rules.drl");
Reader drlReader = new InputStreamReader( drl.openStream() );

// Create the RuleExecutionSet for the drl
RuleExecutionSet ruleExecutionSet = ruleExecSet.
```

```
createRuleExecutionSet( drlReader, null );
// Register the RuleExecutionSet with the RuleAdministrator
String uri = ruleExectionSet.getName();
ruleAdministrator.registerRuleExecutionSet(uri, ruleExecutionSet,
null);

//Get a stateless execution set from this set
RuleRuntime ruleRuntime = provider.getRuleRuntime();
(StatefulRuleSession) session = ruleRuntime.createRuleSession( uri,
                    null,RuleRuntime.STATELESS_SESSION_TYPE );

//Insert the facts - assume that we created these earlier
session.addObject (candyBarOrder);
session.addObject (holiday1);
session.addObject (holiday2);

//Fire the rules
session.executeRules();
```

In some ways the code is more complicated (as we need to specify at the start that we are using the Drools Rule Engine). Like before, once the rules have fired, the updated Java objects will be available for use by the Java program. The Drools documentation gives further information on JSR-94. If you feel you need to use this, there is an alternative API to call the rule engine.

Other rule engines

So, if somebody has gone through a lot of trouble to write the JSR-94 specification for portability (even if you choose not to use it), what other rule engines are available to use? There are literally hundreds of frameworks that claim to embody business rules. But if we filter the list according to those that have a moderate amount of features and traction, either commercially or in the open source community, we get the following alternatives: (Remember that this is not an exhaustive list.)

- BizTalk
- Blaze Advisor
- Jena
- Jess
- JRules
- OpenRules
- PegaRules
- RulesPower

Normally, you'd expect at this point a critical evaluation of the rule engines mentioned in this list—something like 'Jess is a mature Java rule engine with good tool support (for example, plug-ins from Eclipse). It's a commercial product, and the rules are written in a Prolog-style syntax, which can be confusing for many Java programmers.' All of this would be true. However, given my bias (of course, I'm going to recommend Drools on the basis that it's the most mature, open source Java-based rule engine), would you believe any of the analysis?

The best way to summarize is that you should do your own research, and Drools will inevitably be on the shortlist. Some of the frameworks mentioned (for example, Jena) offer basic rules functionality, but it's not their core purpose (for Jena, it's the semantic web). Other frameworks claim to be rule engines, but offer only a fraction of the functionality discussed in this book. Outside Java, remember that Drools.Net offers a rule engine on the .Net platform (although its features are not as mature as those in Drools Java), and Windows workflow (the workflow module that is part of .Net platform) also has a subset of rules functionality.

New API

You may have noticed that the examples in this chapter are using a slightly different API from those in other chapters. The reason for this is that Drools has a new API. Don't worry, all of the previous examples will continue to work as before.

Why change something that isn't broken? The changes to the API make interacting with Drools more 'knowledge engine' based and less 'rule engine' based.

This may seem unusual for a book on rule engines. But a lot of the functionality that is being added is broadening the capabilities of the engine into areas such as complex event processing, solving (both of which we saw earlier in this chapter), and workflow. (We touched upon it in Chapter 9, and we will deal with the extensive improvements in the next section.) Chances are that if you need a rule engine, you'll need (at least some of) these capabilities. So it makes sense to enhance Drools and make the API more generic to accommodate this.

The main parts of the new API that you interact with are as follows—more or less one for each replacement for the Drools objects we used earlier:

- `org.drools.builder.KnowledgeBuilder`
- `org.drools.KnowledgeBase`
- `org.drools.agent.KnowledgeAgent`
- `org.drools.runtime.StatefulKnowledgeSession`
- `org.drools.runtime.StatelessKnowledgeSession`

The notes accompanying the new release have good examples. The main addition in the samples below is that in the new API we need to explicitly state that we're loading a rule file (`ResourceType.DRL`). This is because `KnowledgeBuilder` can also load other resources, such as workflow files. The following sample shows how we would load the chocolate factory from Chapter 6, but using the new Drools API:

```
URL drl = new URL("shipping-rules.drl");

KnowledgeBuilder kbuilder = KnowledgeBuilderFactory.
newKnowledgeBuilder();
kbuilder.add( ResourceFactory.newUrlResource( url ),
        ResourceType.DRL );

//check for errors
if ( kbuilder.hasErrors() ) {
  System.err.println( builder.getErrors().toString() );
}
KnowledgeBase kbase = KnowledgeBaseFactory.newKnowledgeBase();
kbase.addKnowledgePackages( builder.getKnowledgePackages() );
StatefulKnowledgeSession ksession = knowledgeBase.
newStatefulKnowledgeSession();

//Insert the facts - assume that we created these earlier
ksession.addObject (candyBarOrder);
ksession.addObject (holiday1);
ksession.addObject (holiday2);

ksession.fireAllRules();
```

More information on these new objects can be found in the Javadoc at `https://hudson.jboss.org/hudson/job/drools/lastSuccessfulBuild/artifact/trunk/target/javadocs/stable/drools-api/index.html`.

Drools flow—a full workflow engine

Back in Chapter 9 we mentioned that Ruleflow is not a workflow. This holds true, and Ruleflow can still be used to control when the different sets of rules may fire. However, Drools 5 now has a first-class workflow engine integrated into it, plus all of the supporting tools that you'd expect. To remind ourselves of the differences, and what workflow is:

- Ruleflow says what might happen at each stage in the process. The actual rules that fire are selected by the rule engine.

- Workflow says exactly what will happen at each stage in the process. As soon as the workflow reaches a step, we will fire the actions associated with it.

Typically, workflows model the business process. The following sample is from the **JBoss jBPM** (**Business Process Management**) documentation (the other JBoss workflow that Drools integrates well with). It describes the business steps needed to process an e-commerce order.

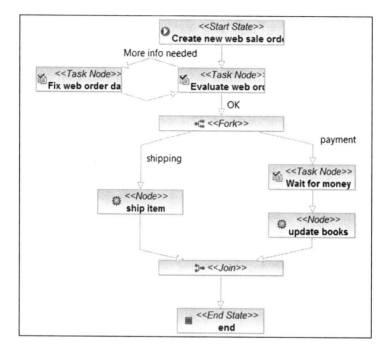

What both Drools Flow and JBoss jBPM provide are Eclipse-based tools to 'draw' the workflow — the image above is an example on one using the Eclipse tools. Using the tool, you then state what Java code you wish to fire at each point in the workflow. (It is easy to write because the Java code doesn't have to worry about what is happening around it, only that it will be told to run in the correct circumstances.) Drools and jBPM also provide a runtime that executes the workflow as the various steps are met.

Drools hooks into the decision-making node for both Drools flow and jBPM, allowing you to make (rules-based) decisions on what path you want the process to proceed.

New features in Guvnor

Guvnor gains a lot of enhancements in the latest Drools release. These include:

- Fine-grained security: You can restrict what groups of users can and cannot do.
- Web-based decision tables: They have a similar grid-like format to that which the Excel decision tables have (as seen in Chapter 8), but are accessible through the Guvnor web interface.

- More powerful scenario-based testing tools: The ability to load files using Windows Explorer, that is, drag-and-drop uploads to Guvnor.
- An editor to take advantage to the declarative modelling/inline beans: There is no need to create JavaBeans in Eclipse. It can be done in Guvnor instead.

There are also substantial under-the-cover improvements to the core rule engine, the net effect of which is to increase stability and performance.

Does this still sound like where you work?

Back in Chapter 1, you may have taken the 10-question pop quiz with the heading 'Does this sound like where you work?' The aim was to show you the problems that Drools can solve. Lets take a look at the solutions.

1. Is Bob in the corner the only person who knows how the system really works? Can the business scale only if we have an expert? Is critical knowledge lost when people like Bob leave?

   Solution: Getting the knowledge out of Bob's head and into a business rule-based system is a scalable, durable, solution.

2. If you're Bob (owning the knowledge), are you sick of people asking you stupid questions? Do you think: don't these people know that you've got a job to do?

   Solution: Write your knowledge as business rules. That way, at the very least it's documented; and even better, it can be run in the rule engine.

3. Are your customers getting a different answer every time they call your company (and getting more than slightly irate about it)? Are you at the risk of receiving a slap on the wrist (or worse) from a regulator or other standards body?

   Solution: Having the company's knowledge in one place (the business rules), and referring to that each time means that clients will get consistent answers.

4. Do you find yourself working around, rather than with, your computer systems? Have you ever thought of pouring coffee into your computer keyboard in frustration?

   Solution: Drools won't stop you from pouring coffee into your computer. But since rules-based systems are more flexible, you should be less tempted to try pouring coffee into your computer in the first place.

5. Are things always done with books, or is there a lot of informal knowledge that is just in people's heads?

   Solution: There will always be an element of informal knowledge in every business. But since rules are much easier to update than code, the balance will be shifted towards documented business rules (a good thing).

6. Did you prepare for a quality (ISO 9001) audit and then leave the process documentation unused on a shelf? Is there anybody around who knows or wants to change this process?

   Solution: If you move your knowledge to rules and workflow, the next time you have a quality audit you just print the rules and send the auditors their way.

7. Is your business knowledge in some format that gives payback? (For example, Electronic instead of that dusty paper copy, and not locked away in unreadable machine-code.) Is this format easy to update? Can everybody use it from one central location (so that copies do not get 'out of sync')? Can you track changes and roll back if you get it wrong?

   Solution: Drools gives a repository to securely store your knowledge and track changes. Even better, it can 'execute' that knowledge (as rules) directly from the repository.

8. Do the right people (and only the right people) have access (both reading and updating) to this information? Does this access need to change depending on the context of what the user is doing at the time?

   Solution: The rules repository that comes with Drools Guvnor allows you to do just this.

9. Do people in your organization work on projects? Do they come together to form goal-driven teams, and then go back when the objectives have been achieved? Do you know how to document the outcome of these projects as rules so that they can be reused both over time and over the organization?

   Solution: The project team (among other things) can generate new or updated business rules. Captured by Drools, these can be shared with the rest of the organization.

10. No task is done in isolation. How do we ensure that tasks and team members collaborate effectively?

    Solution: Rules encourage sharing so that everybody can understand what is going on. Even better, the Guvnor web editor allows many people to contribute at the same time, without needing to install special software.

OK, so our pop quiz was slightly biased (this is a Drools book, after all). But the fundamental problems that Drools solves, and the change that JBoss Drools can make to where you work, should still be clear.

Summary

We've come a long way since the start of this book. Chapter 1 introduced the problem of capturing business logic in a way that is readable and updateable by non-technical users. It introduced Drools and rule engines as a solution to the problem. Chapter 2 showed where to obtain Drools and other open source software, and how to install it on your computer. Chapter 3 introduced the Guvnor web editor, available to help non-technical users write business rules.

In Chapter 4 we began to write our first business rules using the Guvnor editor, and wrote our first JavaBean to support these rules using Eclipse/the JBoss IDE. In Chapter 5 we wrote more advanced rules using Guvnor, rather than the JBoss IDE, to write the business rules due to the increased power that it offers. Chapter 6 continued this thread to give a comprehensive guide to the rules syntax.

Testing the rules written in the previous chapters is the focus of Chapter 7, while Chapter 8 showed how to use Excel to hold both the business rules and the data for those rules. Chapter 9 showed other ways of expressing your rules using Domain Specific Language and Ruleflow.

How to deploy all of the business rules created to date was the focus for Chapter 10. In Chapter 11 we took a view inside the rule engine to help us write better business rules. Finally, in this chapter, we looked at advanced rules concepts, many of which have become available in the latest Drools release.

I hope this book inspires you to use Drools business rules in your project. Good luck and remember to check for updates to Drools at www.jboss.org/drools and code samples at http://code.google.com/p/red-piranha/.

Index

Guvnor testing 146, 147
mistakes 162
unit testing 156
test scenario, Guvnor
running 103
Then part, guided editor
call a method on option 109
insert a new fact option 109
logically insert a new fact option 109
modify a fact option 109
retract a fact option 109
set the values of a field on option 109
toString method, CustomerOrder.java 131
toString mthod, ChocolateShipment.java
130
troubleshooting 57
truth maintenance 234

U

unit testing
about 156, 157
Chocolate Shipments sample, unit testing
158, 159
Junit 157
unit test, need for 157

V

versions, Java
JDK 32
JRE 32

W

web deployment
about 225
Appfuse-Spring-MVC, adding 227
Appfuse framework, downloading 225
Appfuse framework, used 225
code, adding 227
Drools, adding 227
Maven, used 225
web server testing, Maven used 226
working memory
about 230
logging 236
log viewer 238
text-based rule, building 104
working memory log 237

PUBLISHING

EJB 3 Developer Guide

ISBN: 978-1-847195-60-9   Paperback: 259 pages

A Practical Guide for developers and architects to the Enterprise Java Beans Standard.

1. A rapid introduction to the features of EJB 3

2. EJB 3 features explored concisely with accompanying code examples

3. Easily enhance Java applications with new, improved Enterprise Java Beans

---

TYPO3: Enterprise Content Management

ISBN: 1904811418   Paperback: 595 pages

The Official TYPO3 Book, written and endorsed by the core TYPO3 Team

1. Easy-to-use introduction to TYPO3

2. Design and build content rich extranets and intranets

3. Learn how to manage content and administrate and extend TYPO3

Please check **www.PacktPub.com** for information on our titles

Printed in the United States
150069LV00006B/56/P